Writing Exercises
from *Exercise Exchange*

Volume II

Charles R. Duke, Editor
Utah State University

National Council of Teachers of English
1111 Kenyon Road, Urbana, Illinois 61801

These articles from *Exercise Exchange* are reprinted with the permission of Charles R. Duke, editor, and of the University of Vermont and Murray State University.

NCTE Editorial Board: Candy Carter, Julie M. Jensen, Delores Lipscomb, John S. Mayher, Elisabeth McPherson

Book Design: Tom Kovacs for TGK Graphics, interior; Gail Glende Rost for Glende Rost Associates, cover

NCTE Stock Number 59087

Library of Congress Cataloging in Publication Data
Main entry under title:

Writing exercises from Exercise exchange.

   1. English language—Rhetoric—Study and teaching
(Higher)—Addresses, essays, lectures.   I. Duke,
Charles R.   II. Exercise exchange.
PE1404.W72   1984   808'.042'0712   84-91154
ISBN 0-8141-5908-7

Contents

Foreword

It was in 1951, while talking shop with Christine Gibson (then assistant to I. A. Richards), that I first thought of founding a journal which would enable teachers of English to swap actual examples of their teaching practices. She and I agreed that, while discussions of pedagogical theory might be of some value, a direct and simple exchange of exercises which had proved successful might be of greater practical benefit to teachers. I was then a beginning teacher at Bennington, determined to contrive fresh and intriguing exercises which would elicit the best efforts of my very lively students. My models were three superb teachers who had exercised me at Amherst: Theodore Baird, Reuben Brower, and G. Armour Craig. I often exchanged copies of writing assignments with colleagues at Bennington, and although we seldom used each other's devices in our classes, we found it stimulating to see just what each of us was asking of our students. Why not extend this exchange by inaugurating a modest publication which could be circulated among English teachers throughout the nation?

I first wrote a number of friends and acquaintances, asking them to send me copies of their best exercises with a few words of explanation. By 1952 I had acquired enough good material to fill twenty mimeographed pages (the first page of the first issue contained a fine exercise on Adams and James by Professor Craig), and these I bound and sent to every English teacher I could think of. The response was heartening. Within a few months I was able to publish my second issue and to persuade the Carnegie and Lemberg Foundations to underwrite the cost of printing and distributing it to a much larger audience. Harcourt, Brace loaned me their direct-mailing list in exchange for advertising space, and I soon began to receive exercises from all over the country.

Just as I was about to exhaust the Carnegie and Lemberg grant, Fred Cushing of Rinehart and Company wrote to say that his firm would be willing to publish the magazine if it were given the back page for advertising purposes. The resulting amiable association lasted for over eight years (during which period Rinehart merged with Holt and I edited the journal for two years from the University of Alaska, where I was a Visiting Professor). I moved to the University of Connecticut in 1961, and when other duties prevented me from giving the magazine my full attention, Irving Cummings and Thomas Roberts of the University of Connecticut assumed joint editorship. The university supported the magazine for a number of years, until, in 1972, publication of *Exercise Exchange* was transferred to the University of Vermont. There Paul Eschholz and Alfred Rosa served as editors, preserving the original concept and format of the magazine almost intact. Littleton Long of their department selected some of the best exercises which had appeared in the magazine, and his collection, entitled *Writing Exercises from Exercise Exchange* was published by the National Council of Teachers of English in 1976. Now the magazine is under the capable direction of Charles Duke at Utah State University.

I have no idea how many exercises have appeared in this journal during the twenty-seven-year history, but the three hundred mark must have been passed long ago. It is pleasing to think that teachers from all over the world have communicated through this medium (I recently met an English teacher from Sri Lanka who asked me how *Exercise Exchange* was doing) and that students of several generations may have benefited from the collaboration it has effected.

Thomas W. Wilcox
Founding Editor, *Exercise Exchange*
University of Connecticut, Storrs

Preface

What we as teachers do in our classrooms often remains unrevealed, providing us with the paradox of being surrounded by students and colleagues engaged in a common endeavor and yet being quite alone in our work. Although not everyone always can teach another person's exercise well, we can benefit from sharing teaching ideas if only because it permits us to judge what we like and what we don't like, what opportunities we may have missed or what we can gain.

The term "exercise" may suggest to some people the idea of "busy-work," but *Exercise Exchange* over its thirty years of publication has demonstrated that well-conceived classroom exercises are anything but busywork. After all, such exercises provide the proof that researchers and teachers need to support the implementation of new concepts and approaches as well as to reaffirm old ones.

Exercise Exchange over the years has attempted to open lines of communication to lessen the sense of isolation among instructors at different levels and in different areas of the world. Subscribers and contributors come from such places as Australia, West Germany, South Africa, Japan, England, Ireland, Canada, and from throughout the United States. That the "exchange" has been successful is documented in the many notes and letters sent to the editor indicating that authors have heard from other teachers who have tried the ideas published in the magazine and found them useful.

Exercise Exchange does not limit itself to the publication of articles about writing; in fact, the magazine publishes materials related to all aspects of teaching English. However, the collection in this volume focuses on writing, its principal purpose to supplement a similar and very popular collection published in 1976 by the National Council of Teachers of English.

Choosing pieces to appear in this new collection was not easy. Many fine articles have been published in the eight years since the first collection in one volume. In selecting the pieces, I have looked for ideas and approaches which, for the most part, reflect current practices in the teaching of writing, although readers will not find the writers of these articles spending considerable time discussing theory. These authors are first and foremost classroom teachers interested in sharing what works in their classes. As a result, I have made no effort to turn the collection into a textbook nor to present a comprehensive theory of instruction. What readers will find instead is a variety of ideas, suggesting that a multitude of possibilities still exists for teaching writing effectively.

To assist readers in selection, I have divided the articles into six sections: sources for writing; prewriting; modes for writing; writing and reading; language, mechanics, and style; and revising, responding, and evaluating. The divisions are somewhat arbitrary, and some exercises might well have appeared under more than one heading, simply because the writers stress a sequential development of the activities. There is some grouping within each category; for example, a reader will find several articles with a common focus back to back. Otherwise, the pieces should reveal their purposes and levels of difficulty quite easily. The majority of the pieces have been written for use in high school or college classrooms; however, some of the authors come from junior high schools, and readers of *Exercise Exchange* have indicated that the majority of ideas can be adapted for different grade levels without difficulty. As further assistance to readers, each article is preceded by a brief headnote indicating its focus, and each author provides a short commentary to place the exercise in a classroom context. But the most common denominators found in this collection will be the interest in effective teaching, and the record of practical successes in the classroom.

Special thanks for the existence of *Exercise Exchange* go to Thomas Wilcox of the University of Connecticut, who founded the magazine 32 years ago to fulfill a need he found among colleagues. I am also grateful to Paul Eschholz and Alfred Rosa of the University of Vermont, who, when no longer able to carry on the editorial duties of the magazine, suggested that I assume those responsibilities. Without the support of Kenneth Harrell, Dean of the College of Humanistic Studies at Murray State University in Kentucky, and Delbert Wylder, former chair of the English Department at Murray State University, and more recently, Oral Ballam, Dean of the College of Education at Utah State University, the continued publication of the magazine would have been impossible. But most of all, I am indebted to the teachers around the world who continue to send me quality articles describing their classroom achievements and to the loyal band of subscribers who keep renewing. The magazine, *Exercise Exchange,* appears in the fall and spring of each academic year. Those wishing to submit manuscripts or to subscribe may write me at the address below.

Charles R. Duke, Editor
Exercise Exchange
Department of Secondary Education
Utah State University
Logan, UT 84322

I Sources for Writing

In essence, a writing course by itself has no content other than what becomes the source for written expression. If we can accept this idea, we then should feel comfortable seeking as many different sources as possible to provide our students with a variety of writing experiences. But in this search for sources, we sometimes can overlook valuable ones which are easily accessible. In this section, readers will find suggestions about where to look and what might be used: people and places in the community, pen pals, archives, magazine columns, newspapers, and even tarot cards.

For Writing Teachers Only! Suggestions for Student Writing Assignments

Anthony S. Magistrale

More often than we might like to admit, teachers run out of fresh ideas for writing assignments. That is when suggestions like the following may provide the catalyst for developing a new set of writing experiences for our students. Mr. Magistrale contributed this assignment from the University of Vermont, Burlington.

Author's Comment

I have never met an English professor who did not approach the teaching of writing with the noblest of intentions. On the other hand, composition is without a doubt the most difficult and frustrating course to teach in any English department. Moreover, I am not convinced that we are producing better undergraduate writers. To some extent the recent increase in emphasis on college writing and the accompanying deluge of books, manuals, and articles on the subject make the actual task of teaching it all the more arduous. Composition instructors are inundated with conflicting strategies on writing and rhetoric, and while I certainly do not mean to imply that all these pedagogies are inadequate, most tend to place a greater accent on the abstract and theoretical, at the expense of the practical. Nowhere is this influence more pronounced than in the construction of student writing assignments. I note a tendency on the part of many of my colleagues to compose exercises which reflect an over-absorption with sophisticated rhetorical strategy: as if their assignments are meant to be read and answered by other teachers of writing rather than eighteen-year-old freshmen.

I am not, however, advocating a return to antediluvian themes such as "How I Spent My Summer Vacation" or a series of unstructured "free" writing assignments—the latter emerging from the late Sixties and still popular among many composition teachers. Instead, I propose a series of writing exercises designed to avoid the constraints of complicated rhetoric while providing sufficient direction for young writers.

The assignments which follow accomplish four primary goals: 1) Convince writers that they have something to say. This is established by providing writing subjects or themes that are accessible and relaxed, rather than convoluted and obsessed with pedagogy. 2) Produce work that students actually enjoy writing. Perhaps the first obstacle faced by the instructor is the ability to convince students to make use of their imaginations, and in so doing, help them to establish confidence in their own writing abilities. This will not be accomplished if undergraduates are consistently asked to write about subjects which are uninteresting and/or tedious. 3) Demonstrate that good writing does not always have to sound dull or serious. 4) Help acquaint students with their own ability to use various personae. Each of these activities requires the writer to compose from a different voice and perspective, thereby enlarging the student's awareness of tone, style, and diction.

These assignments—whether used as in-class exercises or take-home— are valuable only insofar as they are followed by student/teacher discussion of the idea behind the essay as well as the images expressed in the actual writing. Furthermore, these exercises should be supplemented with traditional assignments: opinion papers and/or research projects, for example. But in an activity as difficult as the instruction of writing, where fresh methods of teaching should be actively pursued, I would like to suggest than any English professor is capable of incorporating some of these suggestions into the syllabus.

Assignment One: What Seems to Be the Problem Here?

For at least the past decade we have been hearing that "Johnny can't write." Robert L. Craig, an official of the American Society for Training and Development, goes so far as to insist that poor writing is a significant "factor in the whole drop in the growth of American productivity." In a brief and concise paragraph or two, speculate on what has gone wrong in the past, who is responsible for Johnny's state of functional illiteracy. Then, for the remainder of the paper, describe the uniqueness of your own situation and needs. What, for example, do you hope to learn from a course in writing? You have already had twelve years of formal education that included writing instruction. Why, then, do you feel the need to take a course basically designed to improve your skills in writing?

Assignment Two: The Goldilocks Legend Revisited

Let's assume that getting started is the most difficult part—how does one attempt to describe something in writing and what is descriptive prose anyway? There's your first question for late night pondering. It would not do to claim that description starts by contemplating your navel. That's a little too close to home. Besides, a roomful of student navels is an awesome sight—although not, of course, anything so awesome as a roomful of faculty navels.

Therefore, let us begin this course by running away from home—in a storybook sort of way. Everyone in this room, no doubt, is familiar with the cryptic story of Goldilocks and the three bears. So, in the interests of your education, why not re-examine that story, with its unyielding plot-to-the-finish, and freeze it at a given moment in time in order to provide that instant some kind of visible reality. (Notice how traditional fairytale books usually leave this job to the illustrator.)

An adult being told the story would doubtless want a full description of the emotional state of little Goldi when she pops awake in Baby Bear's bed and sees three inquisitive bruins standing at the foot. A little kid, on the other hand, would take a savoring interest in her supposed—and delicious—terror, but that sounds a little too exciting to describe and after all we've only just been introduced.

This should help: Pretend that you're telling the story to a child of five—the kind of tyke who, in the interest of realism and putting off bedtime darkness, demands *details:* who stops you dead just as our breathless heroine is about to walk through the door of the bear house. The little kid wants to know, in just so many words, what the interior looks like.

See how you can aid the poor narrator. Sketch out your description all the while remembering that the brat, like your English teacher, won't sit still for too long unless you make it interesting and imaginative. The better to compare results, let's agree on the scene: Goldilocks comes to the door of the Bear family abode and—STOP—enters the house . . .

Assignment Three: To Construct the Perfect Crime

> "I'd put up with her whining and bitching long enough. It was time to do something drastic, to take serious action. I'd tried the divorce routine; she wanted a ton of money and the Sony. She left me little choice, and what choice I had I was prepared to take: she had to die, this weekend. But how to accomplish the deed, and how to get away with it. . . ."

You have been eavesdropping on the very private thoughts of Mr. Bernard Pettibone, wealthy executive and disgruntled husband. His problem is identical to yours: in the next few days you are to construct a murder of your own without actually committing one.

While none of you have actually performed so foul a deed, it is possible to write as though you have. You have all read about murders in

literature—Shakespeare, Dostoevski, Hitchcock are fine, grisly examples—
watched them take place on television, read about them in newspapers and
magazines. Therefore, take your knowledge of murders and murdering,
combine it with a vivid imagination and some careful writing, and go
construct a creative prose murder. It might help to inform your reader
about the circumstances leading up to the event itself, but stress l'object
d'art: focus your major attention on the perpetration of the homicide.
Also, be forewarned that your teacher has an adverse reaction to excessive blood, gore, and guts—thus, strive to keep your murder as clean and
clever as possible. Remember too, the brilliant criminal lives on to take
other, more wonderful English courses. (Special Reading Assignment for
the Week: Bernard Pettibone, *Fifty Years at Attica: Where It All Went
Wrong,* Penal Colony Press, 1981.)

Assignment Four: The Edge of Nausea

> She: "Look, this is important to me, can I trust you?"
> He: "You tell me . . . am I worth your trust?"
> She: "I hope so, but if I tell you about it, will you still respect me?"
> He: "Is it really that important for you that I do?"

The above is a verbatim account of one of the more articulate con-
versations between two main characters on "The Edge of Night," a semi-
literate phenomenon offered every weekday afternoon for the stimulation
of bored housewives, retired senior citizens, giggly coeds, stay-home-sick
career folk, and perverted teachers of composition. As an exercise in
comprehending American culture, watch one of these serials (remember
that there are evening shows such as "Dallas" that also belong to the
genre) for several days—three at least, more if you can stand it—and note
the following in a critical analysis paper:

1) Who are the main characters? What is their social position in the
world (i.e., banker, doctor, candlestick maker)? Do the actors in your
program conform to certain stereotypes in the roles they play? To what
extent, if any, were you able to "identify" with the characters?

2) In terms of the occupations portrayed, are they a fair or unfair
representation? How are the sex roles managed? Do the men and women
play "traditional" roles? Why or why not?

3) While avoiding a boring plot summary, what are the major themes
of your program? Why are these themes stressed at the exclusion of
others?

4) Did your soap opera have any *intended* elements of humor in it? If
so, how did it come off? Laughter is usually avoided in traditional soap
operas. Why?

5) Consider the enormous popularity of the soap opera: Why do Americans take this sudsy world so seriously?

Assignment Five: Do Not Remove under Penalty of Law

Consider please the following words:

High Heels	Waxed Paper
Polyester	Wombat
Superman	Black Eyeliner
Twinkie	Avocado Green
Crisco	Centerfold
Tupperware Party	Inflatable Doll

These words have absolutely nothing in common, really, except that we share an understanding of what most of them mean today. They have cultural significance which we, as members of our "culture," understand, albeit they may give pause to a visitor from Peking or Mars. The idea of this writing assignment is to choose just ONE item from the list above and write a short essay to explain its cultural significance.

You might begin by spending a few moments thinking about what each one of these words has come to represent for you on a personal level. But eventually provide the reader with necessary background information: some related words and contexts and phenomena. How, for example, would you explain waxed paper to a rural Chinese peasant, high heels to a Bushman from Africa?

Crucial Points of Consideration: 1) Some readers know more than others. Be careful to explain your cultural selection as vividly as possible, using examples and illustrations. The basic identity of a Tupperware party is there, but the attentive writer seeks to remind readers of the possible relationship between plastic objects and the individuals who attend these parties in order to fondle them. And then there will be the writer who remembers hearing frightening tales of Tupperware parties suddenly going berserk.

2) Be attentive to your reader. Think of yourself as a cultural guide, about to provide a pleasant and good-natured explanation of some of America's most prized and cherished institutions. Avoid, then, like the plague, neuralgic complaints, easy sarcasm, apathetic dismissals.

3) Do not feel, on the other hand, that you have to approve of the thing/person being described. Your job is not to banish from the earth any of these words. Instead, describe one by accounting for its signifi-

cance. Your perceptions will certainly involve making judgments, but do so only through discriminating intellectual observation, not mere stubborn preference.

4) Context, context, context. What is the exact language you want to provide the readers to help them see and comprehend their way out of their cultural vacuum? Remember too that nothing in this world exists in isolation; even black eyeliner has a proper place of its own, uses and abuses, creates emphasis and misunderstandings, and occasionally clarifies and defines.

Assignment Six: A Visit to the Art Museum

This assignment calls for a visit to your local art museum. In order to allow time for a relaxed and appreciative journey, we will not have class the day before this assignment is due. You can choose to visit the gallery at this time or go anytime between now and the due date.

During the time spent at the museum, keep in mind the following quotation from *Art and Visual Perception:*

> If art could do nothing better than reproduce the things of nature, either directly or by analogy, or to delight the senses, there would be little justification for the honorable place reserved for it in every known society. Art's reputation must be due to the fact that it helps man to understand the world and himself, and presents to his eyes what he has understood and believes to be true.

What, if anything, about the art exhibited in the museum helps you to understand the world and yourself? What are your own reasons for visiting the museum? Use, if you wish to do so, the above quotation and questions to write a paper about the art museum. The subject of your essay is entirely up to you: it may be a theoretical response to the quotation, a particular painting, or some other work of art which particularly intrigued you. On the other hand, perhaps the exhibited art interests you less than some other aspect of the museum—the architecture, the decor, the other visitors, the gallery guards, etc. Feel free to select a topic and an approach that will enable you to give written form to some part of your experience at the museum.

Assignment Seven: They Tried to Tell Us We Had Acne

It is often said that in heaven everyone will get to be Ann Landers at least for an afternoon. But just in case some of you don't want to wait, here's your chance. Below you will find a letter written to Ms. Thelma Gooch, the Ann Landers of Buffalo, New York, and the great upstate New York region. Give this letter your best advice and consideration and write an answer suitable for publication in an advice-column:

> Dear Thelma Gooch,
>
> I am sixteen years of age and very mature in my outlook on life. I have been going steady with my childhood sweetheart since we were both in the same eighth grade composition class. Now Gwendoline and I want to get married. We love each other with an intensity that would amaze you. We have saved ourselves all these years and are willing to make any sacrifice to become man and wife. I am willing to quit school and do any kind of work to support us in matrimony but my parents and Gwendoline's too refuse to give their consent. What, then, should we do? Should we elope and consummate our vows in a cheap hotel? That seems old-fashioned, but so does waiting to become of legal age. We are confused and would greatly appreciate any advice you can give us on solving this problem that is leaving us . . .
>
> (signed) Hot, Bothered, and Impatient

Please remember that the advice columnist is privileged to tell the whole truth, but must do it courteously, even if curtly.

Who Shall Survive?

Margaret Baker

Sam L. Graham

Values clarification exercises have been used for a variety of purposes in classrooms. The authors suggest that they are excellent sources for writing activities. Ms. Baker and Mr. Graham submitted this exercise from Chapel Hill, North Carolina.

Authors' Comment

Values clarification exercises as developed for use in group training can be effectively adapted for a composition course. This fall-out shelter exercise is a very free adaptation of a problem in *Values Clarification* by Sidney B. Simon et al. (New York: Hart, 1972, pp. 281–286). It is particularly well suited as an introduction to persuasive writing, but by changing the situation or the steps involved, this exercise can be varied to meet other composition needs. For example, it can be used to teach classification or comparison/contrast. However it is used, the instructor will seldom find students to be so enthusiastic about class.

The Approach

The instructor begins by dividing the students into groups with four to six students in each group. Then the instructor gives each student a sheet with the following information:

> Your group is part of the War Department. World War III has broken out, and eight people have sought safety in a small fall-out shelter. Then they discover that the shelter has supplies for only four people for three months—the estimated time they will need to stay there. Thus, four people must leave the shelter and face almost certain death. Rather than fighting among themselves, they have radioed the War Department for help, and the matter has been

9

referred to your group. You will decide who will stay and who will leave. Remember, very few people will survive the holocaust, so the four survivors will be an essential part of any new civilization. Discuss the matter among the members of your group and reach a consensus decision. You have fifteen minutes.

This is all you know about the people:

1. an accountant, 25
2. his 22-year-old wife, who is six-months pregnant
3. a U.S. Senator, 68
4. a high school football coach, 36
5. an unemployed waitress, 30
6. a Protestant minister, 50
7. a female college student majoring in psychology
8. a third-year medical student

When fifteen minutes have passed, a member of each group will put the findings on the board. A brief discussion about the results will emphasize that certain issues can be effectively argued in more than one way. After the groups break up, the instructor will hand out another paper which reads as follows:

More information on the people has just come in; this may lead you to revise your group's findings. The final decision now rests with you alone. At the end of the class period, turn in a report for your supervisor in the War Department which explains your decision and your reasons for it.

Here is the additional information:

1. The accountant has a brilliant mind, but he does not work well with others.
2. His wife has had two miscarriages, but they were in the first trimester of her pregnancy.
3. The Senator is an expert on foreign relations. He is in fair health and the father of five children.
4. The coach is in excellent physical condition. Although single, he loves children.
5. The waitress has no high school diploma and almost no job skills. She and her eleven-year-old son are currently on welfare.
6. The minister's wife died last year and he has no children. He is the author of several famous religious books and is widely respected all over the world.
7. The female student has self-destructive tendencies and has used drugs heavily. However, she has been "dry" for six months and is in therapy.
8. The medical student is actively involved in a local Nazi organization. He has an excellent understanding of medicine.

Summation

During the next class period, the instructor may want to read aloud some of the better reports. He or she certainly should follow up the lesson plan with a brief discussion. When this exercise is used as an introduction to persuasive writing, the instructor should ask the students what they have learned about argument. They should have learned that the more information a person has, the better the choices he or she can make; that many issues can be solved in more than one way; and that a writer must defend opinions with sound, rational thought. These points can be pursued further by discussing specific issues faced in this problem. For example, what is more important—that the waitress has few skills to give a new civilization or that she can bear children? Is the Senator too old to begin life anew or will his expertise in foreign relations be needed to work with surviving leaders from other countries? By getting students to think critically about these issues, this lesson plan becomes an excellent springboard for teaching persuasive writing.

Save a Marriage in Your Classroom

Albert C. Yoder

Magazines and newspapers carry various columns which can become
sources for student writing assignments. This exercise provides suggestions for how a particular type of column can be used to generate
a variety of writing possibilities. Mr. Yoder sent this from Southside
Virginia Community College, Keysville, Virginia.

Author's Comment

Students must often be provoked to write or discuss. And if your students are unable to discover interesting topics themselves, you may have
to provide topics or situations sufficiently provocative to motivate them.
A subject most students find interesting is marriage, yet as a specific
topic, it is too broad. But even narrowing the subject to something like
"The Qualities of an Ideal Mate" or "The Financial Problems of Early
Marriage" may fail to engage the enthusiasm of your students. I would
like to suggest that you use the column "Can This Marriage Be Saved?"
which has appeared every month for years in *Ladies' Home Journal*.

Activity

The format for this column is simple. After a general introduction to a
particular couple's problem, one member of the couple is interviewed and
then the other. Finally, the couple's counsellor expresses his or her views
and explains what eventually happened in the marriage. The subject and
format are provocative for several reasons. First, there is a specific "real-
life" problem presented. Since many students will shortly be married
themselves, they find marital problems potentially relevant and probably
more compelling than the general material found in many marriage
manuals. Second, two points of view are expressed and there is often a
fair degree of right on each side. In other words, the issues involved are
not so black and white that it is obvious who is right and who is wrong.
It is this feature which makes the case histories controversial and debat-

able. Some students will side with one party, others with the second; some will offer one solution, others another. The ambiguity of the problems is also close to what prevails around them, and students relate to this sort of realism as well. Because both the subject and the format are provocative, students are easily motivated to write or discuss the cases. There is enough material in each column to support well-developed essays or discussions. The format also forces students to consider both sides of the problem, something they often fail to do when left to their own devices.

There are several types of assignments which could come from these columns. Since there is a good deal of dialogue quoted, students can role-play the husband and wife, and having introduced the class to the problem in this way, you can ask the class to discuss or analyze it in writing. They could also write "mock" letters of advice to the couple, attempting to reconcile them. In addition, the men in the class might assume the role of the husband and the women, the wife (or *vice versa*). They could then write back and forth among themselves in an attempt to resolve the problem. Finally, since the column provides detail, incidents, physical description, and certainly conflict, there are all the elements for a short story or drama.

I have mentioned the column "Can This Marriage Be Saved?" only because it is ideal and easily available to teachers and students; however, there are a number of books on marriage, divorce, marriage counselling, and the like, that also contain usable case histories. After you and your class have read a sufficient number of histories, you might even want to create some fictitious ones of your own.

The activities described can also be related to the *content* of English courses. With the advent of the women's movement, many rhetoric readers now contain essays on feminism, marriage and its alternatives, and male and female roles. And, certainly, much literature concerns male and female relationships.

Composition and Newspapers: Information, Illustration, Stimulation, Evaluation

Marjorie Kaiser

Within a newspaper lies a multitude of sources for writing. Marjorie Kaiser of the University of Louisville, Kentucky, suggests how these sources might be used effectively.

Author's Comment

It has become more and more common in the last several years to find newspapers visible in secondary language arts classrooms. Teachers have discovered what an inexpensive and replaceable source of reading material the newspaper is and have realized the immediacy of appeal a newspaper has for reluctant readers. But in addition to its usefulness in the reading program, the newspaper can also serve teachers in other aspects of language arts—especially in the composition program.

In order to use the newspapers in the teaching of composition, every student need not have a copy, nor is it essential to have fresh copies each day. The only important thing is that we have available several papers, not all the same necessarily, perhaps one very good daily and two or three weekly or small local papers, even school newspapers, and that we have new issues occasionally. Once we have the newspapers in the classroom, we can begin to use them for four different functions in the teaching of composition: information, illustration, stimulation, and evaluation.

Information

The newspaper is a rich and timely source of information, particularly during the prewriting phase of work in composition. Simply locating information in the newspaper on the price of gold, on how to build a picnic table, on the pros and cons of taking large doses of Vitamin C, on election results, on a popular recording artist, on plans for next season's network television, on films and books, or on deaths, births, and marriages in a community may be the first step in finding something to say and developing a point of view. Such information in the newspaper can provide a focus for simple report-writing, for precise writing, for comparison/contrast papers, for process papers, and other types of expository writing. Perhaps the most elaborate scheme for using newspapers for writing based on information is illustrated in the publication *Murder, Mischief, and Mayhem* (Kraus, NCTE, 1978). In this book, the author presents ten "creative research papers" and a guide for helping students complete original research work almost entirely through the use of newspapers.

Illustration

As a source of illustrations of our written language, the newspaper cannot be beaten. Here teachers and students can find any composition concept or technique desired. We can locate examples of effective objective writing in the reporting of news, effective persuasive writing in editorials and so on. We can illustrate effective methods of organization, paragraphing, and support.

In helping students grasp the meaning of style—that hard-to-define quality of writing, we can pull a variety of styles from columns, editorials, features, and even the news for examination. What are the stylistic differences, for example, between a Kilpatrick piece and one by Ellen Goodman or between one local feature story and another? Through comparisons of diction, use of anecdotes, degrees of abstractness, use of figurative language, sentence length, point of view, and many other elements, students could begin to see what makes one style different from another and—perhaps more important—see that decisions about style derive from purpose and audience.

More effective in helping students learn that they can control their own style to suit their purpose and audience are exercises in which they manipulate a familiar story such as a nursery rhyme or fairy tale in a variety of styles. For example, students could be asked to read the following nursery rhyme:

> The Queen of Hearts,
> She made some tarts,
> All on a summer's day.
> The Knave of Hearts,
> He stole the tarts
> And took them clean away.
> The King of Hearts,
> Called for the tarts,
> And beat the Knave full sore.

The Knave of Hearts,
Brought back the tarts,
And vowed he'd steal no more.

Then they could rewrite the rhyme in prose, first as a brief news story using the five W's, then as a feature story emphasizing the psychological background of the Knave, then as an editorial opposing young adult crime or child abuse, then as a personal letter from the Knave to Abby, explaining his side of the story, then Abby's answer, and so on.

In addition to focusing on style, we can use the newspaper to illustrate many other techniques or aspects of composition. Suppose we are trying to help students develop more variety of diction. Some students tend to rely on the same verbs over and over again and often not the most colorful verbs at that. One section of the newspaper, and one often read by adolescents, consistently presents us with a wide range of alternate verb choices for basic action verbs—the sports section. The actions of *win* and *lose* are expressed in a multitude of ways on each sports page. From one sports section alone, students discovered *rips, thwarts, chops down, wrecks, tromps, tops, flies high,* and *zips.* But we needn't turn only to the sports section to find this concept in action. Students could take a simple verb like *says* or *tells* and look through all sections of the paper to come up with a long list of alternatives, each with its own subtle variation of meaning. In one issue of a newspaper, students found *denies, discloses, contends, urges, claims, defends, proposes, states, admits, assures, suggests, warned, emphasize,* and others, and all in headlines only. Creating the list of alternatives and discussing the concept and the individual variations could lead students to a more conscious awareness of the richness of their language and how it can help them toward more precision and color in their composition.

Likewise, students can search for and find illustrations of various forms of figurative language, puns, allusions, and, of course, symbolism, especially in cartoons. Many excellent newspapers are regularly filled with plays on words, punning, and other clever uses of the language, in headlines, in captions, and within stories. And in most papers we can generally find inappropriate uses of language as well as appropriate ones. If we're working on clarity, for example, we can almost daily find an ambiguous headline or caption. Students delight in finding such illustrations: "Grandmother of Eight Makes Hole in One"; "Dealers Hear Car Talk Friday"; "Many Antiques at DAR Meeting"; and, "Normal Girl Weds Oblong Boy."

One final basic concept that newspapers illustrate is that because of usage, our language changes from place to place and time to time. As language changes, newspapers and magazines are the first printed documents to reflect the changes. If we want students to be aware of this concept, of the ways in which we take new words into our language and the word-making potential of the current language, the newspaper, along with television and magazines, provides excellent examples of these processes.

Stimulation

This third function is perhaps the most exciting; the newspaper provides students with many types of items which can serve as stimulation for writing. According to an NCTE statement on standards for writing programs, one characteristic of an effective program is that students have practice and develop skill in many more than one form of discourse (the expository or persuasive essay). Using various sections of the paper, students can respond by writing poetry, drama, short stories, anecdotes, reviews, interviews, letters of all kinds, character sketches, technical reports, descriptions, journal entries, and so on.

Photographs in newspapers can serve as excellent stimulation for a number of different kinds of writing. After removing the caption from an interesting photograph, a teacher can display the photo on an opaque projector and ask students to create the story behind the picture, as a short story or just a very short narrative or anecdote. They could write a letter to a person in a photo requesting more information about the pictured situation. Depending on how self-explanatory a photo is, students could use it for value clarification in a journal entry and perhaps, too, as a topic for a letter to the editor. They could role-play an interview with a person in the photo and then write up the interview. Photos of rural or urban scenes, both black and white and color shots from Sunday magazine sections, can easily serve as stimulation for writing poetry or for writing descriptive passages for tourist brochures or setting descriptions for short narratives or plays. Concepts crucial to the composition process such as the importance of audience and purpose can be learned through the variety of writing exercises possible through the use of photography in newspapers.

Brief news items, columns, features, classified ads, and comic strips and cartoons can also stimulate a range of writing activities. News items can be used as the basis of stories, poems, or satires. Features and regular opinion columns or such columns as Dear Abby or those of medical doctors or bridge experts can evoke letters, reports, journal entries, character sketches, and so on. Even filler items can stimulate additional research and written reports, while cartoons and comics can provide the context for the writing of dialogues, drama, stories, and anecdotes. Classified ads can serve to stimulate the writing of letters of all kinds as well as the creation of poetry, stories, and plays.

In any edition of a major newspaper, a teacher can collect literally hundreds of items appropriate for student response through writing. We and our students have only to start looking; once we are aware of the potential of the newspaper, it is difficult not to be carried away. And this resource, like any other, can be over-used.

Evaluation

The fourth function a newspaper can serve is evaluation. Many composition teachers agree that one of the most difficult aspects of the composing process for students at all levels is the self-evaluation phase. One thing we can be sure of is that we do not learn to evaluate our own work or anyone else's without experience in evaluating. More and more in classrooms everywhere students are trying to respond to and evaluate each other's writing. While this practice may help improve self-evaluation skills, I am convinced that students rarely feel comfortable in evaluating honestly the work of their friends and classmates.

Students seem to view material that appears in newspapers with a very different attitude. Because the newspaper is so daily replaceable, because it is printed on the cheapest possible paper, because the names of newspaper writers, with some exceptions, are either unlisted or unfamiliar, because we cut the newspaper up to make collages and posters and crumple it up to stuff our packages for mailing, and because we wrap our garbage in it, it does not embarrass or intimidate students as evaluating a friend's writing may. Opportunities abound for evaluating the writing found in newspapers. From a simple judgment of the accuracy of a small news item to a more substantial analysis of a significant feature, advertising campaign, or editorial stance on local issues, students can gain experience in developing the skills essential to self-evaluation.

Certainly a prime advantage in using the newspaper for all these functions is that working with this particular medium adds a dimension of reality to the writing experiences we have our students engage in, not to be found through most texts or films. The more real life we can bring into the classroom the less hard all of us will have to struggle to close that gap between the writing our students do and the life beyond the classroom.

Using the Tarot in Composition Classes

Donald C. Samson

Using a deck of cards as a source for writing may not seem feasible, but this exercise outlines a successful method for incorporating a tarot deck into the writing class. Mr. Samson contributed from Meredith College, Raleigh, North Carolina.

Author's Comment

One of the most difficult tasks facing both the beginning and the more advanced writer is developing the ability to know when he or she has been sufficiently specific in a piece of writing, especially in description. And how do we know if we have communicated fully our information? Too often there is a tendency to assume that if the description seems clear and thorough to us, it is so to our readers. Various exercises have been devised to remedy this problem; nearly every rhetoric text has at least one or two. But I would like to suggest a new one, which confronts the problem of clarity and thoroughness in descriptions and at the same time has an added benefit: it helps the students develop their ability to interpret symbols, and see the connection between symbols and their context. The exercise involves the use of a tarot deck in composition classes, in a series of steps which students find interesting and which teachers have found easy to conduct, even without any knowledge of the tarot.

The tarot deck, used in fortune-telling since at least the Middle Ages, consists of 78 cards, divided into the Major Arcana (22 cards, presenting abstractions such as "Death" and allegorical figures or objects such as "The Magician" and "The Tower") and the Minor Arcana (56 cards, 14 each in the suits Cups, Wands, Swords, and Pentacles). A number of tarot decks have been designed, but by far the best is that designed and executed in color by Arthur Waite and Pamela Coleman Smith, published by University Books, New Hyde Park, New York. Paperbacks on the tarot, and Waite's *A Pictorial Key to the Tarot,* can provide instructions for using the cards in fortune-telling, but I have found it best to avoid this use of the cards in classroom situations.

The Tarot Exercise

The tarot exercise[1] consists of a number of steps, outlined below. One of the assets of the exercise is its flexibility; one need not do all the steps, nor need one follow the sequence presented here. But whatever steps and sequences are used, the objectives of the exercise need to be kept in mind:

1. To lead students to recognize the need for clarity and thoroughness in writing descriptions.
2. To provide students with practice in achieving clarity and thoroughness in descriptions.
3. To provide students with practice in interpreting symbols.

The "practice" referred to in Objectives 2 and 3 involves writing descriptions and interpretations which are commented on by other students in the class, and eventually by the instructor, in conference or in suggestions written on the papers. With these goals in mind, then, here are the steps:

Phase One

1. Decide whether to devote one class period or parts of two (or more) class periods to the exercise.
2. Decide how clearly you want to state the objectives to the students. Teachers who have used the exercise tell me that it works best when the objectives are not specifically stated by the instructor; the students come to recognize by themselves the necessity for clarity and thoroughness in description, and they are not intimidated by the word "symbol."
3. Give each student a card, or let each select one from a face-down pile.
4. Ask the students to each write a description of their card, pretending that an artist will have to reproduce it exactly from the description. Ask them to omit from the description any name or number appearing on the card, as this would make a later step in the exercise (9) too easy for the second student working with the card. (This step takes longer for some students than others, and some cards are fuller than others. When some students finish the description, I announce Step 5.)
5. Ask the students to write, on a separate sheet of paper, a two or three sentence interpretation of the card, stating what the card as a whole means to them. (Many students will finish this first phase of the exercise before others; consequently, I begin the exercise with

about 30 minutes left in the class period. Those who finish early I allow to leave early. A time limitation would defeat, for slower workers, the purposes of this exercise.)

6. Collect the cards, descriptions, and interpretations for use in the next class (or, if you choose to do the exercise in one period, in the remainder of the class period).

Phase Two

7. Distribute the descriptions to students other than the original writer. It is best if the first writer and the second, the "description-checker," are not near enough to each other to be able to discuss the card and/or description (this happens in Step 13).

8. Spread out all 78 cards, face up, on a desk in the front of the room.

9. Ask the students to read the description each has, and underline those parts of the description which they think are most important. When each is finished with the description, he or she is to leave the description at his or her desk, come up and pick out the card which was described. The test of the description, and of the second student's work with it in this step, is how easy it is for the second student to pick out the card from the full deck.

10. Ask the students to compare the card to the description, making any changes which they feel would make the description each has more thorough and accurate.

11. Ask each student to write, on a separate piece of paper, an interpretation of the card.

12. Hand out the first interpretations to their authors.

13. Ask the students to return the description, card, and their interpretation to the original author.

14. Allow some time for the students to examine the descriptions, especially the suggested changes, and to compare the interpretations.

5. Ask if there are questions about the interpretations. There always are. Some instructors show the class the card in question by means of an overhead projector, ask them to consider its significance, and then read the interpretations and request others. Common elements in the interpretations appear quickly, and most of the weaker interpretations are recognized by their writers as too literal (this is the most common weakness). The instructor is usually

asked to interpret some cards, and this is easily done by anyone trained in literature.

16. From here, the class is easily led into a discussion of the necessity for clarity and thoroughness in description, and into an examination of particular symbols and of particular associations which certain colors, figures, etc. give rise to. Here the instructor might discuss particular cards, or refer to works the students have recently read, in pointing out the universality and prevalence of symbols.

In subsequent writing assignments, the students could build on this exercise with paragraphs of careful description, or, in a course with an emphasis on literature, they might be asked to read and interpret a particularly symbolic work, such as Poe's "The Fall of the House of Usher" or the Grass section of Whitman's "Song of Myself."

Students at the high school, junior college, and college and university levels have enjoyed this exercise, and profited from it. Some instructors doubt their ability to work with the cards, remembering that even Madame Sosostris, the "famous clairvoyant," couldn't find "The Hanged Man." But I believe it is clear from what I have said here that knowledge of the tarot is not necessary. All that is needed to make the exercise a success is an English major's familiarity with symbols, a deck of tarot cards, a group of students, and a desire to provide instruction which is both profitable and pleasurable.

Note

1. A parallel exercise by T. J. Ray, based on purely geometrical figures, can be found in *Exercise Exchange,* 17 (Fall 1972), 19–21.

Pen Pal Writing

Collett B. Dilworth

We often assume that pen pal writing has to involve correspondence between people separated by considerable distance. This assignment suggests, however, that pen pal writing can be used successfully within a single classroom to foster self-awareness and a sense of audience. Ms. Dilworth submitted this while at the Fayetteville City Schools in North Carolina.

Author's Comment

A primary objective of our language arts program is that "Students should be increasingly willing and able to make use of writing as a means of realizing, ordering, and communicating their perceptions of themselves and of life at large." To this end we have worked to devise classroom situations that foster writing as an act of personal significance. One useful assumption in this undertaking, which seems validated by our experience, is that students have things that they need to say to each other. Other assumptions are that writing, while it limits communication in many respects, is a medium providing unique opportunities to realize and to communicate, and that students can perceive this if given the chance to apply the medium to their most pressing concerns.

Pen Pal Activity

One activity that has been a success in our efforts to exploit these assumptions and to further our objective is "pen pal" writing. This activity is based on the type of writing in which two strangers, taking advantage of specific prearrangements, correspond to find out about each other and to share and explore experiences and ideas. To begin, each student in all of a teacher's classes is assigned a "secret number," and each student submits a description of preferences concerning the type of person with whom he or she would like to correspond. Letters of introduction are then composed, and the teacher matches pairs of correspondents on the basis of student preferences and the teacher's judgment. Many students are afforded several introductory letters to choose from, but no student is permitted to correspond with a member of the class. Anonymity, it seems, is the essential ingredient, and students are instructed never to identify themselves or to inquire after their correspondent's identity. Inevitably, of course, a few students do find out to whom they are writing, and as their interest flags, they are urged to find new pen pals. Correspondents may ask for new partners if both consent, and students do ask to write to more than one correspondent. So far there has been no problem in finding and maintaining partners.

In any case, students write and "mail" at least one letter a week (more if they wish). Mailing is accomplished by putting a letter in a special folder and returning the folder to a box on the teacher's desk. There is a pocket in each side of this folder, one for each of the two correspondents, and so all the letters for each pair of pen pals are kept in a single folder labeled with their secret numbers. Frequently they choose to substitute fictional names for their numbers. Whenever there is time the students may obtain their correspondence from the teacher, and about thirty minutes each week is reserved specially for reading and writing letters.

The teacher's role is that of mail supervisor, privileged observer, and diagnostician. Naturally the letters are not graded, but the teacher does read them with an eye to discovering the strengths and weaknesses of the students' writing. Over a semester the collection of letters for each student provides an invaluable record of the effect or lack of effect of instruction in usage. Furthermore, the letters are very revealing about students' concerns, and they make fascinating reading. Below are given genuinely typical exchanges of correspondence to illustrate the development of a relationship from the introductory letters to a later exchange.

10/9/73
No. 31

O, Yeh,
    What's happening? This first letter is gonna stink, but I'll try to make it worth both of our time.
    My fictitious name is "Dimples." I am 15 years old. I am a Capricorn, January 14, 1958. In a way this is a good idea, but I feel stupid. I hope we have some things in common. As far as sports goes, I like football & basketball. I enjoy just being my natural black self. No offense if you're the opposite race. I get along with everybody. I take myself as being a very mature sophomore. That silly, silly shot should get off.
    Being a girl, I enjoy being around different kinds of dudes. Most I've met are okay, for starts. Dig, friends it's hard to write to some-

one you don't even know, but I hope you enjoy this as much as possible. I hope this turns out to be more of what it is.

Are you going with anyone to the homecoming? I hope someone asks me. Well, the bell's almost ready to sound off. So, I plant you now and dig you lata. Write soon.

"Dimples"
76

P.S. Hope it wasn't boring. If so, I'm sorry.

10/9/73
No. 23

Hi

This isn't how I usually start a letter but once we get to know each other, we will get down to the normal thing.

I guess I am just about an average guy who likes to go play sports and lots of games like chess. I like to go out places and as soon as I turn 16 and get my license I'm gonna be driving my "some what" own car.

Well, I have to go but I would like to know you a lot more than I do now.

Yours truly,
"J. T."

11/20/73
No. 23

Dear Dimples,

I'm glad to hear that blues has left us and I hope it stays where it is.

It's too bad about Ross-Sanford game but those boys came down here for nothing but victory, and they were more "fired up" than Ross has ever been in all our games put together, no joke!

Me and poetry are like hat and coat and I have written plenty of poems, though when my brother and sister read them they just laugh. I think that your poem is beautiful and really together.

The finalists were "bad" and I could have done a better job than what they did even though I think the winner looked alright.

I try and find the book I read it out of and show you or tell you about Areatha, but she has been on it for a long time, try 3 months. I'm short on time so hang loose.

Yours with love,
"J. T."

P.S. I like that last line of that poem the best. You have a very special talent and that's what makes you special to me.

11/26/73
No. 31

Dear J. T.

Thanks for letting me be special to you. I liked your P.S. better than the whole letter. So much for that! Tell me what special talent do I possess?

Right on Sanford was fired up and I think we were scared. Most of the guys still want to play Friday. I was at a party and some of the guys on the team were saying, "We're supposed to be playing now. I felt so bad and sorry for them. I hope we do better in basketball. Do you think the girls are gonna do it? This is the first year Ross has had a girls team. Hope we start off good. I also hope J.V. does well, cause I don't want to cheer for a shrink team. (Dig?)

Hey, since your poetry is so together, write me a few lines to express your feelings these days. Thank you for the compliment on mine. You know you can rap off some beautiful words. I just wish I could meet you.

Next year I'm gonna run for Miss RHS. I didn't have the "dinero" for it this year. Plus a sophomore doesn't have much chance. Maybe your sister's and brother's minds are not mature enough to dig on what you are saying in your poems. Maybe they're too heavy for them. A together person like you can't help but write some together lines.

How was your holiday? I jammed all weekend. Now I can't stop. Hope yours was together too. J. T., do you know whose initials you are using? Or, are these your initials? These initials just drive me crazy, because I used to dig on a dude with the same initials, but he's a senior now. Stay Black and Beautiful and write Dimples.

Affectionately, "Dimples"

If we look beyond the nonstandard usages and the shortcomings in writing conventions in these letters, we can see that this activity has significantly nurtured the development of these two students in the language arts. Their first letters indicate a rather pronounced urge to communicate, and the rewards of their subsequent communications are manifest in the later letters. Specifically, they have established a genuine dialogue based on mutual concern, respect, and affection. Also J. T. and Dimples have become appreciative and supportive readers of each other's poetry, and if he gets around to it, J. T. is liable to turn Dimples on to a book. Indeed, the activity seems ultimately justified by the fact that writing has become an important and effective part of these students' lives.

Writing for a Real Audience

Shirley Nelson

Finding an audience and writing for it successfully are experiences we would like all student writers to have. Shirley Nelson of South Royalton High School, Vermont, suggests using a source to which almost every high school has ready access—the local elementary school—as a means for developing audience awareness and reinforcing the entire composing process.

Author's Comment

I have used the following exercises to help writing students develop a stronger sense of audience. The sequence of activities is divided into three phases—prewriting, drafting, and rewriting—and a fourth phase of publishing activities is added. During the prewriting activities I make appointments for the writers to read their drafts to the children in grades K to 3, the age of the audience for whom they are writing. The writers then use the feedback from the readings to make their final revisions. At least eight class periods are needed, and there are also homework assignments.

Prewriting

First class period. Whole class activity—analyze "Smashed Potatoes: A Kid's Eye View of the Kitchen," by Jane G. Martel. In these children's writings, find and discuss examples of repetition, simile, kinds of details, rhyme, author's attitude and interests—such as personalizing things and events, and faith in parents. Analyze one of Aesop's Fables in the same way, using school library books.
First homework assignment: Rewrite one of Aesop's Fables.
Changes to make:

Change setting to a definite time and place.

Change animal characters to human characters.

Create a conflict appropriate to characters and setting.

Add details, dialogue, suspense.

Second class period. Small group to whole group activity—in groups of three, analyze rewritten fables for the above list of changes. Each group chooses one fable to share with the whole class. Successes are noted by students and teacher.

Drafting

Second assignment: Plan a story for children between the ages of five and eight.
Guidelines:

Topic—should interest children in grades K–3, as noted in prewriting activities.

Setting—either ordinary, or magical, or a combination.

Characters—not more than three or four, either animal, or human, or both.

Plot—simple and repetitious.

Magic—animals and plants can talk.

Moral—intrinsic to the story, not at the end.

Style—short sentences, simple and colorful words, dialogue.

Third class period. Editing workshop. Each student edits three peer stories. Prepare in advance edit slips that list the guidelines, as well as a checklist of mechanical skills, for the student editors.

Rewriting

Fourth class period. Stories are returned to writers with the edit slips of peers and teacher attached. Rewriting begins in class.
Fourth homework assignment: Redraft the stories and add pictures. Writers can either draw their own pictures or ask someone else to read the story and illustrate it.
Fifth class period. Appointments have been made in advance for the writers to read their redrafts to children in grades K–3. Two writers go to each classroom. The host teachers help their children offer suggestions about story and pictures. Writers have been prepared to ask questions about what the children liked, disliked, and understood about both stories and pictures.

Fifth homework assignment: Make a final, typed draft of the story. Try to use suggestions made by the children. Illustrations should be added to the manuscript as it is typed.

Publishing

Sixth class period. Typed manuscripts with the illustrations inserted are shared with the writing class and then submitted to the teacher for evaluation. Last changes/corrections are made.
Sixth homework assignment: Student volunteers photocopy all of the stories. This takes several days.
Seventh class period. Students collect the stories into booklets and bind them in file folders with large paper fasteners. An autographed copy of the booklet is presented to each class by the writers who visited earlier. Members of the writing class are given booklets for their own use, and autographed copies are given to the school library and to members of the school administration.

Feedback and reactions to the booklets are posted in the writing classroom. On one occasion, the students were invited to an elementary school in a neighboring town. There they were the guest-authors for an "I Love to Read Day" celebration.

Utilizing Local Resources in Teaching the Importance of Writing Skills

David Hadley

Often resources outside the writing classroom go unused simply because we fail to recognize their availability. David Hadley of the University of Texas at Austin suggests using personnel from an employment office as a catalyst to promote writing for the real world outside the classroom.

Author's Comment

We hear a great deal about the importance of making writing assignments "real," but we are rarely provided with workable examples. My freshmen composition students suggested a pedagogically powerful assignment, one based on the use of a readily available community resource. The assignment uses students' practical desire to find jobs to teach an important lesson in the power, practicality, and everyday relevance of writing skills. While leading students to understand the importance of the conventions of writing, it simultaneously motivates them to achieve results, not mere completion, from their writing. The task itself is commonplace. Students are asked to write a resumé and a letter of application. It is the approach that I believe important.

The Approach

The secret ingredient in this lesson is the local employment director, a resource available in nearly every community and on most college campuses. I invited our campus director to talk to my classes about writing resumés and letters of application. Upon arrival, he turned out to be a dynamic speaker, one who genuinely excited my students. He brought sample letters, resumés, and heuristic forms designed to help order the information required for writing resumés. He also included a discussion of interview skills. Because he recognized that students were likely to forget important high school and work experiences during their college years, he encouraged them to record and update such experiences on an on-going basis. When they graduated and faced an urgent need to get job applications out, needed information would be at hand.

The placement director provided students with some sound rhetorical advice while discussing tone in their letters of application. He also warned them that any errors in usage could frustrate their efforts to get jobs, thereby helping them come to understand that the conventions of writing are like conventions of speech—essential to master if one is trying to realize an intention through the act of communicating. Furthermore, by insisting that employers are too busy to look at resumés more than a page long, the director encouraged students to work for precise thought and concise expression.

The Follow-up Assignment

Students were asked to write a resumé that was complete, factual, error-free, and no longer than the one page recommended by the placement director. They were also asked to write a letter of application. I told them that the letter could be written to a potential summer employer, someone they hoped to work for after graduation, or to someone with the power to give them the job they harbored in fantasy. Those students who had suggested the assignment revealed their motivation by working diligently to finish polishing their letters and resumés in time to take them home over spring break. It is then that the scramble for summer jobs becomes more intense.

Discussion

This simple assignment teaches many lessons. It is easy to forget that too many of our assignments ask students to practice technique, but ignore their need to recognize and fulfill purpose through writing. When their writing has an actual purpose, both the conventions of usage and the concept of the rhetorical situation suddenly take on real significance.

At the heart of the lesson was the experience of achieving a real purpose through a piece of writing. Those who actually engaged the assignment, and most did, learned the difference between the merely adequate and the absolutely finished. Many students experimented with syntax to make already error-free sentences sound better. Even those students who did not have immediate plans for their resumés were sufficiently involved to want to present themselves as effectively as possible.

In fact, much of the motivation students demonstrated on this assignment may have resulted from the opportunity it presented to discuss and write about the subject they know best: themselves.

Results

The assignment helped students see the importance of those writing skills we normally ask them to practice in isolation from any self-sponsored purpose. It also provided them practice in listening and note-taking. Although I made no formal attempt to follow up on the pragmatic results of this assignment, three of my students did return in subsequent semesters and volunteered the information that their letters and resumés had helped them get summer jobs.

Writing and Career Development

Heidi Koring

By relating writing to the process of finding a job, Heidi Koring shows how students draw from their own backgrounds to create writing that may assist them in locating suitable jobs. Ms. Koring teaches at Lincoln Memorial University, Harrogate, Tennessee.

Author's Comment

Poor writing and speaking skills handicap today's job seekers. Yet composition courses seldom address job-hunting skills directly. Resumé writing, letters of application, and interview strategies are either taught by persons outside the English department or given cursory treatment, stressing format rather than content. As a result, many students are simply not aware of the importance of communication skills as career development tools. Students who are aware seldom make the connection between writing skills taught as career development and those taught as part of the English curriculum. They do not grasp the importance of the Freshman English class, so do not apply themselves to learning skills taught in one of the most important courses they may ever take.

It is possible for the instructor to integrate job-seeking skills within the Freshman English curriculum without sacrificing the teaching of writing and rhetoric. Teaching writing through job seeking using an approach based on Bernard Haldane's S.I.M.S. method heightens student motivation, improves student writing and job-seeking skills, and makes students confident, well-prepared entrants into today's increasingly competitive job market.

The System for Identifying Motivated Skills

Bernard Haldane, founder of Haldane Associates, a career counseling corporation, developed a self-analysis method called the System for Identifying Motivated Skills (S.I.M.S.), which is the cornerstone of the

Haldane program and the first phase of an English course focused on career development. S.I.M.S. is equally effective with persons at all career levels and works well with small classroom groups functioning as subgroups.

Haldane clients begin their self-analysis by isolating and writing about their greatest achievements: experiences when clients felt they accomplished something they enjoyed doing. Achievements need not be work or school related; their impact on others may have been minor. The important factor is the feeling of satisfaction and success that accompanied the experience. Clients then examine their achievements, trying to isolate skills that were important to those achievements. As all the achievements are analyzed, a pattern of motivated skills develops: skills a client is best at and truly enjoys performing. The resulting list of motivated skills forms the basis for an ideal job description and, ultimately, a resumé.

The Achievement Essay

This Haldane exercise is a wonderful Freshman English activity that can be the first step in teaching writing through job seeking. Once the rationale for the exercise as part of a career development process is explained, students enjoy writing essays about their greatest achievements and sharing them with subgroups of their peers, reading them aloud, or passing out dittoed copies. To facilitate discussion, the instructor may use check lists of motivated skills such as those in the books listed at the end of this article. Or students may develop their own list of categories under headings such as Communication Ability [writing, speaking, persuasion] and Personal Strengths [physical endurance, "stick-to-it-iveness," attention to detail]. During discussion, students are encouraged to break down skills to their lowest terms. "Sales ability," for instance, indicated by a successful student club car wash campaign, could indicate "persuasion," "record keeping," "interpersonal skills," and "management."

A group attempt to isolate motivated skills becomes a criticism of student writing. As students and the instructor ask, "What exactly did you do to make this happen?" they are asking for greater clarity and more supporting details within the essay. In many cases students will find it necessary to revise essays to make their achievements clearer. By doing this, they not only improve their written organization; they learn that the process of writing can be used as a technique to clarify one's thoughts and goals. The instructor should assign at least two achievement essays to by analyzed so that students may see a pattern of motivated skills emerge.

Classification Essays

When all the students have written and critiqued their achievements and, as a group process, have delineated lists of motivated skills, they use material from the achievement essays to write a theme called "My Greatest Strengths." This will be a reworking of the achievement essays in a classification mode. Students will write an introduction giving their strengths, then paragraphs devoted to each strength, supporting their assertions with examples from the achievement essays, so they will have the opportunity to rework material to fit a different format. This phase of the course culminates in writing an Ideal Job Description. The Ideal Job Description is an extension of the greatest strengths essay showing how these strengths have practical application. Such a paper would begin like this: "My ideal job would be as a salesman in a farm machinery store. In such a position I could use my abilities to speak persuasively, to explain things clearly, my knowledge of farming, and my understanding of machinery." These essays, as well, should be discussed in small groups: either the original groups or groups of students with similar motivated skills.

Research Essays

Testing the ideal job description against career opportunities forms the second phase of the course, calling for objective writing and some elementary research skills. Students should be introduced to career handbooks in the library like *The Dictionary of Occupational Titles* and *The Occupational Outlook Handbook,* both U.S. Government publications, and Craig T. Norback's *Careers Encyclopedia* [Homewood, Illinois: Dow Jones-Irwin, 1980]. These three volumes plus college-oriented magazines like *Black Collegian* and professional journals give descriptions of many career opportunities. Students enjoy clipping career-related articles from magazines and starting a career file for future researchers. Using these sources, students may explore career opportunities directly through mini-research papers, showing how the careers they are considering will allow them to exercise their motivated skills. They may also discover that a career they were interested in pursuing (for instance, computer programming) calls for skills they do not have (attention to detail).

If possible, students should be encouraged to interview professionals within the community and write a second research paper combining hard data concerning a given occupation gleaned from the above publications with personal insights obtained from the interview. Most professionals are happy to devote half an hour or so to interested students. Students can make contacts through personal sources—neighbors, classmates, community or church groups—or use the alumni or career development office for help. These research papers, like the achievement essays, can be discussed in small groups. Each class period may begin with ten minutes devoted to progress reports in which students tell whom they interviewed and what was learned. Progress reports may be solely oral or read from written essays.

Job-Finding Formats

After students have defined career goals and researched appropriate fields, they are ready to prepare resumés, letters of application, and practice interview techniques. Haldane recommends a functional resumé, one based on motivated skills, rather than a chronological one. Functional resumés are indeed more effective with college students who may not have impressive work experience. Resumés and letters of application should be discussed and critiqued in small groups and, if possible, by a member of the institution's business department or the personnel manager. The personnel manager can also give hints about filling out job applications and interview techniques.

The best way to practice interview strategy is to role play. The instructor can play the role of personnel manager, of course, but the students who have by now done extensive research in different career fields can also function as employers in role plays. Role-play interviewing, like the other activities suggested here, works best in small groups with one person playing interviewer, one playing interviewee, and the others observing and writing critiques of the role play which can then be discussed in class.

Course Procedure

A course following the guidelines above will provide ample writing practice in personal, research, and critical writing. About two-thirds of class time can be spent performing the activities above and discussing one of the texts listed in the next section. One-third can be spent discussing and practicing writing mechanics using any of the many excellent handbook-workbook combinations or writer's guides available and examples from student writing. At the end of the term, students have reached a firm decision about their career directions. They have ample information about available careers and have spoken with at least one person active in their chosen field. They have sample resumés and letters of introduction which they can use as job-hunting tools for a post-graduate career search or a hunt for summer employment, and they have a thorough understanding of the mechanics of job hunting. Most important, they have learned that writing and research skills are a necessity in any career development plan.

Texts and Sources

Bolles, Richard Nelson. **What Color Is Your Parachute?** Berkeley, California: Ten Speed Press, 1977.

An eclectic and therefore somewhat unstructured guide to finding employment, this book draws extensively from the work of Bernard Haldane and John Crystal for its job-seeking approach. Traditional college students find the book's format appealing. The instructor can generate many additional writing assignments from the material.

Djeddah, Eli. **Moving Up.** Berkeley, California: Ten Speed Press, 1978.

An associate of Haldane for many years, Djeddah follows the Haldane approach, gearing it to mid-life career changes. It presents a detailed and effective interview strategy and works particularly well with older students who have work or military experience. *Moving Up* is a very effective text for continuing education courses.

Haldane, Bernard. **How to Make a Habit of Success,** revised edition. Washington, D.C.: Acropolis Books, Ltd., 1975.

Not recommended as a textbook for this course, *How to Make a Habit of Success* presents the clearest description of Haldane's S.I.M.S. approach so is useful for instructors. The book is intended for persons seeking in-house mobility and promotions and for managers wishing to reorganize the staffing.

Haldane, Bernard, Jean Haldane and Lowell Martin. **Job Power Now! The Young People's Job Finding Guide.** Washington, D.C.: Acropolis Books, Ltd., 1976.

As the subtitle suggests, this book is geared to senior high school and college age students. It is much more structured than Bolles's approach. As a result, under-prepared and under-motivated students who might have difficulty dealing with the wide array of material and strategies Bolles recommends will find this volume appealing, effective, and easy to understand.

Forces and Sources:
Beyond the Bookroom Wall

Natalie White

Who knows what sources for writing may lie outside the bookroom walls until we begin to search for them? That search led Natalie White to discover that archives can be sources of enjoyable writing activities. Ms. White submitted this exercise from Albuquerque, New Mexico.

Author's Comment

Every English teacher knows that there are forces. There are pressures. Select from "back to the basics" or the "minimal competency movement" or "individualization of instruction for 35 students in a 55-minute period, contained classroom" yet remember Titles I, VII, IX. Complying with all this at once, a teacher is headed for certain cultural shock.

Forces mounted and finally avalanched into my classroom one day when I was struggling to use one of those new textbooks designed to reach inner-city youth. You know the ones, they have many pictures, few words, some rough and tumble teenagers who deal with drugs, depression, isolation . . . the concrete jungle. It wasn't working. The students had tuned out, bored. I was happy to leave that afternoon and made a sudden change in plans in order to boost my spirits. I went to a library. It's an odd therapy, perhaps, but inexpensive.

It was that afternoon while I was going through archives that the force became a source and I discovered the obvious. Teachers are supposed to consider the student's background and cultural diversity. Through some strange twist of mind, though, we are all taught to do it by using a published text and adapting it to particular needs and situations. But there are things out there waiting to be rediscovered; free things, wonderful things. They may be in your library, in archives, or even in a dusty drawer your great aunt hasn't gone through for years.

The Sources

That afternoon I found old photographs, lots of them. I had a few copied by the library attendant at the cost of ten cents a page. The next morning

38

I made several copies from the originals, using an inexpensive screen to bring out the greys (many of the less expensive copiers in the schools print only blacks). What I was unknowingly beginning to develop was my own inner-city local, original, multi-cultural, *Stop, Look and Write.* I had a picture of the Boss Saloon, the first automobile in the city, prim students in white starched collars and frilly white aprons, stiff, respectable and bored. There was a turn-of-the-century football team, all native Americans; there was a funny little girl, her black shoes worn white at the toes, wearing a ragged dress, smiling as though the world were hers alone.

The next class, students were allowed to select a picture they wanted and write about it, using description or creativity. The responses were exceptional. They were writing about their town; some of them, their ancestors.

The Force

It became a hobby of mine, digging around for useful archives. I finally decided to see if any students wanted to join the hunt. Their enthusiasm exceeded the size of my car, but I took four to the library with me that afternoon. They laughed at me and I at them when we decided to get into the old Albuquerque newspapers, preserved on microfilm. The second time back the students referred to it as going to the silent movies and asked me to sneak some popcorn in so that it would really be like going to the movies. There are few things I fear like the wrath of a librarian, but this was a measure of my dedication.

The students found, among other things, an ad for a liquid that one could drink for an internal ailment or put on an external one. A quick cure was certain whether patient was a person or a horse. There was also an article from the 1890s on the mental differences between the sexes, as well as the story of the first Edison bulb bringing light into the darkness of a Pennsylvania town. We copied these and began to develop exercises with them in small group activities. Some groups made cloze tests for other students to take; some chose to modernize the language of the stories. Some worked on titles, others preferred to allow themselves more imagination and discussed how electric lights had changed the century, how better off we would have been without them.

The students began to discover themselves, their town; and the past, which was so unreal to them, became something they had seen and experienced in a "down home" way. The variety of things available in city, university or state archives is phenomenal. One "low-rider" (I believe they used to be called "hot rodders") spent several days working with a 1913 driver's manual. He set his own criterion for modernizing it, and did some very good work.

Although these news stories and pictures could be grouped into a unit, perhaps with a reading of *Our Town,* I liked using them occasionally. It always made that day somewhat special and the day following it was, then, easier.

The copyright law has been tightened and textbook monies are decreasing. Archival materials can be a positive and enjoyable force for you and your students if you will just break through that bookroom wall, examine available archives, and then do it yourself in the characteristic American way.

Activity-Based Writing

Jo Lundy Pevey

Sources for writing can come from activities which students engage in outside the classroom. Jo Lundy Pevey of Southern Technical Institute, Marietta, Georgia, suggests several possibilities for such activity-based writing.

Author's Comment

To help students who have difficulty generating ideas for writing, I have designed some assignments which avoid the necessity of the students' creating ideas directly from the mind alone; the assignments are activity-based. The students participate in an experience, alone or with someone else, and then write about the experience. In the beginning, fairly specific instructions can be given and class discussions held. Early assignments may be only to record the experience; later assignments may request a reaction to the experience. Finally, a generalization based on the experience or a principle formalized as the result of the experience is stated and discussed by the student. Below is one such assignment.

The Activity

Within the next three days, dine at a place where you have never eaten before. This place may be a restaurant, a friend's home, a picnic area, a main street sidewalk. Pay close attention to details.

A class discussion might result in a body of questions which the students would consider and would use to assist them in looking for details. Such a list follows:

What is the mood of the place?

How is the mood established?

Is there music? other noise? How do these help create or destroy the desired mood?

What is the decor? the theme?

Is there congruency in architecture? in landscaping?

What type of flatware and dishes are used?

What is on the floor?

What kind of and amount of lighting is used?

What is the age range of the clientele?

How are they dressed?

How are they similar to your friends? different from your friends?

What do you infer from their appearance?

What are people doing besides eating?

What do you notice about the service? the food and drink? the prices?

How do you react to the place?

If you are eating with someone else, how does that person's presence affect you?

Is the dining experience satisfactory? Why or why not?

Assignment Options

Compare and/or contrast this experience with your usual dining experience.

Write a letter of recommendation to someone who might be considering dining at the same place.

Write a letter of commendation or complaint to the manager, a letter of appreciation to the hostess, or a letter to the local newspaper.

Use the setting as a background in revealing any personal interaction you had with your dining partner—or what you wish you had had.

Write a short story, using the scene of your dining experience in the opening paragraph, in the conclusion, or in the scene for the turning point of the story.

In detail, describe the behavior and appearance of some colorful character you saw while eating.

Discuss some insight gained from the experience.

Additional Activities

Visit a museum.

Visit a clothing store for people of the sex opposite to your own.

Visit a theatre.

Visit a public park.

Ride public transportation.

Take a walk through your neighborhood.

Take a walk or ride through a neighborhood occupied by people of a socio-economic level different from your own.

Read an article in a periodical which you do not usually read.

Attend a club meeting held for persons of the sex opposite to your own.

Study the advertisements in a professional journal or a work-related periodical.

Hat Tricks for Teaching Writing

Barbara R. DuBois

Varying classroom routine helps to maintain student interest and involvement in a class. The author suggests some ways she has developed to encourage frequent writing in her class using various sources. Ms. DuBois teaches at the University of New Mexico-Los Alamos.

Author's Comment

Since our English 102 has changed from *Writing with Readings in Literature* to *Analytic Writing,* we now emphasize writing and de-emphasize literature. I used to lead discussions about genres; now I need to change class activity from discussion to writing. I used to assign six papers per term, not even half as many as in English 101; now I must assign ten or twelve to satisfy myself that I am teaching writing effectively. Obviously, I needed prewriting strategies. As a woman and an English instructor, I am used to wearing many hats, so I decided to buy one more, a bright red Lobo hat from the college bookstore because the lobo is the UNM mascot. With my new hat, I perform several hat tricks to help my students become accustomed to writing at the drop of a hat.

First Trick

The trick I use most often is to put in the hat small cards with authors' names. Each week I assign four or five readings from *The Conscious Reader: Readings Past and Present,* 2d ed., by Caroline Shrodes, Harry Finestone, and Michael Shugrue (New York: Macmillan, 1978). A class of twenty-five gives me five groups for classwork. The groups have twenty minutes to compose a theme statement and support in response to a writing suggestion from the book's appendix. For example, one group may consist of five students with McLuhan cards: they may like the book's suggestion "Take one or two current television commercials or print ads and demonstrate what they tell us about the values of our society." The group will agree on a theme statement to report to the class.

Of course I remind the students that writing is exploration and that a theme statement may change during the writing, but I do find it worthwhile for them to start with a hypothesis. After twenty minutes, I reassemble the class for groups to report. They always succeed in composing theme statements, but they do not always have time to plan support. The class as a whole then discusses various patterns, and students recall such aids as examples, classification, comparison, and causal analysis.

Second Trick

Some weeks have more time than others, and I use a trick that works with individuals rather than groups. The text has study questions as well as writing suggestions, so I put numbers on the cards in the hat (no, not 6⅞), for example, "Huxley, #2." Each student works alone on a question like "What details would you regard as contributing to the utopian atmosphere?" After fifteen minutes, I call on students for individual recitations of their written answers.

Third Trick

Another trick for an uncrowded week breaks the class into three groups to edit a duplicated student essay that I have distributed several days earlier. One group works on organization, one on support, and one on style. When I reassemble the class, I call for rewriting of any ineffective sentences. I hope that suggesting improvements for a peer's essay will help them strengthen their own work.

Fourth Trick

My fourth trick applies when we have one of our frequent in-class writings announced. On the two previous prewriting days, I put authors' names in the hat, again dividing the students evenly among the readings. But the assignment now is for each student to pretend to be the instructor and invent an examination question; I use in-class essays as practice exams. A student may merely use one of the textbook's writing suggestions, but since I seldom use one in its exact form, a wiser practice is for the student to ascertain the reading's subject and compose a question about the subject; for example, a Thurber essay is about women's liberation, and I might ask a question that is about the topic but that has little connection with the Thurber essay itself.

After twenty minutes, the students sit in pairs and trade questions. Now each student must pretend to be taking the exam. A student must compose a theme statement to answer the partner's question and suggest support if time permits. This has proved an excellent practice for the in-class writing, helping students review content and consider strategies.

Trick Variation

When the students act as if they are bored with my hat tricks, I can use this variation on any trick: I place numbered cards in the hat, and each student draws a different number. The #1 now refers to nothing but choice: the student has first choice in the current activity. If we are composing theme statements, #1 may choose the reading, for which to compose a thesis; if we are answering study questions, #1 may choose a question; if we are practicing for a test, #1 may choose the reading from which to frame a question.

Results

Having tricks always ready reminds me to resist the temptation to lecture, which we do not believe teaches writing skills. Having students write every day, even if they write only tentative theme statements and suggestions, establishes priorities for them and banishes the blank-paper blues. We constantly emphasize organization and theme statement so that students have thought about every possible subject, theme, and approach and have only to choose a favorite, whether at home or in class.

The students never know which trick they will have to play, but they always know that they will write in class, with or without tricks, and they know that practice builds confidence and skill.

II Prewriting

The stage of preparation in writing which we have come to call "prewriting" is an important one. From this stage, writers launch into their drafts, seeking to express their ideas and present their information. The term "prewriting" has come to mean many things, ranging from brainstorming to freewriting, jotting down lists of details to engaging in elaborate heuristic or invention strategies. It also may mean becoming aware of audience needs, establishing a focus or thesis, dealing with preliminary organizational problems, and deciding upon steps for meeting the requirements of an assignment. In this section readers will find a variety of ideas for helping students understand the different aspects of prewriting.

Writing Process/Response Exercise

Donald M. Murray

Many students do not have a clear perception of what is involved in the composing process. This sequential writing exercise introduces students to each stage of the process in one class meeting. Mr. Murray submitted this exercise from The University of New Hampshire, Durham.

Author's Comment

The purpose of this article is to introduce the writing process/response method of teaching writing to students (or teachers) in the first hour of a writing unit or in-service workshop. It is not to produce a polished piece of writing.

The Writing Exercise

Distribute six 3 × 5 cards—salmon, blue, yellow, green, red, and white—to each participant.

Tell each participant to take the salmon colored card and brainstorm specific details about an event, place, or person important to them. Do the same thing yourself. Share what you have written at the end of four minutes, or when half the participants seem to have finished.

Have each participant choose a partner. Have one partner play the role of teacher, the other student. Have the teacher partner ask, "What appeared on the card that you didn't expect?" and respond to the student's answer. In two minutes have the partners reverse roles and ask the same question. Terminate that activity in two minutes.

Tell each participant to take the blue card and start writing about the specific which surprised them, or just to free write. Write yourself and share what you have written with the group after three minutes, or when half the group has stopped writing.

Tell the teacher partner to ask, "What do you intend to develop in the next draft?" and respond to the answer. After a minute and a half have them reverse roles and after another minute and a half end this activity.

Tell each participant to take the yellow card and develop a draft as they had indicated in the conference, or to continue with the subject. Write yourself and share what you have written after three minutes or when half the group has stopped writing.

Tell the teacher partner to ask, "What is the piece of writing telling you?" and respond to the answer. After a minute and a half have them reverse roles and after another minute and a half end this activity.

Take the green card and have the participants follow the piece of writing wherever it is leading them, or switch the point of view and write about the subject from a different perspective. Write yourself and share what you have written after three minutes, or when half the group has stopped writing.

Tell the teacher partner to ask, "What do your readers need to know that you haven't told them?" and respond to the answer. After a minute and a half have them reverse roles, and after another minute and a half end this activity.

Take the red card and have the participants tell the readers what they need to know. Write yourself and share what you have written after three minutes, or when half the group has stopped writing.

Tell the teacher partner to ask, "What questions do you have of me?" and respond to the answer. After a minute and a half have them reverse roles, and after another minute and a half end this activity.

Take the white card and have the participants write a final draft, making it as clear as possible. Write yourself and share what you have written after three minutes, or when half the group has stopped writing.

Ask each participant to read his or her white card, sharing the results of the writing process as you have shared your process with them. When everyone is through, comment upon the diversity of voices, and point out the fact that everyone has written six drafts and passed through an approximation of the process of prewriting, writing, and rewriting, through which most writers pass most of the time. Also point out that each participant has received and run five writing conferences designed to help the writer produce increasingly effective drafts.

Author's Additional Comments

The exercise takes 35 minutes plus time for everyone to share the final card. Participants average about half a minute to read their white cards so a class of thirty can complete the entire exercise in 50 minutes.

Many English and Language Arts teachers have not written recently and have had little training in writing or teaching writing. Few teachers or students have experienced the process of discovery when written language leads to meaning. This exercise was designed to allow teachers to experience that writing process at the very beginning of an in-service workshop. Teachers who found the experience valuable to them began to use the exercise with their students.

It is vital that everyone—the instructor included—simply plunge into the writing process without preparation. The leader's assumption should be that everyone will write, and it is my experience that just about everyone does. I've run the exercise with thousands of students or teachers from third graders to university faculties and only about half a dozen have refused to write. The leader must, however, write and share each draft in process so the participants can hear writing in process, see the awkward and exciting process of language seeking meaning.

The purpose of the exercise is to experience the writing process, not to produce a finished piece of writing; but it is amazing how many participants, under these artificial conditions, hear their own voices for the first time, find topics worth exploring later, and even produce drafts which are moving and effective.

May I See Your License, Please?

Robert Perrin

Students sometimes underestimate the importance of specific details in their writing. Robert Perrin of Indiana State University at Terre Haute shows how a prewriting activity can help students focus more clearly on the importance of detail in description.

Author's Comment

When students describe people in their writing, everyone seems to be the same. People have "feathered hair," "nice clothes," and "athletic builds." These patterned descriptions frustrate me and other writing teachers because they are clichéd word groups that provide only the most general impression of what people are like, and my students have never seemed to realize that they are writing descriptions that are interchangeable and therefore ineffective. A partial solution to this problem is this series of activities I developed for my writing students.

First Activity

I had my students take out their driver's licenses and then asked them questions which drew upon the information they included. They raised their hands in response to the questions, and we kept an informal tally of the results. These were the kinds of questions I used:

1. How many have blue eyes? Brown eyes? Green eyes? Black eyes?
2. How many have black hair? Brown hair? Blond hair? Red hair?
3. How many are 5'-5'4"? 5'5"-5'9"? 5'10"-6'2"?
4. How many weigh 100–115 pounds? 120–130? 135–145?
5. How many are male? Female?

This activity was entertaining because students gladly shared this information—and I joined in, which made my reticent students more comfortable. But more importantly, it allowed me to stress that these

51

general methods of description are not completely accurate or useful—
hence the photograph now required. In this way my students got a better
sense that description must be more particular if it is to be helpful.

Second Activity

I then discussed with my students the sorts of distinctions that can be
made to make description more specific. We worked through some of the
five items from the first activity to make the connections between the
activities clearer. The students came up with these features to describe:

1. Eyes: Lash length? Make-up? Tinted contacts or natural color?
2. Hair: Texture? Style? Length? Attention given?
3. Height and Weight: Proportions? Sizes worn? Ways of moving?

When I asked my students what other features could tell readers about
people, they supplied answers like these: Their skin color and texture, the
clothes they wear, the jewelry they wear, their style of glasses, and their
mannerisms. Most importantly, my students began discussing as many
qualities as possible and jotted them on the board. (They wrote them
down for further reference.)

Third Activity

The third activity for my students was to select a person whom they see
often (even though they may or may not know him or her) and complete
that person's description for a driver's license, using approximate height
and weight. Then they were to make a jotted list of important features
which revealed more about the person. With these lists in hand, they did
some peer evaluation of the materials, helping each other catch those
semi-specific (but clichéd) generalities like "good figure" and "designer
clothes." Then they revised the items on their lists.

Fourth Activity

The final activity was to write a long paragraph (150–200 words) to
describe the people they had chosen. They were to include the basic
information from the "driver's licenses," the specific information from the
jotted lists, and any other information they thought useful.

Summary

At other times in the term, I have modified this activity to include descriptions of places as well, using the kinds of information realtors provide for houses and rooms in their multiple-listing books. That activity also worked well, but I had to familiarize my students with the realtor's pages first. I also tried a book description—using trade descriptions as a starting point. With all of these activities, I tried to lead my students from a general and limited kind of description to descriptive writing which provides more information. Of course, an activity like this one does not make every paragraph or later essay carefully crafted and insightful, but it goes a long way in helping students see—in terms they can understand—that specific and interesting details are necessary for descriptive writing to be effective.

The Significant Detail

Ellen G. Friedman

What happens when writers are not precise enough in their use of detail? This activity dramatizes the need for close observation and reporting in writing. Ms. Friedman teaches at Trenton State College, New Jersey.

Author's Comment

My mother, my Jewish mother, not only wanted us to eat boiled, unspiced chicken, but she was hurt if we did not praise the tenderness of every forkful. I guess I am like her in that; only I push writing rather than boiled chicken down the—I hate to admit it—unwilling throats of college freshmen. At least I do not insist that it has to be spiceless. I am not pure. I sometimes garnish classes with games to entice my students to swallow coherent sentence structure.

Writing the Details

One Tuesday, early in the semester, I was talking about the importance of the significant detail in descriptive writing. The game I organized to teach this principle was suggested by the text, *The Writing Experience* (Schoen, et. al., New York: Little, Brown, 1979). It is a variation of a game I usually play to ease the discomfort of beginning-semester shyness.

In this version, the class is divided into three groups. Each group writes, cooperatively, a description (excluding clothes) of someone not in the group. This task accomplished, two groups stand up while a member of the third group slowly reads the description of his or her group. As they hear characteristics (like long, brown hair) that they do not possess, the standing students sit down. If the description is accurate, only one student is left standing at the end. This is the object of the game. However, if there are several students standing at the end, I have a chance to do some verbal finger wagging about the consequences of imprecise phrasing.

At this particular session, the first two group descriptions left several students standing, and I wagged triumphantly. With the third group, however, the game was working the way it was supposed to. Three students were left.

"Dark complexion," said the reader. One student sat down.

"Short, curly hair," he finished.

A second student sat down and one—the one—remained standing. I glowed with as much satisfaction as my mother did at the moment—faces smeared with forced smiles—our plates were cleaned of the colorless meat.

But my years of literary study have taught me an unhappy lesson: to distrust the comforting appearance and to hunt for the nasty reality. So I took the leap and asked the group who had written the description whether the person left standing was indeed the person described. Then came the inevitable answer, "No."

"Who were you describing?" I asked.

After a rather long, puzzling silence came the meek answer, "You, doc."

The student left standing, a young black woman, vacillating between embarrassment and amusement, said in a teasing, self-righteous tone, "Well, you said curly hair and dark complexion." Indeed so, and we both fit the bill—only my complexion had been darkened by the sun.

Sense Exploration and Descriptive Writing: A Practical Exercise

Donovan R. Walling

Students often hear the directive "Write a description" but fail to understand the elements of effective descriptive writing. The sequential approach presented here divides the task into manageable segments while acquainting students with some basic writing strategies. Mr. Walling sent this from Farnsworth Junior High School, Sheboygan, Wisconsin.

Author's Comment

Unless we specifically think about them, most of us are only vaguely aware of our surroundings at any given moment. We may be peripherally conscious of the warmth or coolness of the room, or of a radio playing somewhere in the distance. But unless some element of our environment thrusts itself into prominence—e.g., a cold draft, a sudden noise—we tend to ignore our surroundings.

In the classroom our students, naturally, react in the same way to their environment. Thus, an elementary-seeming assignment in descriptive writing such as "Describe our classroom," presents young writers with a whole set of difficulties unless they have been systematically taught to "tune in" the surroundings they "tune out" as a matter of course.

Since descriptive writing demands sensitive and accurate observation, a primary task for the writing teacher is to develop students' awareness. This can best be accomplished through a series of exploratory activities which direct the students through the range of their senses. Sense exploration reaches beyond simple, visual observation; it helps students examine stimuli in the areas of touch, sound, smell, and taste.

Descriptive Writing and the Senses

It is important to limit the writing exercise in the beginning, so that it does not become an unmanageable task. With this in mind, the outcome of the exercise should be defined. For this example, the assignment is to produce ultimately a description of the classroom. The description, like the actual environment, must contain elements reflective of each of the five senses. The procedures of the developmental writing exercise are outlined in a series of stages.

Stage One

Each student's task will be to write a description of the classroom. The setting is chosen because it is immediately at hand; it can be minutely studied without inconvenience; and student observations can be readily checked.

To begin the task, students are asked to construct a chart in five columns, one per sense. Under each heading the students then list 2–5 items ("things") which involve that particular sense. For example:

Sight	*Hearing*	*Smell*	*Touch*	*Taste*
people	noise	books	desk	finger
lights	teacher	gum	walls	gum
desks	radiator		pencil	
floor	door			

The items listed answer the question: *What* makes up the environment?

Stage Two

Next, students must explore *how* the items on the first chart affect the senses under which they are listed.

At this point, it is useful to involve students in some kinds of "hands on" activities. Texture rubbings, for instance, are very effective to this end. Students are given sheets of unlined paper which they fold into eight sections. Each section is then used to collect a rubbing in soft pencil or crayon of some surface within the room.

By making rubbings, students visually record tactile sensations. When the scurrying activity ends, students are asked to describe each texture. They must tell *how* it might feel, not what it is. No descriptive term may be used more than once. In this way, students build a vocabulary of descriptive words, mainly adjectives and adverbs—in this example, words related to the sense of touch.

A variety of similar types of activities can be conducted for the other senses. A sound-effects record, for example, can be used for the sense of hearing; a student-produced tape recording can be used in this way. A blindfolded taste test for the sense of taste; jars containing garlic, sulfur, or other pungent items for smell; and so on—all can provide effective means of increasing student awareness of the five senses.

To complete the second stage, students construct a chart parallel to the first chart. In this listing they must place a *how* word for each *what* (item) of the earlier chart. Emphasis is on variety and accurate description. A sample follows:

Sight	*Hearing*	*Smell*	*Touch*	*Taste*
tall	loud	musty	glassy	sweet
bright	howling	powdery	bumpy	rubbery
shiny	banging		smooth	
dull	noisy			

Stage Three

Using the material in both charts, students write descriptions of the classroom. To get them started, they might begin with, "As I sit at my desk, I can. . . ." Using this approach launches them into the writing while allowing them freedom of choice to begin with any of the five senses.

Stage Four

About midway through the writing process, it is useful to stop the students for some "in progress" evaluation. Several students are asked to share with the class what they have written. This procedure gives students an opportunity to evaluate their own writing and to make helpful suggestions to their peers.

It can also be helpful to students at this point to check their skill at recognizing the senses used in a description. To this end, students may be asked to list the five senses and check them off as they hear them used while the teacher reads aloud some descriptive passage. (A selection I've found appropriate is the first four paragraphs of Chapter Five, "The Wine Shop," in the first book of Dickens's *A Tale of Two Cities.* It directly addresses every sense except smell.)

Afterwards, students can discuss how the senses were used in developing the description and how the description could be changed by using some senses more, less, or differently. Students then resume writing, finally revising and finishing their descriptions.

Stage Five

Peer evaluation is utilized by asking students to exchange papers. The student readers construct a check-off chart similar to the one mentioned in the last stage. This chart is used to gauge the frequency of usage of the various senses in the description. The readers also comment on the accuracy and effectiveness of the writing. Evaluation is accomplished through student-student conferencing and, to a limited degree, through student-teacher discussion. When the writers' works are returned, students have the opportunity to revise and rewrite.

To demonstrate the type of development this kind of writing exercise promotes, it would be useful to provide a set of *before* and *after* examples. The passage below was written by a seventh grader in response to the simple direction: describe our classroom.

> It is large. It has five rows of desks. It is carpeted. In the front of the room are chalkboards, and on the side wall is a chalkboard. The room is very decorative, with pictures on the walls and drawings or posters. In the back of the room is a desk and a filing cabinet. The room is fun to be in.

Later, that same student wrote the following description:

> As I sit in my desk, I can see people bending over their desks rushing to get their work done. I can see some people combing their hair and lots of people sharpening their pencils. As I look up from my desk, I can see chalkboards with our work on them.
>
> I can hear the pencil sharpener grinding away every two minutes. I can also hear the crackling of paper and my pencil scraping my own paper.
>
> I can taste the horrible taste inside my mouth from my stale gum which I just threw away. Because it is so close to lunch, I can almost taste my lunch already.
>
> I touch the desk in front of me every time I move my legs. I can feel the hard wood of the back of my chair whenever I lean back. I can feel a breeze every time someone walks by me.
>
> I can smell chewing gum, and I can smell the perfume I am wearing.

Although the writing is far from polished, it is clear that this student has begun to make some real observations. And she has expressed them in concrete terms, for the most part, as a result of exploring each of her senses systematically.

Providing a structural framework (via the five stages) within which to utilize these explorations enables students to record their ideas in a relatively painless, peer-supportive setting.

Sense exploration exercises, such as the one described here, can help students build experimental foundations for future descriptive writing experiences. Such exercises also provide bases for examining sentence structure and variety, word choice, paragraphing, and other composition skills. But beyond these fundamentals, the process of awakening students to their surroundings through sense exploration nurtures a kind of insight which is the key to developing and expanding descriptive writing skills.

Teaching the Thesis Statement through Description

Robert C. Rosen

According to writing textbooks, the focus of an essay resides in its thesis statement. Students who have difficulty understanding the function of such a statement might benefit from the exercise described by Robert C. Rosen of William Paterson College, Wayne, New Jersey.

Author's Comment

The following exercise is a useful and entertaining way to introduce the importance of a thesis or main idea in a piece of writing.

The Thesis Statement Exercise

I begin by choosing one student as a model and asking everyone in the class (the model included) to write in ten or fifteen minutes a physical description of him or her. The model should stand for a second, to reveal height, and should sit clearly visible to all (it's easiest if chairs are in a circle). Some students may think they are finished writing after two or three perfunctory sentences, so it may be necessary to prod them, reminding them that there are four billion people in the world and their descriptions must single out one.

You must, of course, choose your model with care, preferably in advance, and with a substitute or two in mind in case your choice is absent or unwilling to be volunteered. Your model should be confident and not unattractive, to avoid the risk of hurt feelings. You should also be prepared for the possibility that students will suggest *you* as the model. From experience, I'd recommend against agreeing to that.

Ask several students to read their descriptions aloud, and tell the listeners to close their eyes and try to visualize a person as they hear each description. They'll probably find it difficult, because most of the descriptions will simply be lists of facts—brown hair, glasses, white blouse,

Jordache jeans, and so forth. Eventually, though, a judgment or generalization will appear, and you will be able to discuss the difference between objective and subjective description, between fact and opinion, and perhaps also succeed in eliciting some suggestions about what makes a description effective.

Don't carry this discussion too far, however. Instead, hand out a ditto of the following two paragraphs (these are just samples):

A.   Sally Jones has blond hair, blue eyes, and stands about 5′4″ tall. She wears wire-rimmed glasses and a thin gold chain around her neck. Her ears are large, her nose small, and her mouth about average. She is wearing a white blouse, open at the neck, a large red belt, and designer jeans. Her shoes have high, pointed heels, and no back. There is a high school ring on the fourth finger of her right hand and a large, ornate silver ring (it looks Mexican) on the middle finger of her left hand.

B.   Joe Smith looks tired. The medium-length brown hair that only partly covers his head is lifeless and thinning. His gray eyes are only half open, and his lower lids sag down beside his large, pockmarked nose. His large mouth (which he never opens) literally droops at the corners. His face is quite pale. Joe is wearing scuffed brown loafers, baggy tan corduroy trousers, and a faded blue flannel shirt, only partly tucked in.

Read these two paragraphs aloud and ask the students to close their eyes and try to visualize each person. Then ask how the descriptions differ, which is better, and why. With little or no prompting, the class will conclude that B has a main idea, a point to make, and that this holds it together and enables the reader really to see the individual described. The reason, I'd guess, is that we cannot absorb a series of unrelated details, as in A—it's too much to remember at once. The thesis in B gives us something to hang all its details on, something to organize them around in our mind. From here you can easily generalize to the virtue of a thesis in all kinds of writing.

To make the point clearer and to give the class practice creating (discovering?) and supporting a thesis, you should choose a second model, and tell your students to study the model a few minutes in order to come up with a main impression or the thesis before they start writing their descriptions. Tell them to announce their thesis in their first sentence, a topic sentence, and then to select and shape their details as much as possible (without distortion) to support it. Remind them that not *every* detail need prove their point; their goal is still accuracy, not caricature. Again, you should choose a safe model, and also—if you want to try to control the situation—one that suggests several clear theses.

When these second descriptions are read aloud, ask the students to listen for how well the details support the thesis. You might ask to hear all the first sentences before starting, and then select readers to maximize variety. This round of descriptions will undoubtedly be better than the first.

As a substitute for or addition to this second step, you might simply debate how to describe a particular member of the class. Encourage your students to argue for the various theses they come up with. And for each suggested thesis, challenge them to draft as many details as possible into its service. You might also, at this point, mention the possibility of a description with more than one thesis, a description of several paragraphs.

The entire exercise can be done in one class period. And it can be an opportunity to loosen up the class a bit. In any case, you should follow it up with a homework assignment—to describe a friend, or perhaps to describe a famous person, in which case you might read the descriptions aloud next time and ask the class to guess who's being described.

The Value of Small-Group Projects in Composition Classes

Donald Heidt

Because students do not always have an opportunity to share their writing with classmates, Donald Heidt suggests using small-group activities that stress collaborative thinking, planning, and writing. Mr. Heidt teaches at the College of the Canyons, Valencia, California.

Author's Comment

Recognizing that writing is often a lonely activity accompanied by insecurity, I have been working on methods of alleviating both the loneliness and the anxiety. To a certain extent, both are interrelated, since individual students are not always aware how their work compares to the work produced by other students or to the standards by which the instructor evaluates the writing of all students.

Although I've always tried to make my objectives clear to the students, it has become evident that more needed to be done to set the students at ease. To that end, I've started using small-group exercises, an approach that relieves the loneliness and anxiety while simultaneously allowing the students to learn from each other. For these reasons, and for additional reasons to be treated later, there is ample justification for using a variety of small-group exercises in composition courses. Certain types of these exercises—for instance, inductive problem-solving and art/poetry exercises—demand time for prewriting and incubation and therefore take three or four class meetings to complete; but the following exercises have been handled successfully during a fifty-minute period in about the fifth or sixth week of the semester.

Exercise 1: The Party

Objectives: Organization, development, and support of a narrative/ descriptive essay; transitions; point of view; tone; verb tense.

Instructions: Have the students arrange themselves in groups of three or four for the purpose of writing an in-class cooperative essay. As a group they are to decide on point of view, tone, and verb tense.

Situation: Tell the students they have been invited to a party cohosted by Frankenstein and Dracula, to be held either at Count Dracula's hilltop castle in Transylvania or at Dr. Frankenstein's castle along the Rhine in Germany. The students in each group decide among themselves who will describe each of any three or four of the following: the grounds and facade of the castle, the grand hall, the tower room, the dungeon, the kitchen, the dining room, the rumpus room, the secret room accessible only through the fireplace (or sliding panel or pivoting bookcase, etc.).

Comment: Students have completed this task in thirty minutes without difficulty, possibly because they have seen enough horror films and horror film parodies on television and at movie theaters so that concrete detail comes readily to mind. Generally, there will be animated discussion for about five minutes or so at the beginning of the work period, the sound of scratching pens for about twenty minutes, and then a few minutes of discussion concerned with transitions. For the last twenty minutes of the period, the groups read their essays aloud.

Another small-group exercise—this time for groups of two—demands greater analytical skills than does the narrative/descriptive exercise above. The "Situation" part of the following exercise in reasoning is taken from Irving M. Copi, *Introduction to Logic,* 5th edition (New York: Macmillan, 1978), p. 49.

Exercise 2: The Engineer

Objectives: Practice in problem solving, encouraging the student to analyze, reflect, and to develop a critical attitude; practice in writing a coherent, well-supported argument.

Instructions: Group the students in pairs and tell them that the object is not only to arrive at a correct answer, but also to trace clearly and completely the process of step-by-step reasoning which leads to that answer. As each pair completes this task, those two students bring their written argument to the instructor for verification.

Comment: This is an in-class assignment meant for one fifty-minute period. Since some pairs are faster than others, I provide back-up tasks for those who finish early. Those who need additional time, work on the task outside of class.

Situation: On a certain train, the crew consists of the brakeman, the fireman, and the engineer. Their names listed alphabetically are Jones, Robinson, and Smith. On the train are also three passengers with corresponding names, Mr. Jones, Mr. Robinson, and Mr. Smith. The following facts are known:

Mr. Robinson lives in Detroit.

The brakeman lives halfway between Detroit and Chicago.

Mr. Jones earns exactly $20,000 a year.

Smith once beat the fireman at billiards.

The brakeman's next-door neighbor, one of the three passengers mentioned, earns exactly three times as much as the brakeman.

The passenger living in Chicago has the same name as the brakeman.

What is the engineer's name? Write out completely the process of reasoning that leads to your answer.

Summary

When I originally started using small-group exercises such as "The Party" and "The Engineer," my motives were to provide a change of pace for the course and to make students feel more comfortable. During the semesters that I've used this approach, the psychological or affective goals have been at least partially attained. By participating in the small group, individuals feel that they are accepted, that their ideas matter to the others because they need each other in order to accomplish the group's goals. Also, working in a small group provides an opportunity for individuals to express themselves in a non-threatening atmosphere.

Finally, besides diminishing the individual's feelings of anxiety and loneliness in the writing situation, small-group activities have worthwhile benefits on the cognitive and social levels. Since our minds are not shaped by the same mold—individuals have their own experiences, their own values—we see different things in the joint process of problem solving. Shared insights within the group expand the understanding and awareness of each student. It is in a small group that students have the best opportunity to discuss an idea, to sharpen their opinions, to clarify their own points of view. In addition to the cognitive value gained, the students learn something of social value; as a group, they learn that they must set clear goals, take collective responsibility for contributions, learn to listen carefully to each other, cooperate with each other, and arrive at a consensus. For all the reasons cited, small-group projects have value for students in composition classes.

Who Gets the Kidney Machine? Opening-Day Strategies in a Remedial Composition Course

Thomas Friedman

Involving students immediately in developing assertions or "propositions," according to Thomas Friedman of Brooklyn College, New York, is an excellent way to begin a writing course because it leads students to some of the fundamental principles in developing an essay.

Author's Comment

My goals in a remedial composition course are no different from goals in a regular course. I want to help inexperienced writers learn to formulate an idea precisely and develop, explain, and defend that idea fully. While the form of the essay comes by way of Sheridan Baker, the terminology is Kenneth A. Bruffee's. The latter describes his purpose as teaching people to "take a position (the 'proposition'), and defend it (the 'defense')."

The process has to begin with getting students to formulate meaningful generalizations. The difficulty lies in getting students to generate ideas, much less getting them to formulate propositions. Add the special problems of a remedial course, students with special problems, convinced of their own inadequacy, instructors new to the field, trying too hard to be encouraging and sympathetic, and the first day becomes all important. If things do not get started the right way, they might never get started.

Some colleagues have developed various methods for coping with the problems of the first day in these remedial courses. One popular first-day activity has been the initiation of a "rap session" where students discuss both their fears of writing and their previous experiences in writing classes. Helpful as these might be, they are limited in that they encourage students to talk, not to write. A more effective way to "prime the pump" would be getting students to write as soon as possible. Mr. Bruffee suggests a number of exercises which ask students to begin writing by writing. My only complaint against "Reminiscence," "Brainstorming," and the other beginning exercises he suggests is that they take too long to get to the most important part of beginning—the formulation of a statement that takes a position. My opening-day strategy thus consists not

67

only in getting students started but in getting them started in formulating "propositions."

Stimulating Students to Write

After the briefest of introductions which might include name, class, office hours (in essence, factual information about the course, not theory or pep talks), I hand out a sheet[1] with the following information:

1. John Williams—28 years old—professional basketball star and TV personality—last year's MVP—$250,000 salary—married—26-year-old, attractive wife—4 children. John Williams is black.

2. Archibald McFarland III—70 years old—former statesman and diplomat—awarded Nobel Peace Prize—former UN representative, Secretary of State and Governor—many children, grandchildren, and great-grandchildren. Archibald McFarland is a WASP.

3. Rachel Goldberg—26 years old—free-lance writer of some renown—married—mother of 3 children—husband is a paraplegic from birth with a degree in chemistry who has been earning $20,000 per year as a research scientist. Rachel Goldberg is Jewish.

4. Gloria Jones—4 years old—was able to walk and talk at an unusually early age—only child of physician-parents—white.

5. José Rodriguez—24 years old—high school dropout who enlisted—sent to Viet Nam—seriously wounded—developed heroin addiction while in army—kicked habit—has returned to school, received diploma, and won a scholarship to college—18-year-old younger brother lives with him. José Rodriguez is Hispanic.

A question appears at the bottom of the page: "Who should be allowed to use the kidney machine?"

Before dealing with the question, we discuss the biographical information. The objective, at the moment, is not to evaluate but to understand. Abbreviations (MVP, UN, WASP) are defined, along with unfamiliar names (Nobel) and terminology (paraplegic). When I am sure that all the information on the page is clear, I am ready to pose the question.

I inform the class that they are faced with an unfortunate but real situation. Because of a scarcity of kidney machines, men and women must very often choose among a number of people the one to whom the machine will be made available. I ask them to try to make such a decision.

I should point out that very often there are many objections from students. Some say they have to think about it. Others (a surprising number) say they do not want to "play God." I assure the former group that our decision will not be hasty and the latter that they are to concentrate on the one they are saving, not the ones they are condemning. It should be clear, however, that the individual teacher might choose another, less "lethal," question to pose. The primary purpose, after all, is to get students to take positions. In fact, the objection itself should be turned to advantage. After all, the objecting students have taken the initial step toward successful writing—they have taken a position, expressed an opinion, stated a proposition. In any case, if this particular scenario develops, the teacher has, in a sense, been successful in "getting things started," without resorting to either irrelevant "rap sessions" or over-long preliminary exercises.

As students begin to state their opinions, I ask them to write them down, and I follow suit on the blackboard. It is extremely important now to make sure students do not do more than state opinions. The tendency for most will be to say, "I choose X to use the machine," then continue with "because." This "because" should, for the moment, be nipped in the bud. Ask students to present their opinion, but explain you do not want them to "defend" that opinion, not yet anyway.

When students have both stated and written their choices, I explain to them that they have already done one-half of the basic writing process. They have taken a position (called a "proposition" from then on). I also point out to them that most already know what the second half of the basic argument consists of since most of their sentences tried to continue with "because." The "because" is, after all, nothing other than the defense of the position.

What I find exciting about the situation we have reached is that students make their own discoveries. The exercise shows that the written argument they are supposed to learn in this course—proposition and defense—is a process already familiar to them. The key word is, of course, "show" and not "tell." That is what "rap sessions" do, after all. They "tell" students the same things this lesson *shows* them.

The lesson is far from over. While students have become aware of the basic division, they might not be clear about the contents of that second half. What goes into the defense?

The form of the essay I use comes from Mr. Bruffee again, with certain important modifications. Mr. Bruffee diagrams the essay[2] the following way:

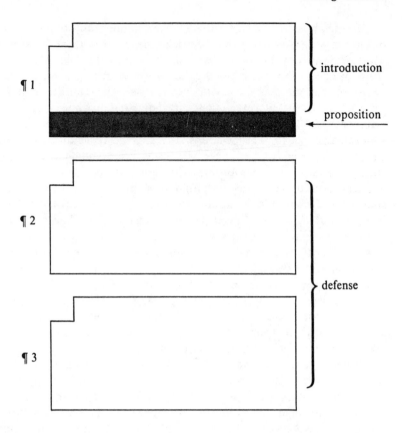

As the diagram indicates, the proposition is followed by two paragraphs of defense. Keeping in mind that this is not the only form in
which to write an essay, I try to get students to use each paragraph to
develop one important reason in support of their proposition.

I then ask them to offer one reason why they feel the particular person
they have chosen for the kidney machine merits their consideration. I
stress that they should offer one reason and one reason only. When two
students offer reasons in support of the same choice, we try to decide
whether the reasons being offered are truly two different reasons or
whether they are really similar to each other. Once again each reason
goes on the board and into notebooks, but while the blackboard has Mr.
Bruffee's diagram which visually illustrates the separation of proposition
and defense, their notebooks are using separate pages for the same purpose. In other words, the proposition goes to the bottom of a page and
the reason begins at the top of a second sheet.

Not only does this form emphasize the separation of proposition and defense, it also prepares the students for other aspects of the essay form. Most obvious is the presence of that empty page. All students know that the page will eventually contain the introduction; few of them are aware, however, that the introduction can be written later. Another advantage of this "loose sheet" essay is that it enables students to change the order in which different reasons are presented. As they become more sophisticated, later on in the term, in the uses of Nestorian order or the strawman defense, they will find that shifting paragraphs enhances their strategy. The loose sheets enable them to do this without rewriting the entire essay. If the classroom is organized along collaborative lines where students work with each other's papers, the loose sheets will come in handy again.

For the purposes of opening-day strategies, however, the one paragraph per page form has more important benefits. After students have formulated one reason in support of their proposition, there is a discussion. If, for example, someone suggested Gloria Jones for the kidney machine because she is "young," we would discuss that argument. The teacher's role might be restricted to demands for articulation and explanation. I am interested in having them develop their reason. After the discussion, I ask students to write developing paragraphs, making sure that they do nothing more than explain as fully as they can the one reason they have chosen in defense. This is how a paragraph defines itself for them. By restricting the entire page for the use of just one paragraph, the student is prevented from beginning a second paragraph under the mistaken notion that the same reason was being developed. I tell them to stop writing when they feel they have explained that one reason. There is no other length requirement stated. Let them leave vast expanses of space. It helps them realize that perhaps more development is needed. And more importantly, I tell them, it indicates that to go on would mean starting a new reason.

When they are done, I collect only the page with the reason. I leave with them their proposition and ask them to write one additional reason at home. The loose sheets, of course, facilitate this assignment. More important, the loose sheets generate the second day's work. When they come to class with that second reason, I ask them to read them out loud. Most of the paragraphs I have gotten lacked any kind of transitional phrase, but some did have a phrase like "Another reason why Gloria Jones should get to use the kidney machine is. . . ." I then return to them their first page and begin a lesson about connective phrases between paragraphs. Because of the division of a paragraph per page, the need for the transitional phrase becomes more obvious and, of course, the division made the separation of pages and hence the overnight assignment possible.

The first day's work ends with a recapitulation of what the class has accomplished. I point out to them that they have essentially written an essay and that the term's work consists of nothing more than perfecting the skills they have displayed on the very first day. At the least, if they can formulate an idea precisely and defend and explain it fully, they have learned the minimum they need for passing the remedial course.

This is not to say that such essentials as grammar and style are ignored. They will be dealt with later. As far as the first day is concerned, however, this lesson has accomplished its purpose. It stimulated students to begin writing, informed them of the term's goals, built up their confidence, and prepared them for the second day.

Notes

1. The idea for the biographical sketches and a question was first suggested at a seminar at Kingsborough Community College, during the summer of 1971, part of the EPDA Summer Institute program. A form of it called "The Fallout Shelter" was used to generate opinions and attitudes among students. A tape of that lesson is available.

2. Kenneth A. Bruffee, *A Short Course in Writing* (Cambridge, Massachusetts: Winthrop, 1972), p. 26.

Composition with Adult Students: Getting Started

Terence G. Collins

More and more people are returning to school to complete their education. Classroom strategies designed for younger students may not work as successfully with these older students. Terence Collins of the University of Minnesota, Minneapolis, suggests a strategy he has used successfully to involve adult students in finding subjects for writing.

Author's Comment

In the recent *Academic Turmoil* (Anchor-Doubleday, 1980), Theodore L. Gross claims that "the entire shape of higher education is changing dramatically. . . . In the last year alone, the student population entering elementary school has diminished by 4 per cent; the projection for the next ten years is 25 per cent. At the same time, the population of people between the ages of twenty and fifty will increase. These figures are significant enough for educators to reconsider the scope and method of their offerings" (p. 221). This is not news to those of us who teach in urban colleges and universities. But what sorts of practical adaptations can we make in our writing classrooms to better accommodate this growing adult college population?

Until more research comes in, we'll have to learn with the seat of our pants. One thing, though, is clear: classroom strategies designed for typically less self-directed 18–22-year-old students are at best marginally effective for more mature students who bring to the composition classroom a rich work history, extensive experience as heads of households, and a cultivated impatience for teachers and tasks which too frequently fail to leave room for differences.

Approach

Assignment design is especially important if adult students are to feel that they can draw on their rich life history as a strength (how often such students see their age as a liability in the youth-culture of college!) and at the same time be challenged in ways which foster growth in their writing skills. Early assignments, given when student uncertainty about educational re-entry compounds any weaknesses in writing ability, play a key role in developing positive attitudes toward the business of writing—and, indeed, positive attitudes toward the self as a writer. Through trial and error and through informal consultation with hundreds of adult students, I've come to several conclusions about the sorts of early assignments which work.

First, such assignments will not necessarily be the type of assignment younger students or I might enjoy. However much I might fancy myself capable of responding enthusiastically in writing to E. B. White's problems with geriatric terriers, I run a great risk in projecting into other mature adults what is at best an acquired taste. Likewise, old standbys like comparison of dorm life and apartments won't have much meaning for the adult student. Rather, I do better when I tap the rich life histories of the students themselves for ideas. Simply by asking for them the first day or night of class, I get folders full of remarkably varied and effective real-life situations which have demanded better writing skills than students volunteering the problem had when they faced the situations. By using such class-generated problems, I am able to assure the students that the skills they are setting out to learn are not divorced from their histories—or futures—and that their precollege experience is something on which they can build rather than something extraneous to higher education.

Assembling such a folder of workable class-generated writing problems is easy. Like the students, I function more or less gracefully in the world of normal adult responsibilities. Drawing on whatever "real-world" problems I'm currently facing, I relate to them the demands and frustrations I encounter as a practical writer; for example, an exchange of letters with a magazine's business office which insists that the three-year subscription for which I've paid has expired, while my cancelled check and I argue that I have half a year to go. With my anecdote before the class, I ask them to include in a one-page self-sketch a description of a recent writing task they've run into, preferably one which they feel defeated them. With only a very few exceptions, adult students have no trouble responding—a result which surprised me at first, since I had come to accept the cliché that today's student writes only to sign her or his name to checks. Moreover, because I collect the sketches and writing problems halfway through the first two-hour class and glance through them quickly at the break, I can use one or two cases immediately.

An example which appears in the folder at nearly every first class session will illustrate. Typically, at least one student will report having been billed in error on a charge account or credit statement. Frustrated by endless minutes on hold or by some other failure to resolve the problem by phone, the student will have been driven, reluctantly, to write. Simple at first glance, the problem sponsors learning in most areas writing instructors see as central to student success and does so in the first class session. Discussion and group composing elicit an initial writer-focused impulse to ventilate frustration. Gentle prodding, however, soon elicits from the group the need for audience definition before writing begins. Audience definition ("some underpaid clerk") leads to a description of the intended reader's needs in the light of the writer's aim (a clear and full description of the error and an equally unequivocal statement of the desired adjustment). Strategies for achieving the desired reader response (vocabulary level, desirable tone, organization of the facts, relevant documentation of claims) follow logically from a discussion of audience. Eventually, the group will reframe the problem as a *writing* problem: how to compose a message which gets a harried high school graduate to see the error of the mystifying computer's ways. And in first-night revision of a group-composed message, fairly subtle issues which have long eluded my "regular" classes emerge spontaneously—how complex can a sentence be and still succeed with a rushed reader whose abilities are unknown? How can connotation of words help me get the adjustment I seek?

Assessment

Naturally, neither teacher nor student will want to work with such materials for more than a week or two. For good or ill, students need to get on with the business of doing academic writing. But by starting with student-generated tasks—have they had to attach an explanation to an IRS 1040? Have they tried making a brief family history for their grandchildren? Have they served on a PTA committee? Have they struggled with the personal statement on the college's admission form?—we can provide adult students with a familiar and supportive transition into college writing. And if the numbers are right, we'll need such transitions more and more in the years to come.

Free Writing That Counts

Carol L. Reinsberg

Much classroom writing is highly structured; therefore, students welcome the opportunity to do their own writing. But teachers have difficulty finding time not only to work such free writing into an already crowded curriculum but also to find ways to grade the results. Carol L. Reinsberg of Springbrook High School, Silver Spring, Maryland, suggests a method she uses successfully to solve both problems.

Author's Comment

Since the late sixties, writers have been preaching a message to English teachers: we must get out of our students' way if they are to develop their writing skills. Free writing rather than structured composition, the articles and books tell us, is the way to unlock a young person's inborn writing talent. Writing without teachers will allow the authentic voice of the creator to emerge. Student evaluation of writing can be more helpful than teacher comments. All of these statements are more or less true, of course. But there is another truth seldom voiced in these sermons, and it is that having produced a piece of interesting writing, a student wants credit for it—teacher credit—*grade* credit. And how can a public school English teacher, already stretched to the limits of time and energy by the demands of a traditional curriculum, manage to sift through the creative efforts of every student, choose the best, and allow the quality of these pieces to be reflected in the final grade?

This question nagged at me when I began teaching English in Montgomery County, Maryland, six years ago. My juniors and seniors often grumbled over the County's composition program with its twelve structured—mostly expository—compositions and recalled wistfully the creative writing they had been encouraged to do in elementary school. I sympathized, while at the same time reviewing the old multiplication problem: 150 students times 12 structured compositions equals 1,800 pieces of writing to correct and discuss, and 150 students times even a minimum number of creative or "free" writings added to the original 1,800 equals teacher collapse.

Impromptu Writing in the Classroom

In response to this problem, I have worked to develop a free writing program that overcomes many of the practical difficulties and creates respect and enthusiasm in students for the craft of writing. I call this program the Impromptu Series, to suggest the spontaneous nature of the writing experience. The success of the series is the result, first, of careful shaping of students' attitudes at the beginning of each writing session, and second, of a method that places much of the burden of evaluation and revision on the student.

The series consists of six to eight free writing sessions scheduled as often as time permits, usually in the second semester. During these periods, students write in any form—narrative, poetic, dramatic, descriptive, expository, impressionistic—although I limit them to two attempts at poetry. They are free to take pieces home to work on them but must bring them back to school, where they are kept in individual folders in the classroom.

On one day toward the end of the school year, I ask each class to review their creative writing folders, making certain that every piece bears at the top a clear statement of purpose, such as "a lyric poem expressing joy at the discovery of love," or "a short story revealing a young person's character as he or she is forced to make a decision," or "a familiar essay whose ironic tone points up the hypocrisy of the student government." I ask each student to polish the best piece, place it first in the collection, and hand the entire collection in to me.

I skim the folder, choosing the impromptu that seems to be second best, and then grade both. (Knowing that I will choose a second impromptu to grade discourages students from using an occasional writing period as a creative rest time.) I am careful to evaluate these free writings in the light of the student's stated objectives, and when I average grades for the last marking period, I count these two grades as an important part of the final grade.

The logistics of the program are meaningless, however, unless during every impromptu session the students are sincerely trying to do the best writing of which they are capable. Here, the readiness is all. On each writing day I use the reliable old device of the stimulus. One time it may be a few minutes of taped music; on another occasion, a silent film or series of evocative photographs. Sometimes I hand out a list of "beginnings"—opening lines from poems, short stories, essays, descriptions. While these stimuli are valuable in setting a mood and helping students to break out of the mundane world of school, they are even more important in contributing to a special attitude, a sense of getting ready for something important.

Establishing this attitude may take ten or even fifteen minutes at first. I begin by placing a sign on my classroom door that reads, "Quiet, please: Silent writing in progress." Next, we give careful consideration to everyone's physical comfort. We decide on the best lighting and adjust the blinds or turn out lights. We open or close windows to adjust the temperature. The basketball player is provided with an extra chair for a leg rest, privacy seekers are encouraged to move to remote corners of the room, floor sitters are given something comfortable to sit on. We talk about the need for everyone to feel alone during the time ahead. Therefore, not only must there be no talking, but there must be no communication, by gesture or look, to break the spell, for everyone is to be enclosed within an imaginary bubble inside which ideas can germinate. To emphasize this point I even ask gum chewers to remove their gum. We agree on the time at which the silent period will end. Finally, they begin.

Aside from the practical value of these preparations, this "countdown" establishes the importance of the task ahead and creates a feeling of excitement—even impatience—as the students wait for the opening notes of the music or first glimpse of the picture. Rarely does a student disturb the writing environment, and as a rule, most want to continue writing beyond the time agreed upon. However, in the first session or two I insist that they stop well ahead of the bell so they can share their responses, and because, like all party organizers, I know the best time to end a party is at the moment when the guests are having a good time.

Since introducing the Impromptu Series I have had more positive results each year as I have learned to devote more time to the establishing of a freeing, quiet environment. I find that in the midst of a six-period day during which students must shuttle from math to gym to locker to cafeteria, my providing them with an emotional space and time in which they can look inward gives them something of value, and this something is frequently expressed in memorable written expression. Most of my students look forward to these opportunities and are disappointed when our crowded schedule forces postponement of an impromptu session.

The Impromptu Series has advantages for me, too. By staggering the due dates for my classes I can grade while students are editing their folders. Moreover, I have found that the time required to grade two impromptus is usually less than that needed to evaluate one standard composition. If the students' purpose is to reveal character through a short-short story, or to create a vivid portrait of a stranger through description, their success, or lack of it, is quickly apparent. More often than not, they are at least partly successful, for they have been free to set up their own objectives and have had weeks to revise and rewrite.

Some of the best impromptus have appeared in the school literary magazine and others have been proudly reproduced by parents. Still others have been reshaped and submitted to contests. One former student came smiling into my classroom not too long ago bearing his college literary magazine, in which his story, born in an impromptu session the year before, was one of the main features.

True, only a few of the impromptus see the light of publication. Nevertheless, every student who takes part in the Impromptu Series receives recognition for creative effort, because a final grade in English represents not only mastery of the County curriculum, but also the student's special vision, freely expressed.

Awareness of Audience's Needs:
A Charade

Ann D. Spector

By writing for their peers, students can gain an understanding of audience's needs. This exercise outlines a series of short writing activities that are designed to reinforce the importance of anticipating an audience's needs. Ms. Spector submitted this from Fairfield University, Fairfield, Connecticut.

Author's Comment

I used this mini-unit to stimulate the class in working effectively as a peer group. Moreover, the task demands that students develop an awareness of their audience's needs by providing an immediate and concrete response.

The Approach

1. One class period, each of three groups was asked to choose a topic for a charade, and then to write its own process, or set of instructions for performing it. The instructions were written in class. Sets of instructions were a single paragraph and took about twenty minutes to write. It's important to remind students that instructions must be strictly behavioral—metaphoric commands, e.g., "grin like a shark," are ruled out. This exercise presented us with our first rhetorical dilemmas; if our charades were to be guessed, we obviously needed to define our audience and limit our choice of topics. We solved these problems by confining ourselves to the titles of popular movies and television shows.

Each group was asked to give its set of instructions to a second group to perform before the third group. The second, or acting, group had no idea what the first group's charade was about; all they had were the instructions for performing it: "lift your right foot," "wave your hand," "grin and shake your head," and so on. The students saw that if their writing was not effective, if their instructions were not clear and concise, if they were too diffuse, if they'd given their audience too much or too little, something too complicated or too simple, then one group couldn't act it, and the other group couldn't guess it. In other words, if they hadn't adequately communicated the information that was necessary for the other two groups to act out and interpret the charade, the process wouldn't work.

2. For the next class, the students were asked to write their own set of instructions for a charade to read to their group. The group had to guess the title from these written instructions. Students were asked to observe the group's responses to ascertain the cause of whatever difficulties the members had in interpreting the charade.

3. For the third class, students were asked to write rhetorical analyses of their own instructions. Since the entire rhetorical process had been very concrete, and apparent, these analyses were easy for a group of novices to write. Moreover, when we discussed what we had learned from the entire process, we were able to abstract a list of criteria which served as the basis for annotating our next set of papers.

Unscrambling Organization

Alan Price

To familiarize students with some organizational patterns in writing, Alan Price uses a classroom game that calls for cooperation and discussion among students as they attempt to unscramble topic sentences related to an argumentative piece of writing. Mr. Price contributed this from Pennsylvania State University at Hazleton.

Author's Comment

Many of my composition students have a difficult time finding suitable plans of organization for their themes. I know that organization is a problem because students tell me so in conferences. Further, I know that it is a problem because I read their essays, and frequently raw material is presented in very rough form.

Organizing the information in an argument (statistics, evidence from secondary sources, personal experiences) is a very complicated process for the best of writers. Students are usually clearer about what blocks the effective organization of an essay than what contributes to it. Some student writers, for instance, become so absorbed in the research effort that they fail to allow sufficient time for organizing, writing, and revising. Many find it difficult to call a halt to a search which is new and exciting. Even those who leave enough time often find that they have worked so closely with their subjects that they are unable to see what should follow. Others become tense when they realize that much of their hard-sought material will have to be excluded. And a few are so sick of their subject after the research that they skimp on steps in the writing process.

Research or brainstorming is fun for most students. It is an open and expansive step where all ideas are fair game. Little emphasis, significantly, is placed on evaluating (or "grading") the information as it comes in. The important thing is to keep an open mind, to let the juices flow.

Organization creates a much different psychological atmosphere. The mood that pervades all of the barriers to successful organization is tension or anxiety. To outline is a constricting process where ideas are sorted and arranged by priority. As the focus becomes tighter within the paper and tighter still within individual paragraphs, student writers begin to tense up. Organizing is a process of grading, or excluding, of arranging and rearranging—a process which takes enormous amounts of mental and psychic energy for the student. Art students are taught in drawing class to squint at the objects before them to get a clearer sense of their form. Squinting at a still-life setup to perceive an outline is hard work and so is squinting at the notes for an English composition.

An Organizing Exercise

How can the composition teacher reduce the tension which seems to be an inevitable by-product of the organization step? A strategy I have found successful in teaching organization is to use a classroom workshop game in which students work in small groups to discover the most effective arrangement for a set of scrambled topic sentences. The teacher should choose topic sentences which are ahead of the pace of the class so that an immediate understanding of what each topic sentence says and where it fits is beyond the quick grasp of most individuals in the class. These topic sentences may be drawn from an essay by a professional writer or an outstanding theme by a student from a previous year; the source is not important. What is important is that the sentences are mixed in such a way that their classroom presentation implies no original order. They could be dictated to the class. I hand out mimeographed exercises (see sample)[1] with sentences typed sideways or upside down.

Once the students have the sentences, they should be divided into small groups of three or four to work as teams. I find that the exercise is most successful if the teacher selects the members of each team. The friendships and groups that have already naturally formed in the class do not usually provide the best mix for this project. The members of the team are going to benefit if each contributes, after all, so carrying forward established patterns of leadership is not very productive.

The teams are instructed to rearrange the topic sentences into an order which will lead to the most effective development of an argument. I allow the teams the rest of that class period to work on possible arrangements with the clear understanding that each team must present its preferred outline at the beginning of the next class period. Many times the exercise is informally carried over to discussions in the library, dorm rooms, or the student union. There is always the risk that the teams will cheat by sharing ideas, but I have found that competition between teams is a stronger motivation than collaboration.

Some teams are marvelously inventive in their approaches to this assignment. I have come upon them drawing elaborate arrows, using

English Composition
Exercise in Organization and Logic

Directions: The following statistics and statements (drawn from an article on the advertising of pet foods) are presented in a random fashion. The evidence needs to be arranged into a pattern which shows a clear line of reasoning leading to a logical conclusion. Working in groups of three or four, you should rearrange these randomly displayed statistics and statements into the outline of an argument.

"When we bring out a new flavor in our pet-food line, they're tested on pet owners rather than pets."

I've heard a woman say that when she walks in at night from the supermarket her husband might not even look up from his paper, but the dog always acknowledges her coming back home.

By 1965, however, the amount of money Americans spent on commercially prepared pet food had risen to seven hundred million dollars. Since then, the business has grown to the point where people are spending two and a half billion dollars a year on this commodity.

With the unceasing advertising barrages on television, and with the emphasis on the virtues of high-priced dog food, it was as if price had become the touchstone not only of the quality of the product being offered but also the quality of the purchaser—as if the social status of citizens could be judged by the expensiveness of the dog food they bought.

Anyone considering this point might bear in mind that no pet food merchandiser ever loses sight of the fact that the customer is not the pet itself but its owner.

It's more convenient for pet owners to open a can or other container than to cut up whatever table scraps may be available.

Pet foods account for five percent of all money spent in supermarkets on dry groceries.

Actually there appears to be some question as to how well dogs, for example, can distinguish between the flavors of the many different animal parts contained in commercial dog food. Basically it's just nourishment to them, and they can get by equally well on a total vegetable cereal diet, although some animal amino acids are desirable as part of such a diet.

These studies seem to agree that a household pet is increasingly regarded as (to use a phrase that occurs over and over in such documents) "a member of the family."

According to current industry estimates there are now between fifty-seven and seventy million cats and dogs in this country—thirty-five to forty million dogs and twenty-two to thirty million cats.

different colors of ink, even cutting apart the original exercise sheet and pasting up a new order. (The manuscript pages of Edith Wharton's novels were cut and pasted several times, and they frequently vary in length because of this organizational technique.) One group has even gone off to the computer center, punched in the topic sentences on cards, and received all the possible orders for arrangement. The teacher should simply provide the materials for the exercise—even to the extent of bringing in scissors and paste and pens with different colored inks—and avoid directing what evolves. The interaction within the teams produces some surprising and creative behavior. One mechanical engineering student, for example, suddenly began drawing elaborate flow charts and diagrams on the blackboard. He happened to see ideas most clearly in spatial arrangements. Once he discovered his personal scheme, his English themes became very tightly structured. The best practice is to keep hands off unless the teams become disruptive.

Attendance at the next class is excellent. Students feel a personal stake in their team's effort. As each team's outline is flashed up on a screen via an overhead projector, the groups begin to argue. Sometimes there are even gracious concessions that one team, indeed, has found a better plan. The entire period is spent discussing questions of emphasis, order, and approach—always referring back to the topic sentences from the assignment.

The next step is to have the students bring their own research notes and tentative outlines for their papers. Once again they split into small groups (usually choosing members from the original team) and this time work through organization problems of a more immediate and personal significance. Is the anxiety gone? Not completely. However, they now feel better prepared to attack the problems of organization with the experience of the scrambled sentence exercise behind them, and new friends and fellow writers beside them.

Note

1. From Thomas Whiteside, "Onward and Upward with the Arts (Pet Food)," *The New Yorker* (November 1, 1976), pp. 51–98.

A Twenty-Minute Exercise
for In-Class Essays

Ronald E. Smith

Students faced with the prospect of writing in-class essays often express bewilderment about handling such a task. This exercise is designed to show students how to organize their time, topic, and writing to meet the requirements of in-class writing. Mr. Smith teaches at the University of North Alabama in Florence.

Author's Comment

This exercise is designed for a community college composition class, but it is adaptable to any class that involves graded, in-class writing assignments. I first began working on the exercise several years ago to help my students prepare for department-required in-class essays. The time limit on the essays was two hours. For anyone who has never had to write in such a situation, two hours may seem like a rather long time, but many of my students complained that they had hardly begun before I announced that it was time for them to move on to their conclusions. Some of the students even failed to complete an essay in the two hours allotted. It did not take many personal observations or student conferences to discover what the problem was. Many of the students were taking up to twenty minutes just to stare at the assignment sheet before beginning their essays, and even then some of the students would experience several false starts before actually beginning to write. In short, much of the class was spending one-fifth, or longer, of its writing time just trying to get started. It was clear, needless to say, that these students were in need of some form of guidance if they were to have a reasonable opportunity to complete their assignments. It was in an attempt to provide this guidance that I developed the twenty-minute exercise for in-class essays. I reasoned that if at least twenty minutes of the students' time for writing the essay was being wasted, they had nothing to lose by spending that amount of time preparing for their assignment in class.

The Twenty-Minute Exercise

The basic outline of the exercise is really quite simple. The students are given a handout that has six timed steps and a list of topics to draw from. There is nothing magic about the topics and any number of substitutions can be made. It is important, however, to have a variety of topics to choose from as this will give the students practice at selecting a single topic from several choices. Although the topics are normally at the bottom of the handout, for the sake of illustration I will put them at the beginning of my explanation of the exercise.

cars	dorm life	music
cafeteria	drugs	Saturdays
college	houses	songs
bikes	hobbies	sports
books	hiking	television
buses	movies	trips

1. Select one of the topics listed above (2 minutes).

    It is important to stress that the two minutes is a time limitation, and it is not necessary to spend the entire time selecting a topic. Students move on to the next step as soon as they have selected a topic—any time saved is used in the next step.

2. Write all that you can think of on that topic (7 minutes).

    The concern here should be with getting information down on paper, not on grammar or punctuation. Also, while the seven minutes is only another time limitation, students should be encouraged to use the full amount of time on this step. For those students who insist that they have all the information that they can think of or that is needed, the instructor should look at their papers before letting them move on to step three. It is helpful to point out that this is not a race or a contest.

3. From the material that you have, select the points that you feel to be the most important (3 minutes).

    All that the students need do here is underline or circle the points that they feel are the most important to the understanding of their topics.

4. Develop a working thesis (3 minutes).

    This is where the students have the most problems, both on the exercise and while writing in class generally. This is where the students really have to decide what to write about—what to focus on. For those students who really have a problem with developing a thesis, I simply suggest that the first few times they use a pattern something like *The purpose of this paper is . . . .*

5. Select the points that can be used in developing and supporting your thesis (2 minutes).

    This is done by numbering the selections or by indicating them in any manner that the student finds to be effective. It is a good idea to suggest to the students that it may be a good idea to take a closer look at those points selected earlier as being important as well as those points passed over. They may find, in light of the working thesis that has been developed, that the importance of these points has shifted.

6. Write a thesis statement that accurately reflects the work already completed (3 minutes).

    This is really nothing more than a check and a possible revision of the thesis developed in step four.

Evaluation

Some instructors may feel that students are losing valuable time if they spend the first twenty minutes doing what I prescribe here. I would disagree, however, for this form of prewriting is really putting the students to work on their assignment, not keeping them from their writing. Instead of just sitting there and trying to think of something to say or where to begin, the students are actually starting on their papers during the first few minutes of class. Although I have no hard statistics to support this method, I do have personal observations that show my students writing from the beginning of the class rather than just staring at the assignment sheet. I also have student papers that show increasing improvement in organization and development on assignments written in class. There is also a good deal of positive feedback from the students based on this assignment. I do not treat this exercise as a panacea, however, for all of the problems that are encountered while writing an in-class essay, nor is it being presented as one. It will not work for every student, but what will?

How to Introduce Introductions and Outlines

Greg Larkin

The roles of outlines and introductions in writing are not always readily apparent to student writers. This exercise recommends a method that shows students concretely the value and function of both. Mr. Larkin contributed this from Brigham Young University, Hawaii Campus at Laie.

Author's Comment

"Introductions and outlines are passé," a student recently told me.

I can sympathize. Long ago, I remember my ninth grade teacher spent the whole year on them. We didn't write anything but introductions all year long. Every day one introduction was due and that was all. Finally after dozens of introductions, we started doing introductions and an outline. But then the year ended. The introductions and outlines had been literally ends in themselves. Today the profession as a whole has swung away from great stress on the absolute necessity of a formal introduction for every occasion. The result is that for many students introductions and outlines are theoretical cargo, easily jettisoned if not functionally related to the rest of the essay.

Can the introduction and the outline be taught not in terms of rigid "rules," but in terms of function? Years ago, when I was student-teaching, my supervisor, VerDon Ballantyne of Brigham Young University-Provo, introduced me to a method of showing students concretely the value and function of the introduction and outline in terms of the completed paper. This method requires only about 5 minutes and a simple child's puzzle like the one below which must be the kind with a frame into which the pieces are set.

A Puzzling Activity

Before class I remove all the pieces from the frame and put them in my pocket. Then I conceal the frame in among my books, in my briefcase, or

frame   fourteen individual
                               puzzle pieces set into
                               the frame

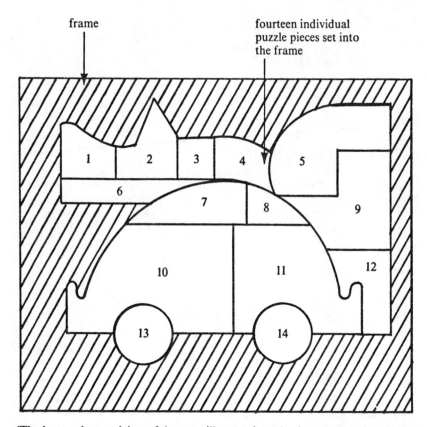

(The key to the puzzle's usefulness to illustrate introductions and outlines is that
the frame's outer edge is perfectly square, but the inner edge, which creates the
indentation into which the pieces are fit, is very irregular. When the student first
attempts to put the puzzle together, the teacher has not told him or her that there
even is a frame. Hence without the frame to establish the boundaries of the
puzzle, it is very difficult to know how to put the pieces together.)

anywhere where the students won't notice it as I enter class. As class
begins, I deposit my books/briefcase (with the hidden frame) over to the
side of the room and place a table or desk at the front of the class. Then I
call one student to come up to help with a "demonstration." As the
student is coming forward I explain that what we are about to see is
related to writing, but that it will not be immediately clear how it is
related. I explain that I will be asking for the relationship as soon as the
demonstration is over.

I then take the puzzle pieces out of my pockets and place them face
down on the table. The student's "demonstration" consists of putting the

puzzle together. I ask the student to explain to us the steps taken as the demonstration progresses. Almost invariably the student's first question is "Can I turn the pieces over?" I ask why anyone would want to turn the pieces over. The answer is usually in terms of "seeing all the parts," "seeing the whole," etc. I then ask the class what that answer has to do with writing. I myself do not answer the question, except to tell the student that if it will help, the pieces may be turned over.

I have carefully selected my puzzle so that the pieces themselves when put together form a very irregular shape, which is only discoverable with the help of the frame. In fact, although it is a very simple puzzle, with only 14 pieces, it is virtually impossible to put together correctly without the frame. The students begin struggling with the pieces, trying and retrying various combinations and generally having a very frustrating time. As the student works, I ask why certain pieces are being put together. The answers are invariably in terms of some pattern, but the student can't see the overall picture and winds up with parts but no whole.

As the time gets longer, the student becomes uncomfortable. At this point I slip unnoticed over to my books and take out the frame. I hold it up to the class (not the student) and ask, "Will this help?" The student is usually so desperate that I have to repeat myself several times before the student sees the frame and, with great relief, takes it, rapidly assembles the puzzle, and retires sheepishly but gratefully to his or her seat.

One variation that can be used effectively is to include an extra puzzle piece among the original fourteen pieces (without of course telling the student that it is extra). If the extra piece is chosen to look quite similar to the correct pieces, without the frame the student has no way to tell which piece is extra, or even that there is an extra piece at all. However, with the aid of the frame, the student is able to discover that the puzzle contained an extra piece.

This simple exercise has always led to a good discussion of introductions and outlining, with the students themselves able to generate the following observations:

1. As with turning over the pieces first, it is a good idea to survey all the parts of a paper before beginning to write.

2. Like the frame, the outline provides a context or frame of reference into which specific smaller pieces can be meaningfully placed. It also provides a means of rejecting unnecessary or irrelevant pieces.

3. Without the frame no basis can be found to judge how "correctly" the puzzle is put together. Similarly, the introduction establishes the rhetorical stance of the essay, which is the basis of most specific choices the writer makes throughout the essay.

4. As the pieces have definite relations to each other as well as to the whole, so the parts of a paper have an internal logic of development. This is seen by noticing various sub-parts within the puzzle's design. For instance, the puzzle that I use shows a car, some tall buildings, and some short buildings, each placed into definite relationship with the others by the frame.

5. As the frame guides the puzzle maker to put the pieces together, so the outline guides the author to write the paper, and the introduction guides readers in their following of the paper.

These points do not teach students how to outline or how to introduce a paper, yet they do show them concretely how an outline and introduction are supposed to function in a paper. I always begin lessons on outlining or introductions with this demonstration because I find it combines a theory or rationale with a concrete example. Students seem much more able to write their own outlines and introductions once they have such a solid frame of reference.

Animal, Vegetable, Mineral:
A Method for Introducing Heuristics

Thomas M. Rivers

Students in the classes of Thomas Rivers learn how to develop their own heuristic procedures for writing. Mr. Rivers sent this exercise from Indiana State University at Evansville.

Author's Comment

One of the problems I encounter in introducing students to the invention stage of composing is that many students are unfamiliar with the complete composing process. Most of their involvement with writing has been with "writing" in the narrower sense of organization, style, revision, and editing. The role of invention has often been excluded from their composition courses. Another problem related to this, i.e., making students aware of the whole process of composition and not just the disposition stage, is that many of our students are overwhelmed by heuristic strategies that are introduced in the prewriting or invention stage. This paper hopes to offer a method for addressing these problems.

The Heuristic Exercise

An ideal way to introduce students to heuristic procedures is to have them develop one themselves. A technique that I have found successful is having them develop a plan for playing "20 Questions." The object of the game is to guess what someone is thinking (the unknown) by asking them questions to which only the answer "yes" or "no" can be given. The object must be discovered within 20 questions. Typically, when we first play the game they are unable to successfully uncover the object—they need a plan, a heuristic procedure for discovery.

In order to successfully develop a plan they need to become aware of three basic processes fundamental to heuristic procedure. These three processes are classifying, sequencing, and questioning. I introduce them to the means, motive, opportunity plan of a detective and show how certain kinds of questions are "contained" within each classification, how they are necessarily sequenced, and how a specialist in each area is capable of asking the best kind of question from the category (e.g., means for a medical examiner). Previous attempts to immediately introduce elaborate heuristic plans (Burke's Pentad or the Young, Becker, and Pike system in *Rhetoric: Discovery and Change*) were premature. It assumed an understanding of classifying, sequencing, and questioning. The value of developing a plan for "20 Questions" is that to successfully play the game students must become aware of classifying, sequencing, and questioning.

The Game

I begin the game of "20 Questions" without giving my students any time to prepare. I explain the object of the game, and we begin. Their questions for the most part are disjointed, random and imprecise—i.e., they do not classify their questions, sequence them or clearly ask them. Either in a given time period (20 minutes) or within twenty questions, they are unable to gather enough information to "discover" the object "hidden" in my mind.

After a few attempts some rules are added to the game. Groups of four or five students are formed. Members suggest the kind of questions to ask in each instance, and, in rotation, one of them decides the question. They write it down, raise their hands, and await my "yes" or "no" answer to their written question. They record each question for each game for future reference. I should mention now the kinds of unknown objects that are permissible. They are not abstractions (colors, virtues, concepts), and they are not unusual (duck-billed platypus). Since the game demonstrates only a discovery aspect (recall) of a heuristic procedure, an unknown object would never be discovered. They can't recall what they don't already know. Finally, they are not specific examples of the object—razor, not Gillette or Cartridge.

Benefits

"20 Questions" introduces students to the objectives of heuristic procedures. The better prepared they are to understand such procedures the better they use them. An ability to effectively use the system in Young, Becker, and Pike, *Rhetoric: Discovery and Change* (YBP) leads to a valid objective of a complete composition course—full exploration and understanding of the experience to be communicated.

A. Learning a System
   1. Classifying—The students keep a list of their questins. They analyze them and note if they can classify certain types of ques-

tions. For example, "Is it used in the kitchen?" or "Do students use it in school?" Such questions can be classified as use questions and quite properly could be used as a classification for generating certain kinds of questions.

2. Sequencing—After the students have come up with four or five categories, they are asked to note whether their classifications follow any sequence (usually they have been random) and whether there is a proper sequencing for them. Typically, they arrive at a system made up of the following sequence:

> Class
> Location
> Use
> Importance
> Physical Characteristics

3. Questioning—At the very heart of any heuristic procedure is questioning. Students learn the importance of precision in stating questions. For example, many times I am unable to answer yes or no to their questions. Furthermore, they learn how their questions often contain hidden assumptions (begging the questions). They may ask, for example, whether a certain object is found indoors (e.g., umbrella). An umbrella can be found indoors, but it is used outdoors. The question assumes the object has a unique location, which it does not. Whether it has a unique location needs to be determined first (where it is used is more germane than where it is found). By asking does it have a unique location they would have learned that it does not and they would move to the next category, use. One of the sub-categories developed for use is where used and it is from this that a more useful question will be generated.

They also learn that their overall knowledge allows them to ask better questions. For example, students who have taken a course in biology will be able to learn more about an object (assume they know it belongs to the class of things called animals) by asking whether it is a mammal. Knowing the phylums, in other words, allows for better questions. A heuristic procedure is not a substitute for experience and knowledge, but allows for a better use of knowledge.

After developing a system the students become more effective and usually within the time allotted or within "20 Questions" they are able to zero in on the "answer" to the "problem."

Before continuing let me briefly note the kind of subtopics that my students developed for some of the categories. The first category entitled class is broken down into living or non-living and depending upon the answer to the questions generated by this subtopic they ask plant or animal if living and man-made or elemental if non-living. Assuming they learn it is an animal, a typical set of subtopics under location is: below, on, or above land, in the water, or possibly domestic or wild. I ask them to develop a set of subtopics for each category, but since "20 Questions" involves much trial and error in getting a useful set of subtopics, I supply them with one after they have made an initial attempt. Remember the object of "20 Questions" is not to become good at playing "20 Questions." Rather it is to introduce students to more elaborate heuristic procedures like YBP or Burke's Pentad. Such procedures are an integral part of the composing process.

B. Promoting Problem Solving

Besides the keeping of journals, I ask my students to write two communications that stem from problematic situations (a method that is well developed in *Rhetoric: Discovery and Change* by YBP). Introducing them to the problem of discovery found in "20 Questions" anticipates the problem solving nature of these two writing assignments. Just as in "20 Questions" they are confronted with an unknown. And just as in "20 Questions" they are aware that a plan is more likely to generate full exploration and a possible solution than exploration of their problematic situation without a plan. Furthermore, introducing heuristics through a problem solving game and the writing on topics stemming from problem situations anticipates some concern over discovery techniques that are not put in a creative context. A fairly typical example of a student problem situation may be trying to discover a way to improve service at the pizza parlor he or she works at. After exploring the problem by using a heuristic plan (I use YBP system as developed in Winterowd's *Contemporary Writer*) the student simulates an audience, purpose and medium— e.g., an evaluation report to his or her employer.

C. Using Brainstorming

Since the students work in groups and discuss the kinds of questions they are going to ask as well as decide on a system for playing "20 Questions," they become familiar with the value of brainstorming. This allows them to observe that problem solving requires more than a mechanistic approach. When they work with their major communications, I also assign them to groups where they use brainstorming to complement the heuristic procedure(s) I use in Winterowd CW— these invention techniques, however, are found in other composition texts.

Summary

As I point out to my students, a heuristic procedure is not a short-cut to problem-solving skills. It does allow students to make the most of what they already know, either to generate new perspectives or to discover information, but it is no substitute for experience and knowledge. A non-reporter, for example, using a system of who, what, when, where, why, and how, may know from the system what is to be discovered, but only an experienced reporter may be able to find all the answers. (We discuss investigative reporting and the film *All The President's Men.*) This point is further illustrated in the detective's system of means, motive, and opportunity. This system generates many kinds of questions, but the experienced and knowledgeable will have the know-how to generate the most profitable questions, as well as answer them (we discuss the TV series *Quincy* and the medical examiner's concern with means and his ability to interpret information). The philosopher's advice that the most important thing one can learn in school is the ability to ask questions is not at issue, but the students must be aware that full exploration will only take place if they can answer the questions they have asked. The student at the pizza parlor who asks how other pizza parlors are run (which is a good question), must also know that the only way to get the answer is to go and look. The invention stage is not just an armchair adventure.

Moving from Prewriting into Composing

Lois Rubin

How does a writer discover content and formulate a way to shape that content into a written draft? This sequence of lessons is designed to equip students with strategies for arriving at an answer to the question. Ms. Rubin submitted this exercise from Carnegie-Mellon University, Pittsburgh, Pennsylvania.

Author's Comment

The following is a series of exercises developed to facilitate both discovery of content and its development into a written draft. The basis of the discovery exercise is the heuristic procedure for exploring experience by viewing it from various perspectives, as presented by Richard E. Young, Alton L. Becker, and Kenneth L. Pike, in *Rhetoric: Discovery and Change.* This work, while receiving great acclaim in the discipline, has met with some concern among teachers as to how to translate its theory into practical classroom experiences. My exercises are an effort in that direction. The method underlying my activity for charting the development of a draft comes from Nancy I. Sommers's "Revision in the Composing Process; A Case Study of Experienced and Student Writers." (Unpublished doctoral dissertation, Boston University, 1979). Together, the exercises illustrate the writing process in action, moving from discovering content to composing it into written form.

Session 1: Discovering Content
(handout, "The Egg")

In one 50-minute class session students are introduced to three perspectives of the Young, Becker, and Pike heuristic, and given the opportunity to try the heuristic out for themselves. As illustration, a handout of notes, "The Egg," is distributed early in the session; these notes explore that object from the perspective of a particle (a static entity), a wave (a dynamic entity), and a field (a network). (Young, p. 122) To give students the experience of using the heuristic themselves, teabags are then distributed, one to each member of the class. Working in small groups, students manipulate the teabags (taking apart the bags from their strings and tags, wetting the leaves) in order to view them from the particle, wave, and field perspectives. One member notes down each group's observations, using the format of "The Egg" handout. Fifteen minutes before the end of the session, students are asked to begin the next phase of composing, selection of information to be included on a paper according to the needs of a hypothetical reader and purpose. Several imaginary readers and purposes are proposed: to describe a teabag for an Eskimo who has never seen one; to persuade a confirmed coffee drinker to switch to drinking tea. After selecting the information relevant to its goal, each group then presents its purpose, audience, and set of information before the class as a whole. The assignment that follows asks students to use the heuristic to gather information about a small object of their choice (cigarette, Coke bottle, brownie), and to bring the information generated to the next class session.

Heuristic for Describing an Object: The Egg

A.   View the object as a static entity, a "particle"

Glowing white, oval shape

Sized to be cupped in your hand

Brittle shell

Inside, clear Jello-like substance, yellow ball sits in transparent pool

B.   View the object as a dynamic process or variable, a "wave"

Upon contact, yellow glob breaks open and spills out in a slime

As it boils, white gel firms in spongy layer, yellow into solid ball

When stirred in frying pan, forms yellow confetti-shaped pieces

As it fries in the skillet, the transparent liquid thickens, whitens and puffs into a bumpy white layer across the pan

When knocked by blunt objects, shell fragments into sharp pieces

Grew from tiny cell in chicken, accumulating yellow and white grains

C.   View the object as a system or set of relationships, a "field" (part of larger system)

Is a complex assembly of interrelated parts, each with its own subdivisions: shell, shell membrane, white, yolk, germ

Has important role for chicken, to form and nourish the
new chicken

Is the most common variety of many types of eggs; those
produced by other birds (ostrich, pigeon, duck, partridge),
by insects (moth, butterfly), by fish (oyster, sturgeon,
shad)

Is important part of man's diet; along with meat and fish
provides a major source of his protein; forms an ingredient in salads, cookies, and casseroles

Session 2: Development of Notes into Draft (handout, "Chocolate Chip Cookie")

At this session the handout is a student's notes, based on the heuristic
discussed in session 1 (with the addition of the category "member of a
class"), and the paper that developed from them. The activity for the
session is to compare the notes with the finished paper in order to trace
the kinds of changes that occur in the development of a draft. As framework for this, I draw on Nancy Sommers's method for analyzing revision,
in particular, the "categories of change": deletion, substitution, addition,
reordering. ("Revision in the Composing Process: A Case Study of Experienced and Student Writers." Unpublished doctoral dissertation, Boston
University, 1979). Specific questions are raised to direct students' attention to the kinds of changes the student-writer made in forming notes
into a draft. Which notes were used; which ones eliminated? What material not present in the notes was added in the draft version? How did
the order of the draft differ from that of the notes? Overall, what form
did the "Chocolate Chip Cookie" finally take? (a personal experience
narrative). What was its purpose and audience? After discussing this
model, students are asked to form their own notes into a draft, the
finished version of which will count as one of the required papers of
the course.

Development of Notes into Draft: "Chocolate Chip Cookie"

I. Notes from the heuristic:
   A. Particle
      Circular in shape, but not perfect; slightly irregular
      Fits in the palm of your hand
      Flat but not thin
      Top surface lumpy, small craters and valleys
      Light earthy color
      Darker brown hills, some exposed, some covered by the
      earthy brown material
      Hills are smooth

Underside flatter; rougher than top; hills are flattened, more like lakes
B. Wave
Bends quite a bit before breaking
Smells like chocolate
Chewy
Chocolate hills dissolve away quickly when eaten
Inside exactly the same as outside
Chocolate and batter blend into one delicious flavor
C. Field
Two major parts make up the whole, chocolate chips and cookie batter
Used mainly as a form of dessert or snack
Little nutritional value
More common during holiday season
One of the more favorite varieties of cookie
Especially appealing to children
Commonly eaten with milk
Best just out of the oven, chocolate chips are melted; especially chewy
D. Member of class, distinct from others
Contains chocolate chips; some have butterscotch chips, nuts or coconut
Not completely homogeneous such as sugar, butter, or ginger cookies
Does not have a filling like the creme in Oreos. Other fillings include marshmallow, peanut butter, fig and other fruits
No frostings, like sugar or cinnamon
Soft and chewy, not hard and crisp
Circular in shape; other cookies are square or crescent-shaped
II. Draft
As I walk into the kitchen, the familiar scent of homemade cookies greets me with delight. I begin my search for my favorite, the chocolate chip cookie. Looking in all the cookie tins, I find the crescents, and some square-shaped cookies, but these are not circular like the chocolate chip. In another tin I find the butterscotch chip cookies and some nut and coconut cookies. But these do not contain the chocolate chips I seek. I allow my nose to follow the smell of chocolate to the top of the oven, where the chocolate chip cookies have been placed to cool. I pick one up, and set it in the palm of my hand. Two major parts make up the whole, chocolate chips and cookie batter. It is circular in shape, but slightly irregular. The cookie is flat yet not thin. The top surface is lumpy, with small craters and valleys running throughout. Exposed are dark hills, surrounded by a light earthy batter, some hills being covered. The underside is rougher in texture and flatter than the top, with the hills being smoothed into lakes. As I break it in half, I notice it bends quite a bit before breaking. The inside looks exactly the same as the

outside. Placing one half in my mouth, I find that it is chewy. The chocolate hills dissolve quickly, leaving a delicious blend of melted chocolate and cookie batter. These cookies are best when eaten directly from the oven. I pour myself a glass of milk to round out my favorite snack.

A single class session features a model which illustrates both the discovery and composing phases of the writing process. Drawing on three perspectives of the Young, Becker, and Pike heuristic—contrastive features, range of variation and distribution—the sample notes explore an activity, exercising at the "Powers Exercise Studio" (Young, p. 55). The paper which results serves as a model of realistic communication, a letter of complaint. After reading the notes and letter, students trace the kinds of changes that occurred in the development of the former into the latter, according to Nancy Sommers's "categories of changes" in revision: deletion, substitution, addition, and reordering. The following questions are raised: Which notes were used, which discarded? What new material not present in the notes was added into the letter? How did the order of the letter differ from that of the notes? Finally, how successful do you think this letter will be in achieving its purpose with the given audience? The assignment which follows asks students to use the given heuristic to discover content about an activity of interest to them, and then to shape this content into a written communication for a realistic purpose and audience.

Notes on "Powers Exercise Studio"

A. Contrastive Features:
    What makes this unit different from other units? What features distinguish it from similar acts or activities?
    Example: How is exercising at Powers different from other exercise programs I have participated in?
    More "gimmicky"—Contests ("Hit Parade of Platters"), before and after photos; posting of success of members, silly sayings along with exercises, social get-togethers ("Awards Night").
    Personalized program—Program of exercises designed exactly for my needs. Members do different things at different times; at the same time women are kicking at the bar, doing sit-ups, floor exercise.
    Flexible schedule—I can go at any time during the day. People come and go all the time. There's no one time when everyone does the same thing, except for group exercises for ten minutes every hour on the hour.
    Environment—Instead of "gym" atmosphere, "glamorous" surroundings: (shag rug, orange striped wallpaper, pink and orange cushioned machines, pink and orange cur-

tains, mirrored walls). Dirtier than bare gym setting—bits of paper in rug, smudged mirrors, dirty curtains; dressing room littered with paper, clips, gum ground into rug; no paper towels in bathroom.

B. Range of Variation:

How does this act/activity vary within itself? How does the experience change from time to time—from person to person?

Example: How does the experience of exercising at Powers studio vary from time to time?

Program changes—Exercises are increased at scheduled intervals throughout the program (from 10–20 sit-ups; from 10–30 kicks). New exercises are added to increase the overall program ("lunges" and side bend machine added after 3rd session).

Personnel changes—Different people on duty each day, different people lead the group exercise sessions each day, (Christen jokes as she directs; Patty runs through the exercises at breakneck speed), moods of personnel change: friendly and helpful when you start the program; indifferent to older members; harassed on a busy day; relaxed when the salon is empty.

Group changes—Some days I meet friends there and spend time chatting with them. Other days, there's no one I know and I merely exchange greetings with the people I come in contact with.

My performance—At the beginning of a new exercise I am awkward, uncertain, in need of help; later I become proficient and can check my accuracy myself in the mirror. On days when I feel good, I exercise energetically and get through the program quickly; on days when I'm tired, I move slowly and ineptly. At the beginning of the program, the employees are helpful, willing to explain; as I become an "old" member, their explanations get briefer and more grudging.

C. Distribution:

How does the act/activity fit into the larger context? Where does it fit in the larger system, in my total life?

Example: What place, role, function does exercising at Powers Studio have in my life?

My routine—I exercise on my non-working days (Tuesday and Thursday) as a change of pace before I start my book work. I do it during easier terms when I'm not overly pressured (when I had projects due every week for Literary Research, I went to the library on Tuesday and Thursday mornings—not to exercise class).

My way of life—Provides a modicum of convenient, regular physical exercise in a lifestyle that is more devoted to mental activity (studying, preparing lesson plans, grading papers). Provides a measure of self-centered activity in contrast to my many other-directed activities (running a household—shopping, cooking, doing erands—child-care—doctors' appointments, teacher conferences).

Environment—located on shopping street in Squirrel Hill, convenient to banks, stores; close to my home; I can walk to it and get the benefit of a walk along with my exercise.

D.   From notes to written statement:

What is my organizing idea? What do I want to say about Powers Studio?

"I think Powers Studio would provide a better service if it concentrated on the essentials of an exercise program rather than the frills."

What is the audience and purpose of my communication?

Audience: Director of Powers Exercise Studio

Purpose: To make them aware of weakness in the program, to encourage them to effect a change in the program.

Letter to "Powers Exercise Studio"

June 18, 1980
Director,
Powers Exercise Studio
Pittsburgh, PA 15217

Dear Sir or Madam:

As a member of the Powers Exercise Studio, I am writing this letter to offer some suggestions for the improvement of your services. The exercise program I'm engaged in at Powers Studio represents a big commitment of my time and energy. As a working person I have little time available for myself. Most of my time is spent either in preparing lessons, correcting papers for my English classes, or in doing the chores that go with running a household and raising children. Between shopping, banking, doctors' appointments, and teacher conferences, I have precious few hours each week for a purely personal outlet. Yet I feel that a program of regular physical exercise is especially important for a busy person. An exercise class which meets several hours a week provides the right solution for me.

Through the years I have participated in modern dance classes, the community center, and privately run exercise classes. These generally consist of a variety of floor and bar exercises performed as a group, directed by a trained phys-ed instructor or dancer. Typically, the classes meet at a regularly scheduled hour several times a week. This year I decided to switch to Powers Studio because of the greater flexibility and individuality your program offers. According to your system I can exercise at any hour I please, on any day of the week, and as often as I wish. I can also follow an exercise program designed exactly for my needs; I do not have to waste time on exercises to reduce my arms if my concern is to slim my waist. Lastly, I am weighed and measured at regular intervals to determine my progress toward my particular goals.

The above are the positive elements that attracted me to Powers Studio. Now that I am a member of the program, I would like to comment on how your facility has met my needs. To my way of thinking, an exercise facility should provide the following basic essentials: opportunity for vigorous physical exercise, supervision by trained personnel, clean and adequate physical plant, and friendly atmosphere. Unfortunately, Powers Studio has neglected or distorted each of the above in favor of alternative goals; you have chosen to emphasize frills and surface features instead of more substantial attributes.

First, instead of presenting exercise in a straightforward fashion, you feel the need to add interest through the use of clever sayings; members are urged to chant as they bend and stretch to such rhymes as, "Cats have paws; dogs have fleas; all I have are two fat knees." While the object, no doubt, is to add humor to the exertion, it works to the contrary in my case; the rhymes make me feel ridiculous. Secondly, the time and attention that I need in the way of supervision from your personnel is allocated instead to public relations. Your employees are too busy recruiting prospective members or arranging social events to be available for counsel on exercising. Indeed, if I interrupt one of them in her "selling" function with a question about an exercise, I receive a grudging response, delivered with a scowl (a striking contrast to the glowing smiles and chattiness bestowed on prospective members). In a program which features close body contact with the physical surroundings, it is important that these be clean and decent. Here again you give precedence to frills over essentials. Your glamorous facade (shag carpeting, striped wallpaper, bright pink and orange curtains, colorful cushioned machines, mirrored walls), is marred by poor cleanliness standards; the rug is littered with bits of tissue, the mirrors are smeared, the curtains are dusty. The dressing room, unseen by prospective members, is both cramped and dirty; the bathroom devoid of paper towels. Finally, while congenial relations with other members of the group make the exercising experience pleasant, extended social contact with them is unnecessary. Yet, you see your function as being that of a social club; you seem to assume that members need you not only for exercise but also for social life. From that follows the many social events you sponsor: "Awards Night," "Hit Parade of Platters," etc. Promotion of these activities takes time and effort on the part of the employees, time and effort which would be better spent in attending to the exercise programs of the members.

In closing, as a working mother, my free time is too limited to be wasted on unsatisfying activities. While the idea of your program is sound, the execution is wanting. Your basic function as an exercise program has been obscured by gimmicks and glamour. A shift in emphasis to the essentials would give me what I entered the program for—an effective physical outlet.

Sincerely yours,

Agnes Aggravated

III Modes for Writing

Students need the opportunity to write in a variety of modes to experience the range of expression that writing can provide. This section offers such a variety. Readers will find approaches that suggest how students may become better observers, thinkers, and researchers as they engage in differing writing experiences. While providing varied modes for writing, these writing experiences also reinforce the importance of audience and purpose, both of which are essential to the successful use of any mode.

Observation and Order in the Writing of Description

Norma J. Engberg

Sharpening students' powers of observation and helping them use those powers in writing comprise the focus of this activity. It is suggested that teachers demonstrate through their own writing process what is involved in effective description and then use this demonstration as a method for helping students become more descriptive writers. Ms. Engberg sent this from the University of Nevada at Las Vegas.

Author's Comment

When we write description, we observe an object or a scene by means of the five senses. We know that the difficulty in this kind of writing lies in finding the right words—specific and concrete—for expressing the sensuous response. At the same time, we make decisions about the arrangement of details, choosing among spatial and emphatic orders. Here the difficulty lies in deciding what to say first and in conveying the reasonableness of this choice to the reader. An emphatic order is often clearer and usually easier to handle than a spatial order because in the latter, the reader expectation makes no one sequence of details preferable to another.

Writing Description

When teaching the writing of description, we want the students to discover by trial and error how to cope with the difficulties inherent in this type of writing. Practice in the writing of description is developed in a two-part assignment. First, I ask the students to concentrate on *observation* in the description of an object; a week later, I talk about *order* in the description of a scene.

In my classroom demonstration which takes up most of the hour, I lead the students through the steps of the prewriting process, proceeding one-sense-at-a-time through the five senses and asking how that particular sense measures an object.

We are most dependent on sight, dependent almost to the exclusion of the other senses. Here the need is to be specific: to measure in inches and feet the dimensions of the object; then to consider how to make these numbers concrete for the reader. Similes work here, but the writer must find new ones to replace the clichés, "big as a barn," "wallet-sized," and "no bigger than a minute," attempts to solve the same problem which through excessive use are now worn out.

Taste is intimately bound up with the sense of smell. Since as children we were warned not to put things into our mouths, taste for inedible objects is a sense our culture has trained us to ignore. Our culture also conditions our response to odor: among non-food items, we are drawn to the sweet-smelling flower, repulsed by the one that smells like garbage, and disappointed in the one that has no smell at all. There is probably more of a reaction to bad smells than to good ones, and we are culturally influenced to try to mask natural bad smells by means of artifical good smells. Even if we are told an item is edible, we are reluctant to taste it if it smells bad.

In dealing with the sense of touch, we search for words to describe texture, temperature, and substance (weight). Again the problem is to be specific: the writer must not be afraid of getting out scales and ther-mometer, and must avoid the clichés of the "soft as silk" variety which obscure rather than clarify this sense.

Hearing, perhaps the most important sense after sight, is also the most cliché ridden. For everyday sounds, the word associated with that sound has become a commonplace, i.e., the wind *blows,* the sea *roars,* the snakes *hiss,* and streams *gurgle.*

Having made some generalizations about the senses, I next write scratch outline notes on the board for specific objects. For this demon-stration, any objects can be chosen, but I pick two—one inanimate, the other animate—that interest *me.* I don't try to guess what might interest my students, and it turns out that since they usually know nothing about the particular objects I have chosen, I hold their attention.

	KETOH*	TIGER SHOVELMOUTH CATFISH
SIGHT	*length:* 4" *width:* 3" *cross-section:* ¼" trian-gular ("carinated" -def?). *cut-out pattern:* combination of rec-tangles, triangles, and s-curves ("corn leaves").	*length:* 22" *girth:* 16" *color:* body: grayish-brown back; white belly and throat; random black, verti-cal ("tiger") stripes 2½"-4" in length. fins: black polka dots on grayish-brown background; white undersides.

	color: dull silver-gray metallic; single pear-shaped turquoise is dark blue-green with blue-black matrix.	head: "shovel" flattened, ½ of body length; random black freckles on grayish-brown background across nose and forehead; brown eyes.
		barbels: 2 brown, 7″ extending out of upper jaw; 2 white, 4″ extending out of lower jaw; 2 white, 3″ from middle of chin.
TOUCH	*texture:* smooth. *temperature:* ambient; cold to the touch, picks up body heat. *substance:* sterling silver; *weight:* 3 oz.	*texture:* smooth, wet, slippery (due to protective mucous membrane). *temperature:* water (76°–78° F.) cold to the touch *substance:* flesh, bones, and blood; weight: 5 lb.
TASTE	smooth, "metallic" (since not something ordinarily put in the mouth, more a matter of touch).	(since—if alive—not ordinarily put in the mouth, same as touch).
SMELL	none.	odor of well-aged water, an environment from which it cannot be separated.
SOUND	(since inanimate, the object must be acted upon—dropped or hit—to produce a "metallic" sound).	no noise if not moving; at night swims and churns up water, slaps surface of water with tail.

Ketoh (alt, *gato*) is a Navajo word for the wrist guard worn to protect an archer's wrist from being burned by the bow string.

As I make up the scratch outline, having the actual ketoh to show and drawing a rough sketch of the catfish on the board as I go along, I point out some of the peculiar problems connected with description of these two objects. Afterwards, we think up questions which we'd like to see the writer answer, and these show students how other, previously studied types can be used to support description. For the ketoh, we ask how it is made (process) and what it is used for (narrative). For the catfish, we ask how it behaves (narrative) and how it is cared for (process).

Just before beginning to write, the students and I consider who our audience will be and what we may expect them to know about our chosen subject. We can write about our object as if for someone who has never seen one and who doesn't know what it is used for. This approach is always a useful self-test for the writer even if the subject is something as common as baseball, hot dogs, apple pie, and Chevrolet. One of the mistakes the writer most easily makes comes from assuming that since the reader knows all about the object, the writer can safely generalize. Another alternative is the riddle: the writer assumes that the reader is familiar with the object but writes in such a way as to keep the reader guessing. In class I read as examples modern English translations of Anglo-Saxon riddles. Of these two possibilities, the students find the riddle form more challenging to the imagination; many choose it, and in writing about everyday household items such as the toothpick, the broom, or the grapefruit, many do well with it.

On the day the students turn in their descriptions of objects, I talk about order practiced in the description of a scene. Again I lead the students through the steps of the prewriting process, considering the advantages and disadvantages of the various kinds of order. Spatial order may proceed from top to bottom, from left to right, from foreground to background or the reverse of any of these. Emphatic order may proceed from biggest to smallest, or from the most important to least important; again, the reverse order is equally possible.

As an example around which to construct scratch outline notes on the board, I bring in an 8″ × 10″ color photograph of a woman on a bicycle stopped beside a thirty-foot saguaro cactus. This picture is chosen deliberately because the largest item—the saguaro—is not, to the human viewer, the most important item. To most people, other people are more interesting than plants.

I first list in a top-to-bottom order the visually striking features of the photograph: clouded blue sky, tip of central saguaro, body of central saguaro with its eight arms, and so forth. This process is repeated, but this time the order is from the bottom to the top. Similar lists are made for left to right, right to left, foreground to background, and background to foreground.

As we talk about spatial orders, we discover that in this picture, foreground to background seems to work best. Then someone points out that actually this order is nearly the same as most-to-least important; thus, the reason it seems most natural is not for spatial adequacy but for its ability to imitate the logic of an emphatic order. We then list on the board the most important to least important features: (1) woman; (2) baby; (3) central, eight-armed, thirty-foot saguaro; (4) bicycle and its fittings; (5) road and gravel shoulder; (6) background saguaros; (7) mesquite and paloverde, individually indistinct; (8) background mountains and clouded blue sky.

It is useful to hypothesize the series of questions that govern the relative positions of the less important. How did the woman and the baby get to the base of the saguaro? By bicycle. How did the bicycle get to the base of the saguaro? By means of the paved road, on whose gravel shoulder this particular saguaro stands. Only after these questions are satisfactorily answered, do we permit our attention to take in the background saguaros, the mesquite and paloverde, the far-off mountains and clouded blue sky. The reverse of this order, least-to-most important, teases the reader; it is not unlike a riddle, but it is more annoying than amusing. To write a description beginning with the least important item first is an affront unless some very good reason for the suspense is incorporated into the description, for example, the mystery writer's scene of the crime in which a description of the body is left for last.

None of these orders—in themselves—guarantees successful descriptions. All of the spatial and emphatic orders in our scratch outlines have been made from the standpoint of the observer looking at the picture from the outside. A different point of view might well make the description more readable. The observer could be placed inside the picture—as if driving by in a car or standing across the road from the photograph's subjects. Alternatively, the observer does not have to be human; we may imagine a bird on top of the saguaro or a lizard on a nearby rock. A third choice would be to make the narrator a participant; the description might be written from the standpoint of the woman doing the pointing. These variations in point of view also affect choice of order: if the narrator is inside the picture, the items will take on a different spatial order from that seen by the narrator outside the picture. If the narrator is also the woman participant, she will not see herself as most important; to her the large central saguaro will be most important.

In explaining my assignment, I ask the students to write two descriptions of the same scene using two different orders, and I suggest that before they do any writing, they outline all the possibilities just as we have done in class. I further recommend that they choose differing points of view as well as differing orders for their two versions since this challenges imagination as well as technique.

This two-part, two-week assignment in the writing of description gives the students a chance to work on both observation and order. As they experiment with the various alternatives, they come to find their own methods for combating the difficulties inherent in this type of writing.

The Great Crisis Telegram:
A Lesson in Conciseness

Timothy Brookes

Composition instructors welcome conciseness in student writing.
Timothy Brookes of Oxford University, England, uses telegrams to
focus students' attention on the virtue of conciseness and its importance in exposition.

Author's Comment

I designed the Great Crisis Telegram Exercise in two parts, one to
promote conciseness and selection of detail, and the other to stimulate
enterprise and initiative.

A Lesson in Conciseness

The first part consists of each student in the class receiving one of two
duplicated sheets describing a series of events, which might go something
like this:

> You are a reporter for the *Daily Objective,* on holiday in the
> Central African country of Lugardo. Having spent several peaceful
> days at the capital, Amnesia, you decide to make an excursion to
> the northern town of Mbengwe. At the railway station, however,
> you discover that the train has been cancelled. According to the
> station-master, "The rebels cut the line." Sensing a story you press
> him for more details, and he tells you that ten thousand rebels have
> been training in the northern mountains for several years, waiting
> for an opportunity to sweep down and overrun the country in ful-
> fillment of an old prophecy. You then make other enquiries and get
> the following reports:
>
> *Police:* There are certainly rebels, but they are in the east, and are
> relatively harmless. They number a couple of hundred. The line
> was obviously not cut, but simply in poor repair, or damaged in
> a landslide.
>
> *Army:* A small band of rebels have been causing trouble in the
> north near the line, but the Army has them surrounded and expects
> a victory any moment. There have always been rebels in Lugardo,
> and there always will be.

Diplomatic Corps Officer (unofficially): The Army is corrupt and may well betray the government. The rebels are Soviet-armed and hope to gain control of Amnesia because of the nearby rich cobalt mines to the south. Official contact with Mbengwe was lost several hours ago. Amnesia, however, is "completely safe."

Amnesian Enquirer: Knows nothing of all of this, but states that several top Army officers were recently murdered without subsequent enquiry; and the paper was forbidden to print the story. Rebels may therefore receive right-wing support. The President, Mr. Joseph Obutu, is generally unpopular because "He smokes big cigars."

You must send off a preliminary telegram at once before the office closes for the weekend, and the message (excluding address, etc.) can only be *fifty* words long. As you enter the office you hear gunfire, although you see nothing; it is coming from just outside the town (and the Army firing range, you know, is miles away). The *Objective* is a scrupulously accurate paper. HOW WOULD YOU WORD YOUR TELEGRAM?

In both pieces the reporter/telegram/newspaper format is the same. I was surprised by how many students were deceived by the red herrings, and how many didn't know how to write a telegram. On the other hand, those who really got interested produced a very concrete and specific telegram. We also had an animated discussion on the news value of a *possible* crisis.

The second half was a reversal of the first. I had depicted two situations, one in America and the other in Tokyo (an earthquake). Those who had composed their telegrams on the first exchanged them with those of the second group, and vice versa. Each student, therefore, had an unfamiliar telegram, and was told to write an article for the newspaper on it. The results were varied. Many merely rewrote the telegram, adding verbs and articles; but others followed my suggestions and produced excellent pieces, complete with historical backgrounds and interviews with the Japanese Consul or Lugardan Ambassador. I was prepared to accept students' breaking the strict rules of fact as long as the material in the telegram wasn't contradicted or misrepresented. Afterwards, we talked for a while about journalism and the need for accuracy, and moved easily into a week on reporting as one of the basics of exposition.

Analyzing a Magazine's Intended Audience (With a Clandestine Exercise in Footnoting Incorporated)

Lynn Z. Bloom

From letters to a combination of inductive analysis and simplified research, this sequence of assignments provides students with experience in identifying different audiences and their needs while developing expository writing skills. Ms. Bloom submitted this exercise from the University of New Mexico, Albuquerque.

Author's Comment

As the audience goes, so goes the paper. Students, even those with some literary experience and finesse, are often nonplussed when asked what audience they're writing for. The insistent questioner will more than likely find the answer to be the offhandedly global "everybody," or the unthinkingly particular, "myself." Prodding may elicit the naively specific: in a class composed equally of 19- and 20-year-olds, "I'm writing for people between the ages of 20 and 30"—which in this case, intentionally or otherwise, excludes the instructor! Or it may call forth the exclusively general: in a class with equal numbers of men and women, "I'm writing for men, because they understand what I like to write about—camping, hiking, motorbiking, and shooting"—whereupon investigation reveals that the women students participate in these activities with knowledge and gusto!

The Audience-Intended Exercise

Students need to become aware of the relationship between one's writing and one's intended audience, of both the obvious aspects and the more subtle nuances. One way to enhance their awareness is to have them determine how they would write three letters on the same subject to three people of different ages, backgrounds, interests, and relationships to them ("My first exam in advanced math," "How I learned to rappel," "The advantages of learning to drive"). I would have high school students write the letters and discuss them in class; college students usually grasp the implications through class discussion, without needing to actually write the letters.

Through this (or a comparable discussion), students become aware of some of the specific characteristics of any audience which they must consider in shaping their argument, determining their level of language, supplying background or clarifying information, making allusions or other references, and the like. Examining letters (real or hypothetical) or textbook readings can help them to recognize the relevance of their own writing of the myriad facets of their intended readers' educational, cultural, or national backgrounds; potential or actual professional, religious, political, or sexual biases; and predominant interests and other values.[1]

Instructors who wish to pursue other theoretical and practical implications of the ways in which works of literature are shaped to accommodate an audience will find helpful Wayne Booth's observations in "True Art Ignores the Audience," in *The Rhetoric of Fiction* (Chicago: University of Chicago Press, 1961; rpt. Phoenix Edition, 1967), especially pp. 111–116.

Then they are ready to write a paper of inductive analysis, in which they determine, in as ample and specific detail as possible, the intended readers of a particular magazine. The following list (to which individual instructors can, of course, make their own additions and deletions) elicits lively and varied analyses, and serves as well to introduce the students to diverse, generally well-written magazines that many of them would not otherwise encounter. My current list (revised periodically) includes these: *Fortune, Harpers, Atlantic, The National Review, New Republic, Dissent, The New Yorker, New York Magazine, New York Review of Books, Scientific American, Journal of Social Issues, Daedalus, Christian Century, Commentary, Esquire,* and *Ms.*

Students must choose a magazine they don't ordinarily read and examine at least three issues, from different years and different months in different seasons. Basing their inferences on the material within the magazine, rather than on their own preconceptions, the students should construct as thorough and detailed a portrait of the magazine's intended readers as possible. They will need to present documented (i.e., footnoted) evidence from the analyzed magazine to support their assertions about the readers' educational level, or range, vocabulary level, predominant interests, cultural background, economic and social status, sex, religion, nationality, age range, and any other characteristics that seem important.

Evidence may be most readily obtained from such relevant aspects of the magazine as its

1. Written content (including subject matter of articles; articles' simplicity or complexity or technicality; tone; point of view; assumptions taken for granted)

2. Literary style (including level of language, amount and nature of slang, jargon, or figurative language, sorts of allusions and quotations, simplicity or complexity of sentence and paragraph structure)

3. Illustrations (absent? if present, consider number, kind, and subjects of photographs, paintings, cartoons)

4. Advertising (nature and cost of goods or services; potential users of—and payers for—these; the various appeals, pitches, logic and distortions thereof, or gimmicks of the advertising)

5. Layout (ratio of illustrations to print, and ads to articles; makeup of the page; face and size of type; uses of color).

Because this assignment is fairly complicated, and because the resulting papers (consisting, as they do, of abundant evidence, amply analyzed) are fairly long, students usually need two or three weeks to write it; in grading, I weigh it accordingly. After the students are fairly far along into the assignment, we usually devote a sorely needed day to the rationale and particulars of footnoting and bibliography compilation. The inclusion of footnotes—I require ten or more different references—and a bibliography make this paper suitable for a term project or a simplified research paper.

This assignment is particularly versatile because of its concerns not only with the manifest topic of intended audience, but with the incorporation of inductive reasoning, analysis of content and style, considerations of logical truths and fallacies, and matters of layout and design. It provides a relatively painless means to teach footnoting and bibliography. Students enjoy this assignment (even though they work hard to fulfill it) because of their intrinsic interest in their chosen magazine, and because of the many aspects—sometimes unexpected—of an intended audience that they discover. They are pleased to be doing "original research"; this assignment is difficult to plagiarize.

This assignment is interesting for teachers and other students to read, because of the variety of magazines analyzed, and because of the diversity of audience characteristics and/or interpretations of these characteristics that the students present. Most importantly, it helps to make the students more responsible writers in many ways, particularly in their attention to the audience for which class readings and writings are intended and in their increased respect for documented analysis and for the mechanics of documentation itself.

Note

1. Walker Gibson's discussion of the relation of reader to author is particularly useful. Throughout *Tough, Sweet, and Stuffy: An Essay on Modern American Prose Styles* (Bloomington, Indiana: Indiana University Press, 1966), particularly in Chapter 2, "Hearing Voices," Gibson explores the concept that "the reader, too, like the author, undergoes a transformation, that he too becomes a kind of ideal or second self as he expresses himself to the expectations of the language" (p. 12).

Written Logodrama:
The Projected-Experience Essay

Robert C. Wess

Exploring cause and effect relationships in their futures seems to work for students in the writing classes of Robert C. Wess of Southern Technical Institute, Marietta, Georgia.

Author's Comment

The following exercise synthesizes ideas gleaned from two divergent sources. The first is Richard D. Kepes's exercise "Write Your Own Obituary" (*Writing Exercises from* Exercise Exchange, NCTE, 1976, pp. 88–89), which asks students to compose their own death notices by "duplicating the obituary writing conventions of the *New York Times*" (p. 88). The second is *Man's Search for Meaning* (Pocket Books, 1959), by the eminent psychiatrist Viktor E. Frankl, in which he describes the logodrama of a suicidal mother despondent over the death of her once-healthy son while her invalid son continues living (pp. 184–186). When asked to project the value of her life from her deathbed, however, she "had suddenly been able to see a meaning in it . . ." (p. 186) through caring for her disabled son.

From the first essay I embraced the notion of future-oriented essays, the method of future self-projection, although the obituary topic did not appeal to me personally. So it was from Frankl's book that I winnowed content. His theory of logotherapy focuses on future happenings, "on the assignments and meanings to be fulfilled by the patient in his future . . ." (pp. 152–153). The creation of the projected-experience essay, therefore, wedded Kepes's futuristic point of view with Frankl's real-life projections.

Exercise One: The Teacher's Task (Optional)

My practice of this exercise took the form of a cause/effect essay. The effect I wrote on was a major life decision—becoming a college teacher—and the causes presented reasons for my choice as seen at retirement. The subsequent essay was entitled "I May Never See My Trophy Case But

Still I Know" (see summary below), which suggested that although the rewards of teaching (its trophies) are often intangible, my reasons for choosing this career-commitment were sound and positive.

Of course, this teacher exercise is optional. Not every teacher will be willing to write the assignment. Since such practice has become more widely adopted, however, especially since the dawn of the Bay Area Writing Project, the earnest composition teacher may choose to initiate the exercise.

Exercise Two: The Class Assignment

Writing the "projected-experience essay" will require a minimum of two class periods. During the first period, the teacher clearly explains the idea of projected-experience writing, how to apply this concept to the cause/ effect essay, and how to apply topic choice to the assignment. The second period will allocate time for students to write their own essay after having had some time between classes to absorb the essay idea and to reflect on their topic choices.

In explaining the idea of projected experience, the teacher clearly delineates three things: the future time orientation, the situation, and the specific effect. Regarding time, the teacher emphasizes the students' task of selecting a certain year of life as vantage point in projecting the essay. Then the student must select a particular life situation (e.g., marriage, career, avocation) to focus on. Here the teacher emphasizes situation-authenticity, one which truly depicts self. Finally, the student must clearly perceive this life situation as an effect brought about by a number of causes. An important part of the writing assignment will be the delineation of these causes. Structurally, the pattern includes real-life "projected experience" as weil as specific causes which led to that situation. The teacher then informs students that one or the other of these causes/ reasons may already have happened in their lives, but some will be projected, having not yet occurred.

The teacher, after providing this theoretical framework for the essay, contributes an example which fits the model. It may be one mentally worked out to be presented orally; or it may be an idea already written out and presented in the form of an outline, thus providing a technique for student imitation. Best of all will be a written example, the teacher's own essay based on real-life projection (see Exercise One). To amplify this last approach, I will summarize an essay which I have written for such a demonstration.

My essay placed me in the situation of a college teacher at age sixty-five, ready to retire after the current academic year. As setting for this situation, I seated myself in the den of my home and began responding to my son's question on why I had chosen teaching as my career. The "effect," of course, was this career choice. The essay included reasons (causes) for my choice of teaching: my aptitude for study, the congenial lifestyle a college teacher enjoys, the gratification of helping others, and the belief that teaching manifests my Life-Calling. The essay concluded with the hope that my sharing of career-choice causes would help my son in his own life plans just as I hoped my teaching had helped students I taught in pursuing their own life goals.

The above explanation and illustration may take thirty minutes of class time. The remainder should be given to discussing student topics. I like to have each student discuss topics with one other student. For the first five minutes one student tells about his or her plan for the projected-experience essay while the other listens and provides feedback. For the second five minutes, roles are reversed. For the final minutes of class, the teacher solicits some of these shared plans for public presentation and feedback. As the period ends, the teacher asks students to reflect further on their topics. In preparation for the next class, they are asked to prepare in writing the structure or outline they will use in writing the in-class essay.

The second class period is devoted to writing the essay. We hope, however, the exercise will not stop there. After the teacher's evaluation, student revision, or both, some or all of these essays may be shared through oral presentations. In this way, students communicate their self-visions to peers, compare and reflect on various life scenarios, and give further consideration to the projected "lives" they have created.

Evaluation

I was impressed with the wide variety of topics on which my students wrote. One projected retirement as a social worker, having "been" a surrogate parent to orphans for thirty years. Another was seen as a retired kindergarten teacher who had opened personal doors (as an older student returning to school) while introducing children to the thrill of learning.

Some students chose sports topics. One mused on the reasons for becoming a champion Olympic swimmer. Another was projected as a retired professional tennis player. A third projected experiences as a marathon runner.

Still others selected more creative topics. Someone envisioned an alien invasion and delineated its causes. Another student visualized atomic devastation. The effect was widespread death, brought about by the 1979–1980 Iranian conflict having mushroomed into worldwide bloodshed. Perhaps the most imaginative of all, certainly the farthest projection, was the student essay which catapulted its creator all the way into the next life, as a saint in heaven. Obviously, for this assignment, the sky is the limit!

Besides the creativity and imaginative vitality which such writing produced, this essay assignment also had practical value for students, enabling them to contemplate and share future life plans. The assignment accomplished a kind of written logodrama, by which student authors could visualize and find meaning in certain major life choices they had depicted for themselves.

If the teacher first performs the exercise, the assignment will also bear fruit in terms of modeling. Insofar as the teacher demonstrates an authentic life decision, to that extent will the student be encouraged to do likewise. Not only does the pattern become a source of imitation, so does the teacher essay, both in its form and content.

Finally, the projected-experience essay may readily be transferred to other modes of writing. For example, a student could describe a future spouse, home, or career. One might personalize the process of becoming a millionnaire, an architect, or a gynecologist. Another assignment would project a future turning point in one's life; for example, narrating a change in careers, lifestyles, or business partners. Some revelatory narratives would surely result. As the reader may see, like the exercise itself, application is as open-ended as the imaginations of teacher and students.

Writing as Thinking:
Solving the Mystery of Deduction

David Schwab

Few people can resist a good mystery. David Schwab capitalizes on that interest to demonstrate to students the importance of deductive thinking in writing. Mr. Schwab contributed this exercise from Northwestern University, Evanston, Illinois.

Author's Comment

As an armchair physician with honorary degrees in video medicine from ABC, CBS, and NBC, I take considerable pride in my ability to diagnose and treat patients portrayed on television dramas. I can spot an aortic aneurysm while the t.v. doctors are still baffled, and, when the problem is routine cardiac arrest, I usually shout "Defibrillate!" before the paramedics alight from their ambulance. I even know when to urge the t.v. hospital staffs to use an electroencephalograph (EEG). The device records the electrical activity of the brain in an uneven scrawl resembling my attempts to jot down snatches of dreams whenever I awake at a predawn hour in a fog of antihistamines. Once, while half-grading my students' compositions and half-watching a t.v. medical team examine the results of an EEG, I was struck by the comparison: the graphs on the students' themes were at least as much an expression of brain activity as the EEG findings flickering on the t.v. screen. The patient on t.v., I concluded, did not have a brain tumor; but a careful diagnosis of my students' writing revealed some marginally comatose cases. Sometime after that experience, I found the beginnings of a cure—a way to stimulate cerebral activity in students (and hence improve their writing).

The idea of giving students a "who dunnit?" to solve is of course not new. To test their students' powers of deduction and expression, composition teachers have gleaned contrived murder mysteries from detective magazines, what used to be called dime store novels, and, most recently, t.v. crime shows. Since English teachers thrive on compiling and revising, many of the plots students are asked to unravel are horrendously complex, convoluted, full of reversals, double identities, double crosses, and improbable coincidences. Students in high school or college, however, should not need the perspicacity of Agatha Christie to write their English papers. The Inspector Clouseaus of the world also need to be accommodated. Responding to this need, I have developed an assignment that is simple enough for almost any student to complete successfully, yet sufficiently subtle to challenge even the most adroit ratiocinator. For the students, solving the "crime" is relatively easy; persuading readers of the wisdom of their conclusions in a clear, forceful essay is a challenge.

The Case

Before I give the assignment, I stress the following points (my parenthetical notes serve as a teachers' guide):

1. Do not assume any facts. (I have had students argue that robbery was the motive because, they said, the victim's wallet was stolen. This was the students' invention. The need to follow directions precisely is even more absolutely necessary than it usually is.)

2. There is no trick to the mystery. Only one person committed the crime; there was no conspiracy. The only suspects are the persons listed as suspects. (The last point may seem obvious, but one college freshman tried to pin the crimes on the coroner.)

3. The victim was murdered; suicide is an incorrect, illogical assumption not supported by the facts.

4. Start with some sort of introduction. (Some students, casting themselves in the role of Inspector, have effectively used a narrative approach.) Do not, however, recopy the facts verbatim. Bring in facts only as necessary to support your arguments. After your introduction, write a paragraph explaining why you are eliminating the person who is the least likely suspect. Explain first why he or she is a suspect; then give your reasons for scratching him or her off your list. Next, argue why one of the two remaining persons is a more likely suspect than the one you have just eliminated, but who, alas, is also not guilty. Finally, convince your readers that the remaining suspect is the murderer—not only because he or she is the only one left—but also for good, logical reasons that you supply.

5. Though the evidence points more clearly to one suspect than it does to the other two, a case can be made to incriminate any of the three. Accordingly, the success of your essay depends less on *whom* you choose than *why*. Thus, your paper can still be fairly successful even if you designate the "wrong" suspect as the murderer.

To whet the students' appetites for sleuthing, I give those instructions to them verbally at the class meeting immediately preceding the one at which they write. On the day they actually do the assignment, I hand out the following information at the beginning of class:

Using deduction as your method of analysis, determine who killed Philo Farnsworth on the basis of the facts given. (Do not assume any facts.) First, state your reasons for eliminating one suspect. Then, explain why you must eliminate another suspect from consideration. Finally, using deduction, determine and explain clearly who killed Philo.

On Friday, April 18, Philo Farnsworth, a thirty-five-year-old professional football player, was found dead in his house on State Street. The coroner reported that Farnsworth had been murdered and that the cause of death was strangulation. The coroner also reported that death occurred between 6:30 pm and 8:30 pm. Police have three suspects in the case. Chives, the butler, always liked Farnsworth. Several witnesses swear they saw Chives running from Farnsworth's house at 9:00 pm on the evening of the murder. Uncle Flatface, a fifty-five-year-old laborer, was inside Farnsworth's house at the time of the murder. Uncle Flatface hated Farnsworth because Farnsworth never gave him any money. Aunt Fungus, an eighty-five-year-old retired schoolteacher who was also inside the house at the time of the murder, had frequently threatened to kill Farnsworth because she disapproved of his habit of drinking too much bourbon every night.

The Trial

I always return the papers at the very next class meeting, for the students are so curious to hear the case explained that putting off this vital feedback would be as unsatisfying, anticlimactic, and unfair as withholding the last page of a murder mystery from one desperate to know the tale's outcome.

My analysis, I explain, is based on three criteria: motive, opportunity, and means. I then take up the three suspects in an order different from the one used in the recitation of the facts (which is, not coincidentally, alphabetical).

I begin with the hapless butler. Chives is the only suspect whose age is not given. One may reasonably infer from his position as butler that he is not young, but his running would also suggest that he is not terribly old, either. In short, Chives may well have possessed the physical strength necessary to strangle a man. Chives, therefore, had the means to kill Farnsworth. The most obvious defense one could make for Chives, however, is that he had no motive: one must take as a given that he "always liked Farnsworth." Yet there is another, more subtle and intriguing argument Chives's defense counsel could use in the unlikely event an inexperienced prosecutor put the butler on trial. The murder occurred no later than 8:30 pm. Chives was seen running from the house at 9:00 pm. But has Chives been placed at the scene of the crime when the crime was committed? The answer is self-evident: opportunity for Chives cannot be established from the facts.

Chives, then, is the first to be eliminated. No, the butler does not always do it. What's that? His hasty retreat? One could surmise that the unsuspecting servant entered the Farnsworth residence shortly before 9:00 pm and found his master dead; horrified, the butler ran from a sight he could not bear to dwell upon. I am not assuming that this scenario must have occurred, but it is consistent with the facts and quite plausible. The argument that Chives is guilty solely because of his theatrical exit is utterly unconvincing in the absence of motive and concern.

Of the two remaining suspects, suspicion falls next on Aunt Fungus. If nothing else, Aunt Fungus had motive. Indeed, no police inspector worth a sixpence could fail to suspect strongly a person who had threatened— not just once but "frequently"—to commit the very act that is the subject of the inquiry. Some will argue that an eighty-five-year-old woman could not possibly have strangled a thirty-five-year-old professional football player. Two lines of analysis. First: while Fungus *probably* could not have committed the deed, the *possibility* cannot be overlooked. Farnsworth drank "every night." Fungus hated his drinking. If she killed him as the result of premeditation, then perhaps she waited until he had imbibed a sufficient quantity of liquor to render him nearly helpless to a surprise attack (possibly from behind) by a spry, monomaniacal enemy. Implausible? Highly. Impossible? Not at all. Second: to those who put sentimentality above logic and argue a) a dislike of drinking is not a good reason to kill someone; or b) the old lady's threats were never meant to be taken seriously, her extreme advocacy of temperance being instead a manifestation of her love for Philo, I would reply a) people are killed every day for motives most of us would consider tragically trivial; and b) repeated threats to murder someone who does indeed turn up murdered can scarcely be dismissed as unique expressions of love. To sum up: Fungus had motive and opportunity, and, possibly, the means to commit the crime. The last premise, admittedly, cannot be firmly established.

The remaining suspect is none other than Uncle Flatface, and he is the killer! He had a clear motive and he had the opportunity to kill his nephew. Also, one can reasonably assume that the fifty-five-year-old laborer had the physical strength required to kill Philo (especially since the victim drank bourbon "every night").

As I explain my analysis, I fill in a chart on the blackboard. The finished product looks like this:

	Motive	Opportunity	Means
Chives			x
Flatface	x	x	x
Fungus	x	x	?

To those who are disappointed because the mystery is so straight-forwardly solved, I offer an ironic twist. Students who become self-conscious about writing in a certain rhetorical mode often lose sight of the objective of their assignment. For example, a student who is overly concerned that the theme be "a cause and effect paper" (whatever that is) runs the risk of concentrating on the means and slighting the end. In handling the Philo assignment, students become so involved in persuading their audience of the correctness of their conclusions that they use deduction as a means to that end, often with impressive results. Papers that, to the students, start out as just another exercise in the use of a rhetorical mode (deduction) often become sound examples of persuasive writing, the means being subordinated to the all-important end of causing readers to nod their heads in silent agreement with the papers' arguments.

In the course of writing the papers, the students are forced to think. The pens moving across the tablets chart the pupils' thoughts in a series of graphs called themes. EEG's should be so indicative of brain activity.

The $500.00 Proposal

Adele Pittendrigh

Developing writing experiences which approximate those encountered in the real world is not always easy. Adele Pittendrigh suggests one way that students can use their own experiences while practicing a kind of writing often employed in professional fields. Ms. Pittendrigh teaches at Montana State University, Bozeman.

Author's Comment

The $500.00 proposal imitates grant proposal writing—a form of real-world writing with a tangible, practical outcome. For students who sometimes cannot see the value of writing "another essay," the proposal offers a chance to practice the kind of writing that is needed in many professional fields and whose value—money for a project—is hard to miss. The $500.00 Proposal allows students to draw on their own experience and to explore their frustrations and complaints about school or a job. Like real grant proposals, the project asks students to go beyond complaining and requires students to think through a clear definition of a problem, a workable solution, a justification for their particular solution, and a method of evaluating the solution should the proposal be implemented. Unlike a real proposal, this project does not require a budget; instead, students must imagine that if their proposal is adopted, they will receive a cash prize for their ideas and a task force will be assigned the job of implementing their proposal. The project can be written by individual students or by teams of three or four students. Student groups, acting as judging committees, can also evaluate the proposals and award the prizes.

Here's the hand-out I give students at the beginning of the project.

The Assignment

Have you ever thought you knew how to improve things at your school or on your job? Often students and workers, who see the school or the

128

job from their own point of view, can see problems and come up with solutions that administrators and supervisors cannot see. Here's a chance to use your expertise to make a recommendation for improving your school or your job.

For Project A

The Committee to Improve Education in Montana (name your own state) is seeking proposals from former or current students for practical ways to improve education in the state. The Committee invites proposals for improving elementary, secondary, or college education. Applicants may suggest changes to improve academic instruction, student motivation, preparation for high school or college, social or recreational opportunities, sports programs, relationships between students and faculty or administration, methods for reducing stress in student life, or any other aspect of school life. The Committee hopes proposals will address significant but often neglected problems. The Committee will award three $500.00 prizes to the authors of the best proposals.

To All Applicants

1) All proposals must be practical; in other words, all suggested changes should be ones that can actually be implemented.

2) Each proposal should show how the desired improvement can be made. If, for example, you propose that there be better communication between administration and students, you need to show specifically how the improvement can be made. A monthly newsletter from the principal, or a role for student representatives on particular committees, or weekly administrative open-houses might be your specific suggestion for reaching your goal of improved communication.

3) Each proposal should be submitted in the form outlined on page 130.

After you have written parts I–IV, prepare a cover sheet for your application that has your name and a short summary of parts I–IV.

Alternative Project B

The Committee for Improvement of the Workplace is considering similar proposals. If you have a job now or have worked in the past, you may make a proposal for improving the place where you work or for improving the quality of the service, product, or method of getting the job done. Follow the guidelines for Project A.

Group Evaluations

If student groups are going to evaluate the proposals, each group should receive the proposals with the cover sheet (including the name of the author and the summaries) removed, and with an identification number assigned to each proposal by the instructor. Students will also need a copy of the criteria for evaluating the proposals and evaluation forms (see page 131) for each proposal they are going to evaluate.

Criteria for Evaluating Proposals to Improve Education

Since the purpose of the project is to identify problems and suggest solutions that will improve education, the most important criteria must be the potential for the proposed change to make a significant improvement in education. Since a task force will be responsible for implementing the winning proposals, it is essential that the members of the task force be able to understand exactly what they are to do; therefore, judges need to be certain the suggestions are expressed clearly in the proposal; judges must resist the temptation to elaborate themselves on what the author has proposed.

The Committee to Improve Education
Application Form

Part I: Definition of the Problem: Describe the existing situation and show that there is a problem.

Part II: Plan of Action: Specify the change to be made, and show specifically what the task force will do to make the change.

Part III: Justification for the Plan: Show how the change you are proposing will solve the problem and improve education. Discuss the probable consequence of making the change.

Part IV: Methods of Evaluation. Show how the task force can measure the effects of the change, if your proposal is implemented, to see whether the change solved the problem.

The groups can then tally the points and either award the highest scoring application the prize or try to reach a consensus within the group. The evaluation forms can be given back to the authors so that they can see how their peers reacted to their writing and how clearly they were able to communicate their ideas.

EVALUATION FORM

Proposal # _____

First, read the proposal carefully; then briefly summarize in your own words the main ideas in each section of the proposal.

    Part I: Summarize the existing problem.

    Part II: Summarize the change to be made.

    Part III: Summarize the justification for the change.

    Part IV: Summarize the method of evaluation.

Assign 0–10 points for each part of the application and briefly explain your reason for assigning the points as you did.

    I. Need for the proposed change.   # of points _____

    II. Possibility of implementing the plan.   # of points _____

    III. Potential of proposed plan to solve
        the problem.   # of points _____

    IV. Method of evaluating the plan.   # of points _____

                             Total # of points _____

Causal, not Casual:
An Advance Organizer for Cause and Effect Compositions

Terry Dean

Although students seem to understand cause and effect relationships in their own lives, they have difficulty applying that understanding in their writing. This model will assist students in making connections between their past experience and the situations they encounter in their writing. Mr. Dean is at the University of California, Davis.

Author's Comment

For many college students, particularly entering freshmen, cause and effect relationships pose problems. To begin with, the word "causal" is perceived and understood as "casual," a mistake often reflected in the level of analysis in the composition itself. Students who manipulate causal relationships reasonably well in their everyday lives become bogged down when asked to write a causal paper. Why? I found that many students had little if any formal instruction in analyzing causal relationships, and when confronted by college assignments, had no ideas where to begin. I have tried to minimize this confusion and bridge the gap between past experience and college assignments by using what David Ausubel calls an advance organizer.[1]

Simply stated, an advance organizer defines and gives examples of the unique characteristics of the concept you are teaching, and it relates this concept to past, present, and even future experience of the student. The organizer provides an intellectal framework upon which to hang the specific details and problems the student will encounter when reading or writing a cause and effect essay. At each step in the presentation of the organizer, the general concept is clearly defined and explained, and related continually to the student's past experience. The process is not an inductive one where students must discover the relationship on their own; instead, everything is laid out as clearly as possible. The assumption is not that students do not know how to manipulate cause and effect relationships; their past experience shows they can. The teacher's job is to make connections between this past experience and the present situation where the student is having difficulty.

The Approach

In presenting the organizer, I try to relate the general concept not only to the composition as a whole, but to the paragraph and sentence as well. To begin, write three pairs of sentences on the board. Those sentences work best that in some way interest the class personally and are fun to analyze.

1. Francisco ran out of gas. His gas gauge broke.
2. Venetia got an A on her midterm. She studied hard.
3. Veda smiled. Mark asked her for a date.

Ask students to copy the sentences down and identify the elements in the causal relationship by marking a C over the cause and an E over the effect. The first two examples pose few problems, but the third can go either way. Next, ask students what words could be used to indicate the cause and effect relationship between the two elements. Put as many words as possible on the board; they will be used later to work with causal relationships on the sentence level. Write two more sentences on the board.

4. Billy Martin was fired.
5. Billy Carter stopped drinking beer.

Ask students to copy the sentences down. Have them write an effect for number four and a cause for number five, joining the sentence they write to the given sentence with an appropriate connector word. Have the students share with the class the various sentences they have written.

Once students can identify the elements in a causal relationship, ask them to define both "cause" and "effect." If the answers are on target, put them on the board. If not, keep probing. A slightly wrong definition is preferable to none. The goal of this discussion is to show that cause and effect are defined in terms of one another. Bringing a dictionary to class and having the students check their own definitions with it is a good way to demonstrate this point. When students realize that a cause and an effect are connected, you can focus on the strength of that connection and introduce the concept of degrees of causality.

I introduce this concept by listing the appropriate adjectives, verb forms, and adverbs that can be used to indicate the various degrees of causality.

necessary	will	always
probable	should	almost always
possible	could	sometimes
unlikely	shouldn't	seldom
no way	won't	never

The example I use to test for degrees of causality is, "what produces good gas mileage?" The causes most frequently mentioned are good maintenance, driving habits, driving conditions, and an economy car. Using the words on the list, see if students can determine the strength of the causal connection in each case and which causes are the most significant. You can go back to the first three sentences you put on the board and make the distinction between single and multiple causes. Stress this distinction because many students fail to consider alternative causes that go back in time and those that exist at the same moment in time. One can explore the possibility at this point of tracing causal relationships from the present moment back to the beginnings of the universe. Nothing is more fascinating than trying to establish historical connections that relate to you personally, and nothing is more difficult than trying to demonstrate the validity of those connections.

Instead of going back endlessly, multiple causal relationships also exist at the same moment in time. Almost any current event that students are familiar with can be used. Here are some causes my students came up with to explain the events at Jonestown:

1. Fear
2. Force
3. Racism
4. Idealism
5. Brainwashing
6. Economics

For both multiple relationships going back in time and those existing at the same time, analyze the degree of causality in each instance and make distinctions between the more significant and the less significant causes. By identifying and defining the elements in a causal relationship, by testing the strength of the relationship, and by distinguishing between single and multiple causes, you have presented the main characteristics of a cause and effect relationship which would be required for most papers. You could, of course, mention that many people doubt the existence of cause and effect relationships altogether, but then students are not likely to have to write causal papers for those teachers. Once students understand these basic concepts, you are ready to make connections between their past, present, and future experience. In each case, call attention to the source of the data used to establish the strength of the causal connection; the difference between the source of data used in past experience and that used in college accounts for many of the problems students have with causal analysis.

To make people aware of how pervasive cause and effect relationships are, I ask them to recall the earliest time in their life when they initiated an action in order to bring about a specific result. Since children learn very early to manipulate parents, students can usually get back to when they were five to seven years old, and sometimes earlier. In each case, test the strength of the causal connection and identify the source of data used to verify it. In all of these situations the data come from remembered personal experience.

A useful example of a causal relationship in the present is "what causes good grades?" If people say that studying causes good grades, test to see if that is a necessary cause. Provided that you have some knowledge of study techniques, you can combine causal analysis with some study skills review. Once you have a list of causes on the board, see if students can decide which are the most significant and which need to be defined more precisely. As you can see from the following list developed in a class, it does not take long to discover the complexity that cause and effect relationships can have.

Causes of good grades:

1. IQ (what is IQ?)
2. Study time
3. Attending class
4. Eating right
5. Enthusiasm
6. Motivation (different from enthusiasm?)

Again, most of the data used to test the strength of the causal connections will come from personal experience, although some students may have additional data from articles they have read on study techniques.

For cause and effect relationships that students will encounter in future college courses, I use actual examples from midterm and final exam questions. One midterm for a history class asked students to analyze how class, sex, race, and ethnicity affected the work options available to working class women in the late nineteenth century. A psychology exam asked students to examine the validity of the hypothesis that people with an extra Y chromosome had a tendency toward violent behavior. Ask students how they would go about testing the strength of the causal connections in these instances. Then compare the cause and effect relationships in these college assignments with those in the students' earlier experience. Is the nature of the relationship any different? Are the causes or the effects any more or less complicated? If you discuss these questions long enough, it will become clear that cause and effect relationships on the college level may or may not be more complex. But the real difference is the source of data used to prove or disprove the relationships. One is not dealing with data from personal experience as much as one is dealing with secondary sources, data from reports and books, data which first must be well assimilated before one can deal effectively with the causal relationship. This means learning and internalizing the required data to the point where it becomes almost as familiar as one's personal experience. For students who believe that if they have read an article or chapter once, then they are ready to write on it, this will introduce the idea of mastering the material before they attempt to test the causal relationships.

It is also useful to challenge the concept of causal relationships that has been presented by examining situations which seem to have the qualities of a causal relationship but which are flawed in some way. The lists of logical fallacies that most rhetoric books contain can be useful, but it is better to make students aware that in order to establish valid causal relationships, they need to ask questions and demonstrate the answers they come up with. Being able to question and prove the strength of a causal connection will be more useful in writing than simply recognizing a *post hoc ergo propter hoc* relationship.

The presentation thus far takes thirty to forty minutes, depending on how freely you let the class participate. In order to change the pace at this point, I have students work on sentence-level cause and effect relationships using the connector words they wrote down at the beginning of the class. I supply them with some information and have them make up the rest on their own, using some cause and effect patterns as a guide.

1. Make up an active voice sentence. Call this sentence X. Finish the sentence using this pattern: X/because Y.
2. Jerry Brown gives a speech — X. Complete the pattern Whenever X/Y.

3. I graduate from college — X. Complete the pattern Provided that X/Y.

4. A doctor discovers a cure for cancer — X. Complete the pattern X/therefore Y.

5. Women may be drafted — X. Complete the pattern Because X/Y.

An alternative to this exercise would be to take a sentence-combining exercise which contained causal relationships and have students do that.[2]

1. Our problems are solved.

2. Calvin chairs the program himself.

3. Calvin keeps his word.

4. Calvin finds someone to chair the program.

For the remainder of the class period (in my case I have a two-hour period in which to work) students can write a short essay analyzing a causal relationship containing at least three causes. As an alternative to writing an essay, one could have previously assigned a causal essay for outside reading and then discuss the causal relationships in the essay. This could be followed up the next class period with an in-class essay based on the outside reading.

The advantage of the organizer is that it clearly defines the elements and steps in the process of causal analysis and allows students to recognize where they need work. For many people it is a tool for working in unfamiliar terrain. By pointing out similarities and differences in past, present, and future experience, it provides a bridge between the known and the unknown and helps to eliminate the "casual" from causal analysis.

Notes

1. Paul D. Eggen, Donald P. Kauchak, and Robert J. Harder, *Strategies for Teachers: Information Processing Models in the Classroom* (Englewood Cliffs: Prentice Hall, 1979), pp. 258–308.

2. Both the sentences to be combined and the causal patterns are from a book to be published by Willis Pitkin. His particular approach to sentence combining emphasizes different binary relationships, in this case cause and effect, and is particularly useful because it can be used to reinforce basic thought processes on all levels of writing: essay, paragraph, sentence. The theory behind this approach is explained in the article, "X/Y: Some Basic Strategies of Discourse," *College English*, March 1977, pp. 660–672.

Values Clarification through Writing

Richard A. Strugala

Using a values clarification activity, Richard A. Strugala of Middlesex County College in Edison, New Jersey, helps his students make connections between thinking and writing. The result is a writing assignment that asks students to define and analyze specific values in their lives.

Author's Comment

The idea for a writing activity based on values clarification originated in a graduate course on group theory and practice. Although the original experience dealt solely with the dynamics of group decision making and individual decisions regarding group definition and priority, I have since modified the original exercise to work in a writing course.

General Approaches

As my freshman composition course proceeds through a developmental sequence of writing tasks, a need for a creative approach to the introduction of expository writing becomes apparent. Since the integration of writing and thinking is recognized as vital in the development of writing abilities, the values clarification experience presents itself as a natural bridge for the students to receive exposure to both processes. It also allows the complete language experience: thinking, speaking, listening, writing, reading. This cross-nurturing helps students to identify, accept, and express their ideas and feelings concerning their values. It further introduces them to the process of self-appraisal and conceptual reflection which is the hallmark of intellectual and cognitive maturity.

The Activity

Students are presented with ten values (freedom, peace, sincerity, social success, faith, wealth, happiness, love, health, friendship) written randomly by the instructor on the blackboard. I emphasize to the class that the order in which the elements are listed does not in any way convey a sense of ordered importance. Individually, working alone, the students are asked to rank order the ten elements from most important (#1) to least important (#10). The students then select a partner and in a limited amount of time (approximately 15-20 minutes) they are required to formulate a composite ranking that both partners agree on. After the working time has elapsed, the students list their composite rankings on the blackboard. The lists are numbered and identified by the first names of the students in the dyads. We then analyze the rankings.

An instructor may utilize any procedure for this analysis. For instance, I begin by examining what values are placed first. Then we usually look at the top three choices across all the groups. An individual value or set of values might be isolated and their placement examined. Some interesting linkages might be explored (e.g., wealth and social success, freedom and peace, love and friendship, health, etc.). One or both partners are asked to explain the ranking of a particular value. An examination/ debriefing of the process for achieving a consensus is also conducted. How did the dyads arrive at their decisions? Were certain values easier to rank than others? (Implicit in this question is whether it is easier to rank extremes than it is to decide the middle rankings.) What role did compromise play in the composite ranking? Did students "trade off" the placement of one value for another? Were there instances of "natural" agreement? Were there instances when no agreement was possible? Why? or Why not?

Since I have utilized this activity for five years, I share the various rankings that have occurred throughout this time span as a concluding portion of the in-class discussion. In examining these past decisions, we explore the impact of societal influences on individual value choices and the implication of developing and integrating individual priorities with those of peers, family, and community.

The Writing Assignment

Based on the individual ranking and class discussion, each student is then required to complete a writing assignment. Within the essay format, students are asked to develop a personal definition for the term "value"; to discuss how they determine whether a concept is of value to them and how they arrive at such a decision; to speculate about the origin of values by probing whether values are learned or biologically inherited; and to examine how society transmits values through cultural, political, and religious institutions. In addition, students are asked to explain the reasons for their first three choices which they listed in their individual rankings. They are asked to present their rationale in a logical and complete discussion and to outline the sequencing of their choices.

Assessment

The in-class discussion and writing activity stimulate a definition and discussion of values as concepts with application to everyday life, career, family, and social concerns. There emerges an articulation of the relationships among different categories of values based on the definitions provided by the students. The assignment encourages students to appraise their judgments in relation to specific times, places, and other environmental and cultural influences.

Using Persuasion to Plan
a Moon Walk

Muriel Harris

As preparation for writing a persuasive essay, students in Muriel
Harris's classes engage in a series of problem-solving activities that
foster awareness of the important elements in persuasion. Ms. Harris
submitted this exercise from Purdue University, Lafayette, Indiana.

Author's Comment

Rhetoric texts used in composition courses usually have adequate discussions of the modes of persuasion used in argumentative writing. However, like most textbook presentations, these descriptions tend to lack
vitality and leave the student without a good technique for turning theory
into practice. In order to breathe life into these descriptions and to
heighten students' awareness of the power of persuasive tactics, we need
to provide an opportunity for students to argue with the natural vigor
they are capable of outside the classroom. Then, when they wish to
examine how persuasion really works, they have a live argument to
analyze. An assignment that I've used, which provokes this kind of cross-
fire, is one that I've adapted from a NASA exercise in group decision
making. This exercise works best when students are not aware of the real
purpose of the assignment until after the results have been discussed.

Being Persuasive

1. The first step is to prepare an exercise sheet which explains to the
reader (in rather vague terms) that he or she has just crash-landed a lunar
landing module on the moon at Point A. In order to survive he or she
must get to the intended landing site at Point B, a task which will require
some traveling across the moon's surface. The heavily damaged module
has only fifteen items which are still usable, and these items are listed on
the exercise sheet. The reader is asked to rank this list in order of importance, assigning the lowest numbers to those items which would be most
valuable to take along. The list includes the following:

A box of matches

Food concentrate

50 feet of nylon rope

Parachute silk

Portable heating unit

Two .45 calibre pistols

Stellar map (of the moon's constellations)

First aid kit (containing injection needles)

Solar-powered FM receiver-transmitter

Two 100 lb. tanks of oxygen

Life raft

Magnetic compass

5 gallons of water

Signal flares

One cs. dehydrated Pet milk

2. During a class hour several days before we begin to work on persuasive writing, I give one of these sheets to each student to fill out. I find that I need to assure the students that this is not a test, but I won't explain or offer any elaboration of anything on the sheet. I also stress that each student must complete the sheet without consulting anyone else.

3. Several days later, I split the class into a series of small groups, and I again distribute those same assignment sheets to each person. This time, however, I explain that the assignment will be tried as a group exercise. Each group is to come to an agreement on their rankings. When all the groups have finished, usually after lengthy (and loud) discussions, I return to the students the sheets they had previously completed on their own.

4. When every student has both sheets in hand, individual rankings plus those decided on in the group, I ask everyone to compare the lists to see how different the rankings are. I then ask students to think about why or how they were persuaded by others in the group to change their original ordering. How, I ask, was each person persuaded to assign numbers which were different from personal decisions made earlier? If the group decisions are similar to the student's original sheet, how did that person influence the group to accept such an ordering?

As various students begin to offer explanations of what happened, I list their comments on the board. In their own terms, students mention that they were persuaded by someone who seemed to know what he or she was talking about (i.e., the power of the authoritative voice); they admit to changing their minds after being given facts about the moon's atmosphere, temperature, magnetic fields, etc., that they hadn't previously known (i.e., the use of facts to persuade). Usually, examples of deductive and inductive reasoning are mentioned, as well as some appeals to emotion. Textbook discussions of questionable tactics such as "the bandwagon approach" come alive as students consider whether or not they were being manipulated into going along with the rest of the group.

When we've exhausted all the modes of persuasion that had been used in the group decision-making process, we are ready to turn to our textbook discussions. We examine the way in which the text describes what has already been mentioned, and we look at other strategies that hadn't been used, such as knowing the audience the writer is aiming at, are also discussed in relation to the students' recent experience in persuading each other to make decisions. When the students turn to their own persuasive writing, they usually have a fairly clear idea of how to use strategies of persuasion.

Persuasion for Survival

Kathleen Kelly

Kathleen Kelly of Babson College, Wellesley, Massachusetts, offers an approach which introduces students to Rogerian argumentation and then has them demonstrate their understanding of the Rogerian principles by using them in letter writing.

Author's Comment

Many composition texts have begun to include chapters on Rogerian argument as a way to teach argument and persuasion. (The classic discussion appears in Young, Becker, and Pike, *Rhetoric: Discovery and Change,* 1970.) The Rogerian approach to argument helps novice arguers avoid two major traps into which they frequently fall:

1. That of treating the opponent's position from the outset as if no one could possibly hold it; and

2. That of offering their own position with no awareness of the objections to which it might be open.

The Rogerian strategy for arguing demands two things from writers:

1. That they suspend evaluation of the opponent's position until they can understand it from the opponent's point of view; and

2. That their own position be built upon values and knowledge they share with the opponent.

The Assignment

An excellent essay assignment consists in asking students to write their own Rogerian arguments in letters, trying to convince others they know to change their mind about an issue of some significance to them. My students have written letters like these:

A letter to a friend convincing the friend not to fire a good employee who blew his or her stack at the supervisor;

A letter to a tennis coach convincing the coach not to be such a severe taskmaster in the first weeks of practice;

A letter to a friend convincing the friend that one can stop smoking; and

A letter to a friend convincing the friend that duck hunting is not a cruel and mindless sport.

Preparation for Assignment

Students, however, often find it difficult to really suspend evaluation of the opponent's position and to empathize with that point of view. This is when the following incident described by Bruno Bettelheim in *The Informed Heart* becomes a powerful example of Rogerian strategy in action. (This incident is excerpted in Young, Becker, and Pike, *Rhetoric,* though not in the section devoted to Rogerian argument; many teachers familiar with the text have thus overlooked the excerpt's usefulness here.) In the incident, Bettelheim is a prisoner in a Nazi concentration camp. Bettelheim needs treatment in the camp's medical clinic, but has to persuade a sadistic SS officer to admit him. Bettelheim's appeal to the SS vividly demonstrates that even an arguer facing an opponent's deadly hatred can "understand the situation from the opponent's point of view" and "appeal to values and knowledge one shares with the opponent."

from *The Informed Heart*[1]

. . . In the winter of 1938 a Polish Jew murdered the German attache in Paris, von Rath. The Gestapo used the event to step up anti-Semitic actions, and in the camp new hardships were inflicted on Jewish prisoners. One of these was an order barring them from the medical clinic unless the need for treatment had originated in a work accident.

Nearly all prisoners suffered from frostbite which often led to gangrene and then amputation. Whether or not a Jewish prisoner was admitted to the clinic to prevent such a fate depended on the whim of an SS private. On reaching the clinic entrance, the prisoner explained the nature of his ailment to the SS man, who then decided if he should get treatment or not.

I, too, suffered from frostbite. At first I was discouraged from trying to get medical care by the fate of Jewish prisoners whose attempts had ended up in no treatment, only abuse. Finally things got worse and I was afraid that waiting longer would mean amputation. So I decided to make an effort.

When I got to the clinic, there were many prisoners lined up as usual, a score of them Jews suffering from severe frostbite. The main topic of discussion was one's chances of being admitted to the clinic. Most Jews had planned their procedure in detail. Some thought it best to stress their service in the German army during World War I: wounds received or decorations won. Others planned to stress the severity of their frostbite. A few decided it was best to tell some "tall story," such as that an SS officer had ordered them to report at the clinic.

Most of them seemed convinced that the SS man on duty would not see through their schemes. Eventually they asked me about my plans. Having no definite ones, I said I would go by the way the SS man dealt with other Jewish prisoners who had frostbite like me, and proceed accordingly. I doubted how wise it was to follow a preconceived plan, because it was hard to anticipate the reactions of a person you didn't know.

The prisoners reacted as they had at other times when I had voiced similar ideas on how to deal with the SS. They insisted that one SS man was like another, all equally vicious and stupid. As usual, any frustration was immediately discharged against the person who caused it, or was nearest at hand. So in abusive terms they accused me of not wanting to share my plan with them, or of intending to use one of theirs; it angered them that I was ready to meet the enemy unprepared.

No Jewish prisoner ahead of me in line was admitted to the clinic. The more a prisoner pleaded, the more annoyed and violent the SS became. Expressions of pain amused him; stories of previous services rendered to Germany outraged him. He proudly remarked that *he* could not be taken in by Jews, that fortunately the time had passed when Jews could reach their goal by lamentation.

When my turn came he asked me in a screeching voice if I knew that work accidents were the only reason for admitting Jews to the clinic, and if I came because of such an accident. I replied that I knew the rules, but that I couldn't work unless my hands were freed of the dead flesh. Since prisoners were not allowed to have knives, I asked to have the dead flesh cut away. I tried to be matter-of-fact, avoiding pleading, deference, or arrogance. He replied: "If that's all you want, I'll tear the flesh off myself." And he started to pull at the festering skin. Because it did not come off as easily as he may have expected, or for some other reason, he waved me into the clinic.

Inside, he gave me a malevolent look and pushed me into the treatment room. There he told the prisoner orderly to attend to the wound. While this was being done, the guard watched me closely for signs of pain but I was able to suppress them. As soon as the cutting was over, I started to leave. He showed surprise and asked why I didn't wait for further treatment. I said I had gotten the service I asked for, at which he told the orderly to make an exception and treat my hand. After I had left the room, he called me back and gave me a card entitling me to further treatment, and admittance to the clinic without inspection at the entrance.

Discussion

In discussing Bettelheim's action as Rogerian strategy, I ask students to explain what they think Bettelheim learned about the SS by watching the officer respond to the other Jewish prisoners: "The more a person pleaded, the more annoyed and violent the SS became." This leads us to discuss the Nazi propaganda the SS may have been steeped in, his probable reasons for wanting to believe the propaganda, and the way he understood his role in the prison camp. How do they think, I ask the class, the SS understood and justified to himself what he was doing?

We then turn to Bettelheim. Why did Bettelheim's strategy to do no pleading and show no pain surprise the officer and lead him to treat Bettelheim differently from the other Jews? What were the values Bettelheim showed he shared with the officer?

The passage can also lead to a discussion of ethical questions. By trying to understand the SS's motives, do we automatically sympathize with them? Approve of them? Forgive them? When we argue with an opponent whose values (as we understand them) we condemn, how do we avoid becoming either blindly self-righteous or mindlessly tolerant of evil?

Whether or not Bettelheim's account is used to lead into a more extensive discussion of the ethical issues in communication, the passage from *The Informed Heart* brings the principles of Rogerian argument home to students dramatically. Sometimes, knowing how to persuade can be a matter of life or death.

Note

1. Reprinted with permission of Macmillan Publishing Co., Inc. from *The Informed Heart: Autonomy in a Mass Age* by Bruno Bettelheim. Copyright © 1960 by The Free Press, a Corporation.

"Not Yet Convinced?" Another Approach to the Persuasive Paper

Stanley Sulkes

Instructors interested in placing more emphasis on primary research material will find this activity useful. Stanley Sulkes outlines an approach that helps students identify their own research topics and then develop the primary research material to support a thesis. Mr. Sulkes teaches at Raymond Walters College, Blue Ash, Ohio.

Author's Comment

In the past I have considered a persuasive theme to be one of the most useful papers for students to write. Its value lies in its broad applicability both to other sorts of college assignments and to the kind of writing that will be required of them beyond the academic setting. Yet the results are often uninspired and evaluating these papers proves problematic, since I am often uncertain over who actually wrote them. Any theme on the downing of the Korean liner, the situation in Lebanon or, worse, a stance on abortion is apt to be a rehash of yesterday's newspaper editorial or last week's *Time* magazine. Typically, one suspects that many students choose political topics not because they are interested in such material but simply as a reflexive reaction to the word "argument." So the results are often dull.

The Approach

I have discovered that a more effective paper usually results when students are encouraged to argue over some issue in the school, even better in their English class, with the research being performed right in the room. Such research can be exciting for students, and it need not consume much time.

The invention phase can be quickly handled by means of a method outlined in Laque and Sherwood, *A Laboratory Approach to Writing,* (NCTE, 1977). The teacher writes a word on the board (in this case "English class," followed by "men," then "women"). The student is given

148

30 seconds to generate a list of words by free association. The response to "English class" might be "expense," "work," "teachers," "grading," "homework."

Each person attempts transforming one into a research question, without concern for its plausibility. Examples:

Do teachers here give too much homework?

Are certain kinds of tests unfair?

What is the maximum number of hours that one can work and still achieve passing grades?

Is journal-writing a waste of time?

Does revising produce better papers?

This is the best means I have found for helping students quickly create simple research topics. Allowing them to devise implausible theories seems to liberate their imaginations, and relieved of the pressure of being "right," students are able to generate a sizable number of projects. Generally, at least one will be promising.

Eventually, the thesis is scrutinized for plausibility, after which students devise questionnaires followed by interviews to test their hypotheses. Questionnaires must take no more than four minutes to complete and must be approved by me in advance. They are then circulated by means of ditto masters, with two or three surveys on each sheet. I warn students to conceal at least temporarily any hypotheses they may have drawn so as not to skew their findings. In addition, I keep track of individuals working on the same issue so that later their findings can be compared. The individual nature of the topics lends itself best to working with students by means of individual conferences, especially in helping them create testing instruments. Some elected to test members of this class, some of another class, some fraternity and sorority organizations, some family members.

A sampling of the kinds of theses they eventually adopted follows:

Grading in practice is consistent with established standards. (Another of my classes where the grading was done by a colleague yielded less complimentary results.)

More effective use of text assignments needs to be devised. (Many students not reading models in text.)

Many students dislike journals but believe it helps them practice grammar and punctuation! (A complete surprise since the aim I announced was to encourage creativity.)

Alcohol abuse is only a marginal problem among students in this class. (Though two students admitted drinking 7 days a week.)

A method should be devised to allow students to confer with one another while the teacher is holding individual conferences.

Fifteen hours seem to be the practical limit for full-time students who wish to keep their average over C. (One young woman maintained a B- average while working full time. Interviewed, she acknowledged surviving on three to four hours of sleep.)

High schools need to do a better job preparing students for college level English. (This was the most articulate paper of a frustrated, unskilled writer.)

The cost of creating more study space in this building would be justified.

Summation

At best this assignment is not only effective for students and interesting to teachers (you'll get a wealth of data regarding what class methods work and what don't, and why), but also in some cases it may even serve to enlighten students. It was rather sobering for one youth to discover, after disregarding what his teachers and counselors had been telling him, that working thirty hours and attending college full time might be incompatible . . . that is, if he needed more than four hours of sleep. Polling his classmates and interviewing a few allowed him to calculate how slim were the chances of succeeding if he persisted in working full time.

Though I have used the method outlined above only for persuasive papers, it should work equally well with the information paper, given the kinship of the two rhetorical modes.

From Catnaps to Essays:
A Saga

Linda Shadiow

Creating a realistic sense of audience for argumentative writing can be difficult. This exercise provides a writing sequence that forces students to examine each other's arguments and develop effective counterarguments. Ms. Shadiow sent this from Arizona State University, Tempe.

Author's Comment

Teaching students to write essays that contain specific rather than general details has always taxed my missionary zeal. A few Freshman English class periods ago, I sensed my zeal waning as the students greeted my familiar sermon about using words and examples to "show" rather than "tell" with well-rehearsed nods, tolerant sighs, and catnaps. I needed to discover a way to help them see the power of specific, detailed writing. In a moment of inspiration I announced "The Cat Paper." (Dozing students smirked at the irony—and at my weak imitation of a few Steve Martin punch lines.) I explained that the appropriateness of the title for the assignment would become clear later on, and I announced that their essays were to contain a straightforward, gut reaction to a controversial topic.

The Approach

The following class period I distributed a detailed assignment sheet:

> Pick a controversial topic you feel strongly about. Write a brief paper that expresses your feelings and your reasons for them. Make it straightforward. Be very accurate about what you feel and why.
>
> Pretend someone has asked you to explain your feelings. You don't have time to do research or to look up any handy-dandy quotes. You do have time to organize your thoughts and explain your own personal reasons for those thoughts. Your paper will be read by someone else, but you will not have a chance to explain anything beyond what you have written. No one will cross-examine you.

> Choose a topic that is very specific and that you feel strongly about. What is it that you could get into a heated argument over? What topic could you do a twenty-minute free-writing on?

The assignment sheet also included a list of contemporary and perennial topics such as the 1980 Olympic boycott, the draft, and abortion. Since we had been working on papers that involved library research, footnotes, and bibliographic notations, they grinned at their good fortune. Some of my zeal returned.

When they turned the papers in at the end of the week, many students expressed appreciation for getting the chance to blow off steam and get credit for it. During the writing conferences that followed, we formulated a "for" or "against" statement and wrote it at the top of the paper as a shorthand guide to the stance the writer expressed.

After all the "Cat Paper" assignments had been evaluated, I crossed out the writers' names and xeroxed one copy of each essay. Armed with these duplicate anonymous essays (sealed in individual envelopes marked with a name other than the writer's), I went into class and distributed the next assignment sheet: "The Cat Juggling Paper."

> You will be given someone's "Cat Paper" where a number of points have been made in order to support a specific stance on a specific issue. Your assignment is to take that gut reaction paper and to write an accompanying essay for the purpose of making the individual think differently about the same topic. Read the paper, not the arguments, and spend time in the library looking up facts and figures that will help you construct an essay that will convince the writer to reconsider the position.
>
> You must only work from the paper, not from any amplification of arguments the author might give to you. It doesn't matter how you feel about the topic you are researching; you may agree completely with the person who wrote it, but you have to take an opposite view.
>
> When you complete the assignment, it will be given to the person who wrote the original paper. That individual will have a chance to respond to your presentation of the opposite view. Similarly, you will receive a "Cat Juggling Paper" from someone working on your "Cat Paper."

Then I distributed the sealed envelopes to the students and explained that the writers' names had been omitted so they could work with the written presentation rather than an oral one. They were awake and eager to begin.

During the next week we looked at argumentative essays and talked about alternate ways to organize a persuasive paper. Most of the students didn't know whose paper they were working on (or who was working on theirs) until the "Cat Juggling Papers" were turned in. As they came to class that morning, they were anxious to find out the effects of their essays—each constructed with specific details to support their views—on the classmate who originally wrote on the opposite side of the same issue.

First I returned everyone's original "Cat Paper" so the writer could refresh his or her memory on how the point of view was explained. They were then given the "Cat Juggling Paper" that had been written exclusively for them. They read these essays much more intently than they read my class handouts; I saw heads nod and shake as they concentrated on the researched papers. As soon as they finished reading, they recorded their reactions on a response sheet:

After reading your paper and considering your argument,

I learned that . . .

I was surprised that . . .

I now know that . . .

I realize that . . .

I think that . . .

I wish that . . .

They spent the last part of the class period talking over their responses to both the arguments and the writing. By working through the development of both papers and evaluating the results with each other, their enthusiasm and intensity replaced my handouts and sermons. They were reinforcing the importance of specific details in each other's writing, and some students admitted to thinking differently about an issue because of the details which showed rather than told them that another side of the controversial subject existed. The missionary zeal was now theirs, not mine. And none of us were catnapping.

You Too Can Write a Science Book for Children!

Herman A. Estrin

Developing writing situations in which students can test their abilities to communicate their own knowledge to a real audience sometimes poses problems. Herman A. Estrin, however, has found one solution. He has his college students, most of whom are engineering majors, use their technical knowledge and write for a children's audience. Mr. Estrin submitted this from the Newark College of Engineering, New Jersey.

Author's Comment

"My first reaction to writing a children's book was a fear of the unknown, for to dabble within the mental state of a child seemed impossible." Such was the reaction of one student to the exercise which follows, but it turned out to be hardly so formidable and very exciting indeed. There is a genuine need for meaningful children's literature, especially in the science area; and students reacted most enthusiastically to the challenge of making art and language work effectively with scientific material to produce a valuable combination of the arts and sciences.

Writing for Children

1. *Read science books for children.* All public libraries have these books in the Children's Department. You should become acquainted with the series "Let's Read and Find Out," published by Thomas Crowell, New York. The following books are in this series:

Before You Were a Baby

High Sounds, Low Sounds

Your Skin and Mine

Why Frogs Are Wet

At the Drop of Blood

Shrimps

Hear Your Heart

How You Talk

Ladybug, Ladybug

A Book of Mars for You

2. *Try to answer these questions* as you read these books:

   a. *Content*—What is the overall content of the book? How would you evaluate the scientific information in the book? Is the subject matter timely, relevant, and useful to the reader? Comment on the introduction (preface) and the conclusion. Does this book reflect the needs and the experience common to all of us, and yet does it have a spontaneity and freshness?

   b. *Format*—What size is this book? How many pages does it contain? Describe its print. Does each page have "white space," or is it full of printed matter? How is color used throughout the book? Discuss its use of illustrations, pictures, charts, and graphs. Can you recommend additional graphic aids? If so, what kinds and why would you recommend them?

   c. *Style*—What kinds of sentences are used throughout the book? Cite some examples.
      How does the author use figures of speech? Cite some examples.
      Does the author use parallel structure? Cite an example.
      Does the author use repetition judiciously? Cite an example.
      How would you evaluate the vocabulary of the book?
      Does the author explain difficult terms? How does he do so?
      Does the author make the reader use his eyes and ears to understand the content of the book? How does the author do so?
      Does this book have humor? Is it direct and obvious?
      Children love the tastes, smells, the colors of things. Does the author use as much sensory detail as possible? How would you use more sensory details?

   d. *Evaluation*—If you were to write a book on this subject, what approach would you use to arouse the interest of the reader? How could this book be improved? Did you learn any new information from the text? Did the author reach the intended audience level?

3. *Select a subject about which you have a thorough knowledge and which would "grab" the child's interest.* Children are interested in subjects concerning ecology, astronomy, and geology. Also, they love to read books about animals—snakes, frogs, bees, and shrimps—for example. In addition children are interested in books about the construction trades,

science mysteries and riddles, and science fiction. Remember that you should write about a subject in which *you* are especially interested.

Students have written the following manuscripts which suggest areas other students may wish to explore:

Ecology Series

What Is Water Pollution?

Ocean Ecology

Why You Can Build Sandcastles

Where Is Down the Drain?

Our Beautiful Dams

Traffic Jams

The Solution to Pollution

Where Are Our Beaches Going?

A Loud, Loud World: Noise Pollution

Alice in Garbageland

Science Series

Let's Learn about Electricity

Kinds of Telescopes

Highways

The Children's Book of Roads

Earth's Friendly Blanket

What Makes It Rain?

Rocks Are Everywhere

On a Journey to the Moon

Did You Ever Look under Your Street?

Henry Meets the Rockheads

Hobby Series

The Soccer Game

On the Art of Fencing

Skin Scuba Diving

How to Keep Tropical Fish

How Would You Like to Travel?

Career Series

What Is Surveying?

The Engineering Tree

How Would You Like to Be an Engineer?

The Adventures of an Engineer

4. *Use the following facets of style in your book:*

   a. white space
   b. vivid colors
   c. subject-verb-object sentences
   d. simple, short sentences
   e. judicious use of repetition
   f. humor
   g. large print
   h. sensory details (taste, smell, sound, and touch)
   i. vocabulary adapted to the reader
   j. attractive, meaningful illustrations
   k. figures of speech, especially similes and metaphors
   l. parallelism

5. *Some of the better papers may be worthy of publication.* If students desire, they may check the following items before sending the manuscript to the publisher:

   a. Place your name and title on each page of the manuscript.
   b. Use a paper clip to fasten the manuscript.
   c. Include a self-addressed, stamped envelope.
   d. Present a neatly typed or printed manuscript.

This assignment helps teach students the values of a particular job and of showing a young child ideas and ideals of engineering. The practical aspects in life must be shown to children in the younger years so that they can make a successful choice of vocation or profession.

The Beginning and End of Writing: The Relationship of Writer-Subject-Audience

Marjorie Smelstor

What choices must a writer make in terms of tone, diction, and organization when composing? Marjorie Smelstor of The University of Texas at San Antonio outlines a sequence of writing assignments, each calling for a different mode, causing students to vary their choices to meet the purpose of each assignment.

Author's Comment

In an effort to emphasize the importance of seeing writing as a dynamic interaction among writer, subject, and audience, and attempting to situate the writing process within the so-called "real world," I recently structured a composition class around the question of how each piece of writing, with its distinct purpose and audience, impels the writer to struggle over a variety of considerations—considerations of tone, diction, organization, approach, to name a few. In our reflection, discussion, and writing, my class and I carefully examined the context within which a communicator operates and how that context alters the message that is finally communicated. What follows is a brief description of the major types of writing done in the course—from journals to research papers—and the various audiences for whom the students wrote.

Design of Course

1. Type of Writing: Personal Writing   Audience: Self

We began by writing for ourselves—in our journals—and we continued this kind of personal, expressive writing throughout the semester because it gave us opportunities to experiment and daydream. Further, in this kind of writing the conventions and rules are least demanding, so the students gain confidence in the writing experience itself without being paralyzed by a fear of "making mistakes." Though we experimented with "free" and "focused" writing in our journals, the most meaningful writing experiences resulted from the focused assignments, including one I borrowed from Ken Macrorie. In his book *Uptaught* (New York: Hayden Book Company, 1970, p. 128), he describes the success he had from using this passage from *Walden* with his students:

> Shams and delusions are esteemed for soundest truth, while reality is fabulous. If men would steadily observe realities only, and not allow themselves to be deluded, life, to compare it with such things as we know, would be like a fairy tale and the Arabian Nights' Entertainments.

Macrorie asked his students to spend the weekend recording fabulous realities, and his students came up with some of these:

> A young lady's fifty-cent check to the Optimist Club bounced.
>
> A man returned to his parked car to find its hood and fenders gashed and crumpled. On the dashboard he found a piece of folded paper. Written in a neat feminine hand, the note said: "I have just run into your car. There are people watching me. They think I am writing down my name and address. They are wrong."

I tried the same assignment with my students, and their realities, while not quite so colorful as Macrorie's students', were still fabulous:

> An antiquated grandmother comes in the H.E.B. grocery store where I work. She wears a scarlet red mini-skirt, a platinum blonde wig, black patent leather boots, and uses a cane.
>
> Yesterday I met a man named Joe Blow.
>
> On Main Street, a doctor's office is flanked on both sides by funeral homes.

2. Type of Writing: Description   *Audience: Class and University of Wisconsin/Potential University Students*

After emphasizing expressive writing, we moved into what James Britton, in *Language and Learning,* calls participant's use of language or what James Moffett, in *Teaching the Universe of Discourse,* views as Drama—recording What Is Happening—or what others call Description. We identified two audiences for this: first, the known audience of our own class, and, second, an unknown audience of other students.

In the first instance, after agreeing that we as both writers and audience needed more help with our powers of observation, we decided to turn to what some call the demon of non-observation—TV—for practice. Each person carefully and actively watched some TV hero or heroine and wrote a descriptive paragraph of the character without naming them.

Sharing our descriptions, we evaluated the effectiveness of the communications by seeing if we, as audience, could identify the character, and if we could, by what verbal symbols and concrete language we did this. As we compared the visions of the audience with those of the writers—we examined audience response—we considered how descriptive language can accomplish the mission Joseph Conrad articulated for writers: "My task which I am trying to achieve is, by the power of the written word, to make you hear, to make you feel—it is, before all, to make you *see.*"

Another experience in writing to and for our class was an *Underground Guide to Shopping in San Antonio.* After each person contributed an entry, carefully giving both factual and descriptive information, two people edited the publication, one copy of which went to each contributor. The project forced us to weigh the balance between "editorializing" and presenting facts, between presenting common knowledge and providing new information. Because our class was its own audience, we could talk over questions among ourselves, an opportunity that greatly facilitated the project.

Communicating in this way with a known audience was relatively easy compared to the next task: writing to a class at the University of Wisconsin. Each group of writers—ours in San Antonio and the one in Wisconsin—was asked to describe its university and environs so that the distant audience, unfamiliar with both a different type of university and "foreign" territory, would gain knowledge and appreciation of the faraway place. After several class days of prewriting, which involved reading and evaluating a descriptive article from *National Geographic,* as well as discussing our variant views of UTSA and San Antonio, we began our drafts. We confronted numerous obstacles: How much or how little information about our location should we provide? What tone should we assume: humorous, reflective, personal, analytical? How much jargon could we use (would our dairyland readers understand "rednecks" or even "armadillo races")? The experience was so engaging and the level of enthusiasm so high that the class decided to photograph themselves—in full Texas costume—as well as the campus and the city. Their words, however, were worth more than a thousand pictures, they believed, so the photographs were mailed *after* the more important verbal communications.

As a variation of this plan, another class did a similar assignment for potential UTSA students. Describing the university to high school students who might be deciding about coming to our school, the freshmen writers saw their papers as useful recruitment resources and donated them to the university's recruitment office.

3. *Type of Writing: Process and Analysis*   *Audience: Class*

Survival manuals were our next effort. After reading an article about blue jeans—why they are popular and how to buy just the right kind— we planned a manual that would do the same thing; that is, explain the *why* and *how* of a variety of current fads, including discoing, backpack- ing, fixing natural foods, jogging, buying a CB, decorating a van. In previous assignments, we had considered questions of tone and diction, and now we added another concern: finding the most effective way to organize what amounted to two rhetorical modes in one paper, process and analysis. In small workshop groups, the students helped each other, always remembering that their peers would be reading this manual and that the purpose was to explain why and how to understand, for example, the physical fitness fad. The final publication, edited by two members of the class, was a tribute to the group's individual and collaborative efforts.

4. *Type of Writing: Persuasion*   *Audience: An Identified Leader*

The penultimate assignment was persuasive writing. Each student chose some person in a leadership position—a former or current teacher, a city councilman, a religious leader, a parent—with whom the writer felt some strong disagreement. Writing a letter to that person about the disagree- ment was a difficult task, for it involved arguing a position logically and persuasively, as well as trying not to alienate the audience through inap- propriate tone, diction, or other stylistic techniques. Most students actually mailed their letters, and since no one reported any retaliative response, the communication must have been at least that successful.

5. *Type of Writing: Research Paper*   *Audience: Class*

The final writing assignment, required by the nature of the freshman composition course, was a research paper. While this might seem the least likely assignment to be informed by a sense of audience (other than instructor), quite the opposite was true. We spent a great deal of time selecting the topics that would be interesting to most people in the class, since we all would be talking about and reading at least some stage of everyone's paper. With only one general restriction—that the topic deal with popular culture, a pervasive reality that touches all of us—the stu- dents chose a wide variety of topics, some of the most interesting being Clark Gable, Marilyn Monroe, Arnold Palmer, science fiction, photog- raphy, automobiles, motorcycles, and billiards. We also devoted many class sessions and much conference time to consideration of purpose: to analyze—for our class—a subject about which we knew a little but not as much as we'd know at the end of our research and analysis.

After choosing the topics and discussing purpose, we struggled over the tone, trying to find ways to be both familiar and formal. We agreed that readability, a key factor in all writing, was especially difficult to maintain in a paper citing primary and secondary sources, but that it was essential to a successful communication. Clearly the element of audience was paramount in this; if we were pedantic, "chatty-kathy," or enmeshed in sources, we would lose our audience. The class recognized that the success of this communication—as it is in all writing—would be the degree of engagement among audience-writer-subject, the communication triangle which forms the basis of rhetorical theory. As they wrote this assignment, at the end of the semester, the students realized that the theory had become so much a part of their writing that it vitalized even this sometimes deadly assignment, the research paper. We ended the course where we had begun, writing to and for an audience, and as T.S. Eliot said, we saw this "as if for the first time."

A Business Writing Sequence for a General Writing Course

Karen L. Pelz

This sequence of assignments, which calls for different modes as
well as different purposes and audiences, is appropriate for business
English and communication classes as well as for composition
courses. Ms. Pelz teaches at Western Kentucky University, Bowling
Green.

Author's Comment

More and more college teachers trained in the teaching of literature
are being asked to teach courses in writing, even in many cases courses
in writing designed for students outside the traditional liberal arts curriculum. My purpose in creating this sequence of assignments was to
create writing tasks that would be both interesting and teachable for the
traditionally trained instructor and useful for students planning a career
in some aspect of business. I also aimed for a sequence that would be
pedagogically sound, based on the expressive to transactional model proposed by James Britton (*The Development of Writing Abilities, 11–18,*
Macmillan, 1975) and involving a variety of modes and audiences to
provide the student with a wide range of rhetorical experiences. The
writing tasks range from informal description to formal exposition, from
autobiography to argumentation. In my own classes, assignments 2, 4,
and 6 are discussed in a workshop format, with several student papers
duplicated for the entire class to respond to.

Sequence

1. Write a letter to a friend describing a summer job you heard about
that you think would be just perfect for you. Describe exactly what you
would be doing as part of this position and why you are so enthusiastic
about it.

2. Write a letter of application to the company or organization, applying for this job you would like to have. You can invent whatever qualifications and experience you think you would need to be considered a

prime candidate. Include with your letter a resumé detailing your education and experience.

3. To prepare yourself for a possible interview, write a description of what you imagine the company or organization to be like that may offer you the job. You may want to do some library research for this project. What does the company or organization do? What kinds of people work there? What are their backgrounds, training, and experience? How do your qualifications fit with theirs? What qualities do you suppose the company looks for in its employees?

4. The company responds to your letter of application, stating that they are interested in considering you for the position. In order to get to know you better, they would like you to write an autobiography and a statement of why you are interested in this particular job. What will you tell them? Respond to their request.

5. You got the job! After you are there for a month, your immediate supervisor asks you to write a progress report detailing what you have managed to accomplish in your first month of employment. What kinds of things should go into a progress report? How much should you say about the job and how much about yourself? Should you talk about the things you haven't done yet as well as the things you have? Write a progress report.

6. After two months on the job, you are told by your immediate supervisor that you are doing a fine job, but the president of the company or organization is considering doing away with your position after you leave because of budget limitations. Write a report to the president, the purpose of which is to convince the president that the job you do for the company is a crucial one and that the position should not be eliminated.

7. It is the end of the summer, and you are leaving your job to return to college. You have enjoyed this work, and you think you might like to return to this company or organization after you graduate from school, perhaps in a higher position. Write a letter of resignation in which you convey this idea to your employer.

Summation

In this exercise students are presented with a coherent and unified sequence of assignments so that when they have completed it, they have a sense of having worked on a project that is meaningful and useful to them. They have gained experience in a number of writing tasks that have specific application in the larger world outside the halls of ivy, yet the tasks have involved them in skills that are generalizable to a large number of rhetorical situations. Equally important, they have produced papers which writing instructors can evaluate for specific characteristics of tone, language choice, clarity, logic, coherence, and development and which they can also enjoy reading.

Rhetoric of the Printed Media:
An Approach to Composition

Robert Perrin

Using a theme called "the rhetoric of printed media," Robert Perrin
suggests how an entire writing course can focus on the effectiveness
of language in the media and on building students' skills in analyzing such language use. Mr. Perrin is at Indiana State University,
Terre Haute.

Author's Comment

When I started teaching freshman composition at the University of
Illinois I followed the departmental recommendation and used Decker's
Patterns of Exposition 6. I found the essays to be varied and enjoyable,
but my students did not. They didn't respond to essays I had them read—
ones by Catton, Huxley, and Orwell—in part, I think, because the essays
seemed sacred and removed from their own experiences. After all,
weren't the essays chosen to be anthologized? Weren't they introduced
by terse paragraphs establishing each writer's authority? To my rather
insecure freshmen, these essays must have seemed at once alien and
above criticism.

Because my students seemed so reticent about critically evaluating
these bound essays and because I had to admit that the essays didn't have
much in common with the kinds of reading they would need to do as
professionals, I started to think about another focus for my writing
course. I began to think about a composition course with a thematic
focus that might interest my students more.

Eventually a thematic course emerged which I have called The Rhetoric
of the Printed Media. I have been able to offer the course to advanced
placement students and have been especially pleased. The course has
proved interesting to my students and has, at the same time, allowed me
to emphasize writing skills and writing analysis in a traditional manner.
The course has also freed me from painfully constructing sets of writing
assignments which included one topic of personal interest, one topic of
political interest, and one topic of social interest. The media focus also

allowed students to address their writing to whichever media interested them most, although my rhetorical focus was always clear.

Procedure

My explanation of the course is this:

> We are influenced each day by the printed media—by the language its writers use, by the format in which those writers present information, and by the advertisements which surround the articles. In this course we will attempt to analyze the media by its readerships, its assumptions, and its methods. A wide variety of subject matter will be covered, but we will focus our attention on the effectiveness of the media's persuasion—that is, on its rhetoric.

This explanation suggests, I think, a broad-based appeal for the course and at the same time presents a focus which is very much in keeping with the standards of most composition departments.

In choosing a textbook for the course, I was faced with a minor problem—finding a book with a range of media articles that would allow my students to begin applying critical skills without requiring them to "track down" a periodical at the same time they were learning techniques of writing. I eventually found *Mass Media and the Popular Arts* (ed. Frederick Rissover and David C. Birch, McGraw-Hill). The text is useful because it provides a wide range of articles treating subjects like political advertising, sexual stereotypes in magazines, and persuasive techniques used by the media. Especially useful is a series of articles on the Attica Prison Riots, which allow us to discuss stance, use of support, and tone. As we progress in the course, and as the students' focus on stance, content, organization, sentences, and diction becomes clearer, I allow them to select their own periodicals, subject to my approval. As might be expected, the most consistently chosen periodicals include *Cosmopolitan, Esquire, Newsweek, Sports Illustrated, Time,* and *U.S. News and World Report,* with an occasional *MS* and *New Yorker.*

Early in the semester my assignments are generally tied to the articles in *Mass Media.* I provide the topics and my students practice writing techniques. Then I free them to use whatever magazines or media they wish, although I still provide some guidelines like these:

> Find a recent issue of a magazine which has a wide distribution and select a kind of advertisement which appears at least three times. Construct a thesis which clearly states your view of these ads and support your argument with specific examples.

Considering the impact which commercials have on television view-
ers, the Federal Trade Commission banned cigarette advertising on
television. Select another product which you feel should not be
advertised (in magazines or in newspapers) and construct an argumentative paper which supports your case.

Steve Shapiro, Francesco Scavullo, Norman Rockwell, and Ansel
Adams have all done paintings or taken photographs which have
appeared on the covers of national magazines. Of course, not all
covers are so artfully designed, but for the most part publishers
want effective covers. Select a magazine (identify it clearly in your
paper) and explain why magazines intended for newsstand sale need
these carefully designed covers.

With these kinds of assignments my students are able to focus on the
magazine which interests them, and I am able to sit down to grade papers
which are as individual as my students and yet are unified in approach.

When we began working on research (at the University of Illinois a
research paper is included in the ten papers which a student must complete in a semester), I was especially pleased because the printed media
provided my students with the chance to do original research if they
wished. The simplest and most traditional approach I present, and which
a few students choose, is a research paper drawn from an assortment of
sources (four books, three periodicals, two newspaper articles, and one
additional source). The papers which are researched in this way treat
subjects like "The Making of a Successful Talk Show Host," "Subliminal
Seduction in Liquor Advertising," and "Carl Sagan and the Popular
Press." All of these papers are respectable and interesting pieces of student writing. However, the most interesting and more original papers are
related to the media in individual students' fields of study. For these
papers I suggest that students select a key periodical in their subject area
and scan every second or third issue over a period of ten years. Once they
have done that, they are to focus on a particular subject—advertisements,
editorials, feature articles, whatever they wish—and construct a thesis
which reflects the change they have noticed. Then they are to return to
the issues of the periodicals and take a more complete sampling. (They
can modify the thesis, of course, but not change the area of focus.) The
range of paper topics and the originality of the students' interpretations
made grading these research papers surprisingly pleasant. Here are a few
of the papers that have been submitted:

"Look, Look, See Dick Dominate Jane"—a paper by an elementary
education major who discussed featured cartoons in three major
children's magazines from the sixties.

"Good Vibes"—a paper by a music major on changing advertisements for amplification equipment.

"The Master Builders"—a paper by an architecture major discussing the changing image of architects in *Architectural Record.*

"Bare Bones"—a paper by another music student (trombone major) on the modification of one company's trombone advertisements over a thirty-year span.

After they have completed these papers I feel that they have learned the rudiments of research and have learned something about their respective fields—for most of them confess to having been "side-tracked" by articles while they were scanning the periodicals. Consequently, I feel that the research papers which were focused on the printed media have been valuable for them, while at the same time they are interesting for me.

Evaluation

I have to admit that at first I was hesitant about imposing a media focus on a composition course. I thought I might try it for a semester or two and then probably return to a course based on Decker or some other general reader. That hesitation has disappeared. It has disappeared in part because my students have found the materials interesting and clearly related to the kinds of reading they will be doing long after they have finished my composition class. Further, a media focus does not prevent me from dealing with writing skills in a systematic, traditional way. But most importantly, this media focus has allowed me to bring together my students' interests in their own reading materials and my interest in their writing. The results have been satisfactory for them and for me.

Choosing a Career:
A Research Project That Works

Adele Pittendrigh

Selecting a career often seems to pose a dilemma for students. This sequence of activities combines students' exploration of career choices with research skills. Ms. Pittendrigh contributed this exercise from Montana State University, Bozeman.

Author's Comment

Last quarter, two groups of students in my freshman writing class agreed that the most serious problem facing college freshmen today is choosing a career. Other problems that the students identified—the draft, the threat of nuclear war, inflation—were all considered less important because they affect individuals less directly and personally. "Besides," one student said of those other problems, "you can't do anything about them." Students admitted anxiety, frustration, and fear that they might not make the right career choice. Many felt that they did not have sufficient information on which to base their decisions. Even students who knew and had known for a long time what field they were going into wondered whether they would be happy and successful in their fields.

The Project

To help students explore this problem, I turn "career choice" into a research project. The project, which takes about three weeks, involves self-assessment exercises to help students discover their career interests, including free-writing assignments for exploring expectations about a chosen field, library research, an interview with a professional in the selected career field, and finally the production of a paper focusing on what students have discovered about their career field. Throughout the project, students are guided by two primary questions: How do my expectations about a chosen career match up to the reality of that career in the working world? And, am I likely to be successful and happy as a _____? I divide the project itself into four stages:

(1) Self-assessment

First, I have students begin to assess their career interests by imagining which groups they would join at "The Party," a career self-assessment exercise adapted from John Holland's, *Making Vocational Choices: A Theory of Careers.*[1]

The Party

Below is an aerial view (from the floor above) of a room in which a party is taking place. At this party, people with the same or similar interests have (for some reason) all gathered in the same corner of the room—as described below.

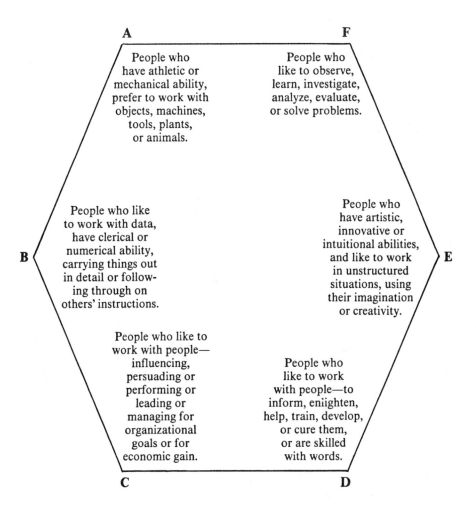

1. Which corner of the room would you instinctively be drawn to, as the group of people you would most *enjoy* being with for the longest time? (Leave aside any question of shyness, or whether you would have to talk with them.) Write the *letter* for that corner in this box:

☐

2. After fifteen minutes, everyone in the corner you have chosen, leaves for another party crosstown, except you. Of the groups *that still remain,* now, which corner or group would you be drawn to the most, as the people you would most enjoy being with for the longest time? Write the letter for that corner in this box:

☐

3. After fifteen minutes, this group too leaves for another party, except you. Of the corner, and groups which remain now, which one would you most enjoy being with for the longest time? Write the letter for that corner in this box:

☐

After students make their decisions, I divide the class into discussion groups according to the choices made on "The Party" exercise. Within the small groups, students discuss why they chose as they did and begin exchanging ideas about career interests. After students have done some preliminary thinking and talking, I pass out Holland's correlations among groups at "The Party," characteristic traits of persons choosing each group, and characteristic occupations suited to those personal traits (Appendix). I then ask students to discuss with their groups the match between their choices, their personal traits, and their career interests.

The small groups also develop a list of job factors that are important to them. To facilitate discussion, I pass out a partial list of factors frequently cited as important for career satisfaction and ask students to add to the list. A finished list might include such factors as salary, job security, opportunity for advancement, opportunity for working independently, clearly defined responsibilities, variety of day-to-day activities, job environment, status, location of jobs, availability of jobs, opportunity to work near family, and so forth.

After each small group discussion, I ask the students to free write about their career expectations—what they imagine their work and lifestyles will be in a chosen field. The free writing helps students develop interview questions and also serves as a starting point for papers that contrast initial impressions of the career with what students discover through their research, or for papers that show in what ways the student is likely to succeed in the chosen career.

(2) Library Research

I then ask students to go to the library to discover as much as they can about the careers that interest them. Most students have already chosen a career to investigate by this stage; others choose after the library research. Students don't need to make or pretend to make an ultimate decision, but should know that skills used in this project are useful for making the series of decisions leading to career choice. I give students a bibliography of resources for career information available at the library. Although students use the library for background on their career, this information is used primarily to develop interview questions since the real core of the students' research is the interview with a professional in the field.

(3) The Interview

The students work in small groups to develop interview questions based on the previous group discussions, the free writing, and the research. Interview questions are shared with the whole class and new questions are added. Some general questions can be used by all the students in their interviews: Would you describe what you do in a typical day? What were your expectations when you started your career and how realistic did your expectations turn out to be? What is the most serious problem you have had on your job? What do you like best about your job? What kind of a person does it take to be happy and successful at this job? Other kinds of questions are, of course, career-specific, but students can nevertheless share them with the class. All students should also be aware of simple follow-up questions—Would you tell me more about _____?—that can make the interview more productive for the student.

Students identify someone working in the field who is willing to be interviewed. I encourage students to find someone outside the university, unless they are interested in teaching or research. When no one is available, then students interview an instructor or an advisor in their field. Often two or more students can collaborate on an interview. I encourage women students entering non-traditional fields to interview a woman if they can and to find out if there are any special problems or advantages for women entering that field.

(4) The Research Paper

Once the interview stage is completed, students write a paper based on what they learned during the project. Most papers answer such main questions as: Were my expectations realistic? Am I likely to succeed in this career? The information gathered in the first three stages of the project can be used to support and answer both questions. I give students outstanding papers from other classes to read and use as models if they wish. Before the papers are handed in, students make two copies that are first circulated within the group and then within the class. Students say they learn from reading each other's papers and that they like having the class as the audience for their own papers.

Conclusion

Many students do their best writing of the quarter on this project, partly, I think, because the project has practical value for them. Equally important, the writing generated in this project combines writing based on personal experience with writing based on research. The transition from self-centered writing to research-based writing is often difficult, even for the most skilled student writers. The project invites students to combine their histories, opinions, and values with data gathered in an interview and then produce a purposeful and significant piece of writing.

Notes

1. John O. Holland, *Making Vocational Choices: A Theory of Careers* (Englewood Cliffs, N.J.: Prentice-Hall, Inc., 1973). "The Party" itself was adapted by Dr. Peggy Leiterman-Stock of Montana State University's Office of Student Affairs and Services.

Appendix

Holland's Groups	Characteristic Interests
Realistic (Party group A)	Activities that involve the precise, ordered use of objects, tools, machines, and animals and includes agricultural, electrical, manual, physical and mechanical things and activities. Example: Working on cars
Investigative (Party group F)	Activities that involve the exploration and examination of physical, biological, and cultural things to understand and control them; sometimes includes scientific and mathematical activities. Example: Reading fiction
Artistic (Party group E)	Activities that involve the use of physical, verbal or human materials to create art forms or products; includes activities and things related to language, art, music, drama, and writing. Example: Listening to music
Social (Party group D)	Activities that involve interaction with other people for enjoyment or to inform, train, develop, cure, and educate. Example: Entertaining guests
Enterprising (Party group C)	Activities that involve interaction with other people to reach organizational goals or economic gain; leadership, interpersonal and persuasive activities included. Example: Working for a community action or political organization
Conventional (Party group B)	Activities that involve the precise, ordered use of data, i.e., keeping records, filing materials, organizing numerical and written data; clerical, computational, and business. Example: Working as a treasurer for a political campaign

Holland's Groups	Characteristic Personal Traits	Characteristic Occupations
Realistic (Party group A)	Present-Oriented Thing-Oriented (rather than people or data) Conforming Practical Shy	Engineering Skilled Trades Agricultural and Technical
Investigative (Party group F)	Analytical and Abstract Rational Critical Intellectual Introverted	Scientific, Analytical and some Technical
Artistic (Party group E)	Creative Expressive Rely on Feelings Imagination Non-Conforming Idealistic	Musical Artistic Literary and Dramatic
Social (Party group D)	Sensitive to needs of others Friendly Outgoing Persuasive Tactful	Teaching Ministry Social Welfare and Other "Helping People Occupations"
Enterprising (Party group C)	Aggressive Self-Confident Ambitious Sociable Persuasive	Sales Supervisory and Leadership
Conventional (Party group B)	Practical Conforming Efficient Orderly Set in Ways	Accounting Computational Secretarial and Clerical

The Whole Is Not Equal to the Sum of the Parts: An Approach to Teaching the Research Paper

Bryant Mangum

Instructors are searching constantly for ways to make research skills an integral part of a writing course. Bryant Mangum suggests a sequence of assignments focused on biographies that combine literature, writing, and research skills. Mr. Mangum teaches at Virginia Commonwealth University, Richmond.

Author's Comment

When a colleague recently asked me to talk informally to a group of instructors about my approach to teaching the research paper in our freshman composition course, the first metaphor that came to my mind was "the absinthe chaser." I encourage students to find interesting slants and exotic perspectives on the "facts" that they have uncovered. Their ways of synthesizing the material, the frameworks that they construct, become the chaser for the facts; and unless the framework is more than a mechanical gluing together of factual details, the paper will be dreary. Unlike absinthe, it will be far from exotic, seldom worth waiting for. I emphasize the package that the facts are placed in, but I am equally concerned with teaching actual research techniques: systematic ways of locating source material and of cataloguing it for use in a paper. Therefore, my approach to teaching the research paper is a two-part one: to encourage the students to make a science of developing research-gathering techniques and an art of blending the gathered material in a way that the paper will be more than the sum of the facts.

The Approach

To accomplish these goals I use biographies. I like biographies, which alone is not a sufficient justification for using them, though I am convinced that one probably teaches writing skills most effectively when one feels passionately about the vehicle being used; but most important, I use them because I believe that a good biography is as good a research project as one is apt to find. Carlos Baker's *Ernest Hemingway: A Life Story,* Arthur Mizener's *The Far Side of Paradise,* Joseph Blotner's *Faulkner,* and Richard Ellemann's *James Joyce* are excellent examples. Thus I select a good biography for the main text and it becomes the model for research. I arrange the assignments in a way that students are acquainted with many of the problems all biographers, all researchers, are apt to encounter before I have them study the model.

The assignments are divided into four parts: two assignments which lead up to the biography, the biography itself, and finally one that becomes an attempt to apply techniques learned through the study of it to a general non-biographical research project. This final one becomes the 2000-word research paper. The first group of assignments clusters around a persuasive writing objective and teaches students to evaluate secondary sources as well as use them in the context of their own ideas. Students first write a persuasive paper without using outside sources; the next paper, still persuasive, incorporates the ideas from an article of someone else who agrees with the student; the next paper includes an opposing view, and so on. The first three or four papers, therefore, in addition to being persuasive are also miniature research projects which are designed to teach note-taking, summarizing, paraphrasing, document-ing, and other techniques to be used later on in the semester.

In the next group of assignments, the students apply the mechanical skills they have learned to a more personal kind of research project: a biographical theme written by one student in the class about another. The students move with this assignment in the direction of the research model, the book-length biography; and to accomplish this they do five brief written exercises. Each student provides the biographer with a resumé, a statement of personal beliefs, an artwork considered by the student to be revealing of the student's personality, a fifteen-question questionnaire whose questions originate with the class, an impression sketch written by a third party, and two letters—one written by the student and another to the student. The author of the biographical theme must digest the material, take notes on it, formulate a thesis about the subject, and support it through footnotes to the sources. When this paper is complete, the student-subject of the theme becomes its chief critic, judging how accurately the writer used the material. A third student can then read the paper, learning something about critical reading and eval-uation of another's use of source material. But the chief function of this assignment is to acquaint the student first hand with some of the prob-lems that the author of the biography, to be read next, encountered in assembling the material. If the student learns from this exercise that source documents are often open to interpretation and that it is the responsibility of the researcher to give the reader clear directions that will enable the reader to see the sources, the student is ready for the model, the biography.

To lead up to the main text I select several other biographies designed to illustrate various kinds of documentation, from clear to confusing— and use of source material, from reliable to unreliable and from responsible to irresponsible. My purpose here is to show that while several types of documentation are acceptable, some are better than others; and some are unacceptable in responsible writing. The first biography that I use for illustrations is Thomas Beer's *Stephen Crane,* which is packed with information about Crane. Much of it, though, must be regarded as suspect: Beer has no footnotes and reportedly destroyed all of the sources, many of them interviews with and letters from people who knew Crane. Students are easily impressed through exposure to this book with the frustration that results from working with non-verifiable information. I usually ask students to create in their minds an image of Beer burning the sources and to connect this image to any "non-verifiable" evidence that they might be tempted to present in their own research paper. Then I move into R.W. Stallman's *Stephen Crane: A Biography,* a book that is demonstrably unreliable, partly because Stallman silently incorporates some of Beer's assertions into the book and presents them as facts.

The second kind of biography is one whose sources are mountainous but which uses a footnote system sometimes so difficult to follow that one is occasionally cut off from the source material by the apparatus used in documenting it. The best biography that occurs to me for this is Carlos Baker's *Ernest Hemingway: A Life Story,* an exhaustive study whose absence of footnote numbers in the text makes it difficult to know where the information comes from. Thus, while the book will always remain an indispensable resource document to anyone interested in Hemingway, it is less useful than it might have been, no doubt, because Scribner's feared the effect on book sales if the biography had included raised footnote numbers in the text. Students exposed to Baker's biography will, I hope, never again face the decision of where to place the footnote numbers without remembering that the note is for the convenience of the reader; it should lead the reader with as little confusion as possible to the source of information. And Baker's book is useful for illustrating at least one other major point: the fact that sometimes gaps in research projects must be filled with information from less than ideal sources, and when they are, the reader should be clearly warned. For instance, Baker relies on Kitty Cannell, mistress of Harold Loeb, the real life counterpart to Robert Cohn in *The Sun Also Rises,* for much of his "factual" information about Hemingway in the "Sun Ascending" section of the biography. The question to be raised in the student's mind is whether or not Miss Cannell could ever have been an objective or reliable source of information after the negative picture of Loeb that Hemingway painted? And how accurate are recollections forty years after the fact?

Therefore, with practical knowledge of the problems that can arise in writing a biographical study gained from actually having written a short "biography" and with a warning from the Beer, Stallman, and Baker books that sources must be verifiable, the student is ready to study the model and to do original research which requires that the student validate sources used by a biographer, measuring the author's conclusions against one's own. For this purpose I use Nancy Milford's *Zelda,* a good research project which reflects some of the problems of documentation already seen in the Beer, Stallman, and Baker biographies, but which finally constructs as accurate and intriguing a picture of Zelda Fitzgerald as one could want. I have students read it backward, from the footnotes at the end to the front, though they read only selected portions. After describing several debatable conclusions drawn by Milford, I have the students select one of them that will be their topic. I try to select problems that can be, at least partly, resolved by reading the Fitzgeralds' letters on the subject, entries in F. Scott Fitzgerald's *Ledger,* passages from Zelda's novel or stories, etc. Thus they are working mainly with primary documents and are finally using the secondary one, *Zelda,* only after verifying its sources and accepting or rejecting its conclusions. Did Zelda have a romantic affair with Edouard Jozan while Fitzgerald completed *The Great Gatsby*? Nancy Milford says "yes"; Sarah Mayfield, author of *Exiles from Paradise,* says "no"; the sources—Zelda's letters, Zelda's novel, Fitzgerald's *Ledger,* Fitzgerald's letters—are accessible to students, and they are open to interpretation. The collection, presentation, and interpretation of the "facts" constitute this 1200–1500 word paper, and it should be more than the sum of its sources. The dimension added to the facts is what gives life to the subject, and Milford's book provides not only a source for comparison but a good model to emulate.

After the *Zelda* model, most of the controlled research ends and the student is asked to pursue any subject related to the 1920s that now is of interest because of the exposure, through *Zelda,* to the time period. Predictable choices would be flappers, prohibition, visual or verbal art, psychotherapy, interior design, women's roles, etc. If there were another semester of freshman English, the next step would be to write on any subject in any time period. Presumably the student would move toward his or her own discipline, scrutinizing the sources there as carefully as was done in examining the sources thus far.

It is true, of course, that the composition course I have described is one that I enjoy teaching, in part, because the books used are ones in which I am especially interested. But it is not a course designed only for myself. My idea was to select a model that was an example of sound research and one which would at the same time be interesting to a large number of students. *Zelda* fits both of these requirements and its subject is one that students have found interesting enough to read footnotes first. Any model that fulfilled these two requirements would work. There are contemporary biographies which would, perhaps, even be of greater interest to students, while there are more "scholarly" biographies that might better illustrate more precise kinds of documentation. But I have found that regardless of the biography used, this genre lends itself to teaching the things that are most important to me in a research paper course; I want to encourage students to believe that they can contribute something original and new to existing knowledge with their research because I believe that they can. I find that a good way they can learn to do this is by taking apart a biography and learning from the dissection sound research techniques that they can carry back to their disciplines. If it is an interesting biography, they will enjoy doing it and learn the techniques in the process; if it is also a well-written one they will have a good model for making an absinthe chaser.

The Post-Mortem Plan: Teaching Writing across the Disciplines

Julie Klein

The need for the development of students' thinking skills cuts across all disciplines. Julie Klein of Wayne State University, Detroit, Michigan, suggests a procedure she uses in an interdisciplinary course to foster thinking and writing skills concurrently. By making students more aware of how to develop their thoughts in writing, she strives to improve students' performance on essay examinations.

Author's Comment

Hunter Gatherers seem so carefree, and there [sic] only work was to find food. It wasn't such an easy work, but they were quite good at it . . . Plus the Hunter Gatherers had a lot more leisure time than we do, and I really like what little leisure time I get. Hunter Gatherers seemed a lot stronger and healthier than people today. They had stronger teeth, and didn't catch a lot of diseases so they didn't have to bother with doctors, dentists, etc. If they did see the medicine man, he would more than likely cure them without needles and surgery.

The comparison above appeared on the examination of a Wayne State University undergraduate enrolled in a required Humanities-Social Science sequence for Engineering students. Along with fellow students, the student had been asked to weigh the advantages and disadvantages of life in a Hunter-Gatherer society, an Agrarian society, and an Industrial society. Clearly, there are problems with the comparison. To begin with, there are grammatical mistakes, but those could be corrected with a little practice and careful direction. Much harder to solve are the problems of critical inquiry, the problems in *thinking* which by default create problems in writing. The student exhibits a pervasive inability to "think historically" in the transpositions of contemporary conceptual approaches to and linguistic labels for work, leisure time, and health. In turn, that inability creates impediments to making other kinds of socio-cultural judgments.

In a collective "post-mortem" appraisal of this exam, classmates suggested its errors and vagueness could be remedied by more precise and sustained use of sociological, anthropological, and economic perspectives. They suggested that the student is headed in a potentially fruitful direction, evidenced by the awareness of the work/leisure split in contemporary life and the institutionalized nature of modern medicine. However, without establishing some fundamental definitions, the writer loses even the most correct suspicions in a jumble of recollected details. There is an alarming universality about such problems. The inability of students to use and perceive language with effectiveness is not the concern of the English Department alone. When students have difficulty distinguishing fact from opinion and interpretation, it cripples their efforts to work across the face of the university, in the Humanities, the Social Sciences, and the Sciences. What is at stake here is not Composition 101 but good composition. Reasoned critical thought is a fairly universal goal and clear expression is, therefore, an essential subject across the disciplines.

Fond as we are of justifying exams as "learning devices," few of us really do use them as well as we might to teach both writing and course content. For understandable reasons, few instructors are willing to sacrifice an entire day in their already-crowded syllabi to engage in close scrutiny of exam results, let alone talk about writing throughout the term. What usually transpires after an exam? In some cases nothing happens, save paper shuffling and mild-to-bold castigations. In other cases, there is a modest attempt to indicate the "right answers." To excuse the inattention by arguing that exams are after all pressured writing is a shallow justification. After they leave school, students will at some point have to write under pressure again. Moreover, exams will remain major tools for evaluating students' knowledge. English teachers feel an increasing responsibility to teach effective exam writing, while their colleagues in other disciplines continue to complain about students' exam writing. To help both groups to teach good exam writing, I shall describe a systematic procedure for leading into and out of exams, fondly dubbed the "Post-Mortem Plan" by its practitioners.

The Plan

To illustrate the Plan, let me draw examples from the second semester of the year-long sequence for engineers with which we began. That course, "The Impact of Technology," brought together several faculty from different parts of the University. As faculty we shared large plenary-session lectures twice a week, then assumed individual responsibility for smaller discussion workshops twice a week. The course exposed students to significant examples of the impact of technology upon society and key arguments about moral/ethical issues in science and technology. Our case studies included alienation in the workplace, multi-national corporations, the Manhattan Project, individual incidents of product liability, PBB poisoning, genetic engineering, and exponential growth. By intention it was an interdisciplinary course, since the assembled staff shared intellectual and pedagogical convictions about approaching such problems and indeed the question of knowledge itself through multiple perspectives. Our lectures and readings ranged across many disciplines: literature (with Vonnegut's *Player Piano* and *Cat's Cradle, Brave New World,* and science fiction), film (with documentaries and "Dr. Strangelove"), economics, industrial technology, history, psychology, sociology, political science, law, chemistry, biology, engineering, and physics.

In the biweekly workshop, it was a struggle just to keep up with the main syllabus, a fairly universal burden for teachers. However, to provide a framework for our study, I set the following broad goals for the semester:

The Theory: Conceptualization
    We were to make an intellectual inquiry into the ways we acquire, conceptualize, and reshape knowledge.

Time Method: Expression
    We would resort constantly to "writing out" our deliberations, speculations and interpretations. This took three forms: "rough drafting" our thoughts, preexam "contract" practice, and postmortems on exams.

Helping students to develop the critical ability to examine conceptual and linguistic assumptions in intellectual disciplines is difficult. Not all intellectuals can see them in their own fields, let alone in others. Nevertheless, raising questions about how people work in their various specialties is a valuable investment of time, not just for the immediate understanding of one subject but for their life-long ability to make judgments and perceptions. An introduction to thinking about the nature of knowledge can be a valuable way to get students thinking about the axiomatic assumptions of a single discipline or the broadly dispersed disciplinary sources upon which most composition teachers draw.

They may not know the word "epistemology" but they can certainly be taught to have epistemological sensitivities which will make their thinking and writing more critical. In any course I introduce subject matter by using a sequence of queries and exercises:

Step I
    What do you know about this [subject, concept, idea, or thinker] already? How did you attain that knowledge?

Step II

How do professionals [historians, chemists, scientists, anthropologists . . .] go about studying this?

What kinds of questions do they ask? What kinds of questions don't they ask?

Step III

How would a different professional look at the same material?

Step IV

What, therefore, should we set up as criteria for study [historiographical methods, the "scientific method" or theories in affective criticism . . .]?

What happens if we exclude other modes of analysis? How will that shape our subsequent knowledge?

To illustrate: let me recall our discussion of the Manhattan Project.

Step I. We began our study of the Manhattan Project by *brainstorming* for five minutes. Brainstorming is an old pedagogical technique, to be sure, but it remains one of the best. Whether a class is in a slump or just not ready to deal with a topic, their act of brainstorming while the instructor writes the results on a chalkboard is very useful. In this case students came up with enough words and phrases to fill the board: snatches of prior history lessons, terms from physics classes, descriptions of Hiroshima from a student whose father was among the first occupation troops. With all eyes on the board, we discussed how students' views had been shaped and how the actions of participants in the Project were shaped by their desire as physicists to solve specific scientific problems and to move from a scientific puzzle to scientific knowledge.

Step II. We categorized the items in our chalkboard list by considering which problems were generally thought to be the province of physicists, which concerned political scientists, what preoccupied philosophers and what comprised the "expertise" of military personnel. That discussion enabled us to enlarge upon our understanding of how people think because they are trained to particular ways and from what positions their thinking on a problem might tend to begin.

Step III. With the help of writings by Laura Fermi and Robert Oppenheimer, we sorted out the different positions on the Manhattan Project, particularly the controversies about how the bomb would be used and the evolution of scientists' concern.

Step IV. Our ability to conceptualize the issues involved and to justify our conclusions about the impact of technology in this case study were aided by such a breakdown of motivations, interests, and reactions to the dropping of the bomb, a subject covered at length in a plenary-session lecture. As we tried to reach conclusions, we stopped discussing and began writing.

Rough Drafting (the first writing)

Rough drafting out our thoughts was a frequent resort, especially when discussions revealed conflicts or contradictions. During our study of the accidental poisoning of Michigan residents due to the substitution of Firemaster (a free-retardant formula with PBB) for Nutrimaster (a cattle growth formula marketed in a 50-lb brown bag similar to the Firemaster bag), we were struggling with the complex issue of complicity. After ten minutes of trying to sort out the mistakes, cover-ups, political interpretations and conflicts in laboratory tests, students were frustrated. Offering once more to serve as their scribe, I suggested they write a one-paragraph summary of the reasons for this terrible accident. It took twenty minutes for them to write collectively the single paragraph. However, they were pleased with the results, for they had posted statements, revised them where necessary, and censored hasty generalizations. It was an enormously satisfying exercise.

As usually happens with this exercise, they had to keep backing up: to curb overgeneralized assertions, to correct errors, to extend shallow cause-effect relationships. Sentences 2 and 3 usually move more quickly than 1 because students become enthusiastic, though they still need to back up. Here is an example of such a rough-drafting, with eliminations crossed out and additions set above the line.

(first attempt)
The government was most responsible for the foul-ups.

(second attempt)   causes of
There were many reasons for the PBB tragedy.

(Students had trouble deciding which reason to place first. One of them suggested the way to generate material for Sentence 2 would be to stop for a minute of brainstorming. This is what they came up with.)

Original Cause
Michigan Chemical Company
*(bag mix-up)
*(poor labelling)
*(tenacious chemical which stuck to machines)

Sources of Confusion

*FDA safety levels set too low

*legislative arguments over who should pay victims

*general unfamiliarity with the PBB chemical

*conflicting test results (differences in Michigan tests vs. out-of-state tests)

Cover-up

*Farm Bureau sluggish (claimed feed ok)

*government response slow

*FDA and others concerned with quarantining of farms, not solution to overall problem

*bureaucratic delays

(With the list before them, they backed up once more to write a new first sentence.)

There are many levels of complicity in the PBB tragedy: business, government, political management and scientific procedures.

(Then they proceeded to build individual sentences to illustrate the levels.)

For the students, such an exercise shows how writing can facilitate thought, not just serve as a requirement to be performed for judgment upon three or four dates in a course. For a teacher, it provides an opportunity to put conceptual goals on the line: to help students test the validity of their assertions by making them *visible* in written form, then to make warranted revisions. Practiced collectively, it gives students a chance to pool their information and to enjoy solving problems together.

Pre-Exam Contract Practice (the second writing)

Whenever we reviewed for a forthcoming exam, we began always by categorizing the massive amount of information for review. After that we went to work directly on answering probable exam questions. On the basis of their review, students designed the most "logical" and "fair" questions to be expected. With the questions posed, we set about writing introductory paragraphs for each question, using a contract method to ensure clarity and to establish a checklist for writing and proofing the body of the answer. For their term papers, I had prepared an Introductory Page Contract which students themselves modified for exams:

The Introductory Page Contract

In order to keep yourself on track while writing and to keep your reader informed about your purpose *and* how you will meet that purpose, make a CONTRACT with the reader on the first page. Set up the expectations that you will share with the reader. Be sure to include the following on that page:

1. **statement of topic:** what it is you are investigating
2. **statement of the problem:** why the topic is important (its moral/ethical/technological significance)
3. **statement of method:** how you've gone about your investigation (source, goals, and any limitations)
4. **statement of organization:** how you've set up your presentation of evidence and conclusions, and why you've used this approach
5. **any qualifying remarks:** any special expectations the reader should have or any qualifications you need to make.

The Exam Contract

In order to focus directly on the question and to make clear your strategy for answering that question, make a CONTRACT in the first paragraph of your answer. Set up the logic of your answer by including the following:

1. **statement of focus:** what the scope of your answer is (works to be discussed and reasons for choosing the examples)
2. **statement of thesis:** what key arguments you will make
3. **statement of procedure:** how you will structure your argument and why you've chosen this approach
4. **any qualifying remarks:** any special points you wish to make or assumptions the reader must be aware of.

Where there is generally only enough time to draft introductory contracts for one or two questions, this exercise reinforces the importance of planning and developing clearly formulated arguments for exams as well as papers. Moreover, the class enjoys the same kind of joint writing and revising that they have been sharing in the Rough-Drafting process.

In writing a question about PBB, to recall the above example, students zeroed in on the issue of what lessons we had learned for future application from a past tragedy. Using the EXAM CONTRACT, they wrote the following, with deletions and revisions indicated:

we can learn from
There are many lessons for the future the PBB tragedy:

the need for
about the need for responsibility in business, control of

government regulations
government offices, problems which arise from our

the need for tough safety standards
dependence on science, how chemicals can be mishandled or

the need for thorough testing procedures
misunderstood. I will discuss the causes of PBB poisoning and

first the original cause and then the series of mistakes and cover-ups
the cover-ups. Then I will suggest what alternatives might have

lessened the damage.
kept it from getting worse. My sources are the Detroit Free Press

I will use Dr. Maier's review of the causes,
articles, Dr. Maier's lecture, and our class discussion.

Free Press discussion of cover-ups and bungling.

While this CONTRACT could still use some improvement, the students made prudent changes and their final exams were strong. Both exams and essays are often crippled by vague opening (a lack of clear purpose) and weak structure (absence of a tight and logical sequence). Setting the contract up as a checklist for each paragraph in an exam or essay enables a student to test the effectiveness and contribution of single paragraphs to the overall purpose.

The Post-Mortem (the third writing)

If possible, I return all exams the next class period, certainly no later than one week after the exam, both to capitalize on the students' factual recall and to keep major conceptual concerns alive and constant. Passing around anonymous copies of students' exams is hardly a new idea. However, we try once more to engage in a collective writing exercise which tests information, conceptualization, and expression. There are certainly good reasons for using an "A" exam and an "E" exam, but I have found it more productive to distribute copies of "B" and "C" answers to the same question. This way students are forced to concentrate on the relative strengths and weaknesses in arguments that are neither indisputably excellent nor woefully incompetent. Students can combine strengths from separate exams while purging their weaknesses. *Making* the exams stronger rather than just talking hypothetically about probable strength is the goal.

Again we work collectively, though with a somewhat altered agenda:

1. We read copies of anonymous exams.
2. We itemize strengths and weaknesses.
3. While I serve again as scribe and guide, students revise weak sentences.

These revisions do consist, as one might expect, of adding examples. However, we also fine-tune CONTRACT paragraphs, strengthen conclusions, and assess the balance of generalizations and specifics.

When I originally began using the post-mortem plan, I did only STEP III, the exam post-mortem. However, STEP I evolved from my conviction that good writing and thinking must be on-going topics in any course. STEP I, ROUGH DRAFTING, was born of a moment familiar to most teachers: students were mute, so stuck on a problem that they were growing disinterested out of frustration. ROUGH DRAFTING not only picked up their spirits but led them to become fascinated with a problem which a few moments before had very little fascination for them. STEP II, the EXAM CONTRACT, was a logical extension.

Given that examinations will probably remain one of the chief means of testing comprehension in most courses, it behooves us to deal in such comprehensive fashion with exams as acts of communication. With some hope, we can look to their next exams and papers for improvement. Yet, with some humility, we ought also to look beyond courses and exams, to ponder seriously how well our students will be able to test and evaluate the forms of knowledge they will encounter beyond their school years.

One lamentable truth of learning is that facts are forgotten. Worse than that, what survives very often is an atmosphere marked by distortions. Once a student passes through the doors of the classroom, such impressions and atmospheres are rarely laid open to the kinds of challenges and rethinking that constitute genuine critical thought. While it is not a panacea, teaching writing at one of the most forgotten points—the exam—might reinforce the means and urgency of critical expression. It might give a sharper critical methodology and justification for a writing task which many students either abhor or fear. It will also demonstrate that essay exams are not arbitrary monsters invented by teachers. Writing a good exam involves using universal principles of critical thought and persuasive expression which students will need well beyond their exam. To fail to discuss these issues at exam time is, then, a serious omission.

IV Writing and Reading

One of the primary ingredients of any English class is reading, and a natural extension of this reading is writing. Such writing may be to discover or report meaning, to engage in personal response, or to create a literary form. Articles in this section offer ideas about developing students' appreciation of literature, about using reading as a springboard for short stories, poems, and essays, and about helping students to write critically and analytically about their reading.

Practically Literature:
Or How I Learned to Stop Worrying
and Love the Course

Valerie Goldzung

The study of literature has traditionally spawned the writing of critical analysis essays. Valerie Goldzung suggests, however, that literature ought to be viewed as an excellent stimulus in writing classes for exploring many forms of written response. Ms. Goldzung submitted this exercise from Springfield College in Massachusetts.

Author's Comment

One of the problems with using a reader in a composition course is the temptation for both teachers and students to talk about the themes and ideas in a work they are reading rather than to use it as an aid in discussing rhetoric, or, in an introductory course in literature, as a way to concentrate on forms. After all, it's much more fun to talk about "life" than literary and rhetorical abstractions, even if you're using examples. One of the ways I've tried to enliven discussions of rhetorical and literary problems of form and style is by using the things we are reading simply as common material for imaginative productions of the students themselves—short stories, skits, interviews.

I had always been struck by the ability of students, myself included, to write with color and concreteness when consciously developing a circumscribed persona, and found this increased as the materials one might work with—the plot, the characters, the language—were further limited. The game-like aspect of composing, the conscious delight in solving arbitrary problems of a size you can handle and discuss, stimulated imagination and decreased personal anxiety.

I usually emphasize one particular form in class discussion at particular times during the semester, and encourage each student to try out that form during the term. But I don't twist arms. Small exercises in class can provide all the students with some practice in the less exotic forms of exposition and argument. And if they become good narrators, describers, or dramatists in the course of a single semester that's better than having them become grumpy or cliché-ridden essayists and disclaimers.

I no longer feel guilty for not explicitly dealing in class with the four levels of discourse, or the eight ways to organize an expository theme, or the difference between restrictive and non-restrictive modifiers, or of becoming frustrated by trying to make sure the students get the historical and literary pinups to go with the readings. I have actually come to enjoy reading students' essays, each of which is different, and which, good or bad, stimulates my own imagination as possible material for future classes. I've even done some of my own assignments for fun!

I don't pretend this is a new approach, or even unique; I think it occurs to us all at times. It's just a matter of getting over feeling guilty or suspicious about consciously using an approach that's so personally enjoyable. Below is a sample exercise that utilizes this idea.

Sample Exercise

Read John Updike's "Ex-Basketball Player."

Updike himself transposed characters, theme, plot, imagery from one medium to another as a skilled "professional amateur" (as he liked to view himself). His poem "Ex-Basketball Player" was reworked five times—twice as a novel and three times as a short story.

Following Updike's example and practice, look at the images, characters, setting, and facts for possible plot development in the poem as providing material for compositions of various types. Notice how the nature of each medium or form of discourse demands that different elements of Flick's experience be emphasized; how your own experiences and responses to life and language transmute the elements provided in Updike's poem.

Below are some suggestions for this assignment. Remember to utilize what we have discussed about each particular form.

These are only suggestions—you may develop your own narrative, description, skit, exposition, or argument that takes off from the experience of the poem.

1. Narrative:
   a. First person—Compose a monologue by Flick at work, or taking his coffee break, or telling someone of his past victories.
   b. Second person—Catch the waitress telling someone (girl friend, customer) about Flick.
   c. Third person—Tell the story using basically the same point of view as in the poem.
   You may use dialogue in any of these and may extrapolate from the incidents in the poem.

2. Description:
   Describe the diner, the town, the gas station, Flick, Mae—or any combination of the above—from a stranger's point of view.
3. Drama:
   Use the character of Flick as described in the poem, and have him talk to the present high school "star," or with an old classmate who is now a successful businessman, or with his boss, or Mae.
4. Interview:
   Interview Flick for the sports page of your high school newspaper on the occasion of his class's 10th Year Reunion.
5. Expository Essay:
   a. A character in one of Updike's novels who is very like Flick says, "I once played a game very well. I really did. And after you're first-rate at something no matter what, it kind of takes the kick out of being second-rate." Write an essay in which you explain why you agree or disagree with this point of view. You may support your ideas with specific references to "Ex-Basketball Player" as well as your own experiences.
   b. Compare the ideas on early success presented in Updike's poem with Housman's "On an Athlete Dying Young."
   c. Define "success" using the experiences and values expressed in Updike's poem, supplementing them (or contradicting them) with your own experience.
6. Argument:
   a. Prepare a deductive argument proving that "Living in the past will only lead to unhappiness."
   b. Argue the point that high school curriculums foster competition without teaching skills or sophisticating the student's values.

Writing from Literature

Donald R. Gallo

One common written response to the reading of literature has been the book report. Donald R. Gallo of Central Connecticut State University, New Britain, suggests that teachers explore more of the possibilities for writing from literature rather than about it. The activities he suggests can be done with a class-assigned book or in conjunction with independent reading.

Author's Comment

The following activities are based on several observations and assumptions: 1) Writing too often is taught in a vacuum; 2) students are often required to write on topics they know little about and couldn't care less about; 3) "academic" writing often has greater legitimacy than "creative" writing, especially because of the basic skills emphasis of recent years; 4) students almost always write for one audience: a nebulous, general, no-one-in-particular reader who is usually only the instructor.

Writing *from* literature, instead of only *about* literature, can provide creative approaches with academically respectable topics written for specific alternative audiences. Thus, academic skills are not sacrificed to interest; and writing can be both academic *and* creative. The activities listed below can be done in conjunction with the study of a single assigned book, or—in junior and senior high school—they can take the place of the traditional book report on outside reading.

These topics are only suggestions. Some are for well-known classics; others are for more contemporary teenage novels. Each topic can be modified to "fit" different pieces of literature or to accommodate students of greater or lesser sophistication.

The first activity is the easiest. One can see why it works well with junior high school writers, but many college writers can enjoy and benefit from it as well. Be careful not to reject it because of its simplicity and seemingly non-academic quality.

Classroom Exercise

1. Pick a book you've read.

2. Pick a key character from that book: e.g., Patty Bergen from *Summer of My German Soldier;* John or Lorraine from *The Pigman;* Holden Caulfield from *Catcher in the Rye;* Sophie from *Sophie's Choice;* Biff from *Death of a Salesman.*

3. Choose one major problem that character has: e.g., Lorraine's feeling that her mother picks on her; Sophie's concern about Nathan's rages and his callous treatment of her; Biff's inability to express his feelings to his father.

4. Write a letter that your character might write about that problem to Ann Landers or Dear Abby.

5. When the writing is finished, place all the letters in a pile and scramble them.

6. Blindly select a letter from the pile, making sure it's not about the same problem you wrote about. (A different character, where possible, is also preferable.)

7. As if you are Ann or Abby, write a response to the problem expressed in that letter.

The chief advantages of this activity are its brevity and simplicity, and almost every student type is familiar with the length and kinds of letters which appear in the daily newspapers. Note, also, that in order to do this seemingly trivial assignment well, the student must have read the literary work carefully enough to understand the character's problem and emotions regarding it; must understand and be able to reproduce the language, sophistication, style, and possibly dialect of the character; should be able to reproduce the typical Dear Abby letter's format and response style; and, writing as Abby or Ann, ought to exhibit a tactful, thoughtful response to the character's problem. The assignment is thus creative in that it requires some originality and a voice not usually called for in literary analysis papers; it also has an academic legitimacy in that it requires analytical skills, a proper form, and convincing description as well as analysis.

Other Topics for Writing from Literature

1. A *newspaper account* of events from the book—e.g., a sports report of Alfred's big fight in *The Contender;* a society column about a

big party in *The Great Gatsby;* a feature story on the rodeo exploits of Thomas Black Bull in *When the Legends Die.*

2. A *letter* from one character to another—e.g., from Holden to his brother to describe his adventure in New York City from *Catcher in the Rye;* from Slim to George two years after the ending of *Of Mice and Men.*

3. A *script* for the Evening News—either radio or television—about an incident from the book—e.g., the discovery of the hiding place in the Secret Annex in *Anne Frank;* the death of Adam's father and mother in *I Am the Cheese;* the assassination of Caesar in *Julius Caesar.*

4. An *entry in Who's Who* for a main character—e.g., Shane from *Shane;* Atticus Finch from *To Kill a Mockingbird;* Zhivago from *Doctor Zhivago.*

5. A *letter of recommendation* for a character—for a job or "Man of the Year" or some award—e.g., for Brother Leon for a teaching position in a new school from *The Chocolate War,* for one of the doctors from *Hiroshima;* for Beth in *Ordinary People.*

6. A *eulogy* for a character—e.g., father in *Sounder;* Kizzy in *Roots;* Paul Baumer in *All Quiet on the Western Front.*

7. A *citation* from the mayor or a civic group to praise a character's actions—e.g., for Ben's heroism in *Deathwatch;* for Sidney Carlton's sacrifice in *A Tale of Two Cities.*

8. An *obituary* for a character—e.g., for Haven Peck in *A Day No Pigs Would Die;* for Willy Loman in *Death of a Salesman.*

9. A *plea* from a character to a television audience for understanding of his or her motive for acting in a certain way—e.g., Raskolnikov in *Crime and Punishment;* Miro in *After the First Death;* Tess in *Tess of the D'Urbervilles.*

10. A *newspaper editorial* about an issue (or theme) in the book—e.g., teenage violence in *The Outsiders;* the practice of weaseling dogs in *A Day No Pigs Would Die;* censorship in *Fahrenheit 451.*

11. A *personal letter* to a character in the story—e.g., to Holden in *Catcher in the Rye* to explain how you feel about your parents in comparison to his feelings about his; to Nurse Ratched in *One Flew Over the Cuckoo's Nest* about her treatment of the inmates.

12. A *questionnaire* administered to the public about an issue from the book—e.g., the mistreatment of dogs in *Call of the Wild;* test-tube babies in *Brave New World*—and then a *report* on the findings.

13. A *dialogue* between two characters, either from the same novel or from different ones—e.g., a discussion between John and his mother in *The Pigman;* an accidental meeting outside a bar between Jay Gatsby from *The Great Gatsby* and Willy Loman from *Death of a Salesman.*

14. An *interview* with a character, with you as interviewer or with someone else as interviewer—e.g., you interview Charlie in *Flowers for Algernon;* Gloria Steinem interviews Hester Prynne from *The Scarlet Letter.*

15. A *psychiatrist's report*—e.g., on Tony in *Then Again, Maybe I Won't;* on Katsuk in *Soul Catcher;* on Kurtz in *Heart of Darkness.*

Several Activities for a Single Work

Each of the above activities seems to be limited to a single work of literature. In fact, several different activities can be assigned for a specific book. Students can be required to do all of them or to select one or more from a suggested list. Three sets of assignments follow:

A Separate Peace

1. A *diary entry* for each of several days to record Gene's feelings about some of Phineas's actions—e.g., the war games, the pranks, the athletic activities, the fall from the tree.

2. A *letter home* from Phineas describing his first impressions of Gene; or from Gene describing one of his encounters with Phineas.

3. A *newspaper account* of Phineas's fall from the tree.

4. A *eulogy* Gene might write for Phineas's funeral.

5. A *questionnaire* that might be distributed to the boys at the school to determine their interests: fill out a copy as Phineas might have, or as Gene might have, or as other characters might have.

6. A *citation* from the town to the student body for their help during the snow removal.

When the Legends Die

1. An *editorial* about the treatment of Indian kids at a BIA school.

2. An *advertisement* (ironic) for the Indian school.

3. A series of *newspaper accounts* of Tom Black's rodeo exploits.

4. A *letter of recommendation* for Tom Black to become "Cowboy of the Year."

5. A *personal letter* from Tom to Mary Redmond, written after he returns to the mountains.

6. An *obituary* for Red Dillon.

Macbeth

1. A *script* for the CBS Evening News recounting the murder of Duncan, or of Banquo, or of the death of Macbeth.

2. A *psychiatrist's report* on Lady Macbeth.

3. An *entry* in *Who's Who* for Macbeth.

4. An *ultimatum* from Macduff to Macbeth to surrender.

5. A *diary entry* of one of the murderers about the events leading up to the murder of Banquo.

6. A *suicide note* from Lady Macbeth to her husband.

7. An *obituary* for Macbeth.

8. A *recipe* for a witches' brew.

Verbal Addictions

T. J. Roberts

Rather than always having students write critical essays about authors and their works, T. J. Roberts suggests having students explore their verbal addictions, which allows them to draw upon their own experiences with reading. Mr. Roberts contributed this from the University of Connecticut, Storrs.

Author's Comment

Students need to talk about this assignment in class before they set to work on it. My practice now is to distribute the assignment in mimeographed form to my students about two weeks before the essay is due and then to have a half-hour discussion in class on the assignment at the next class meeting. On the whole, this is probably the best-liked of all the different problems I have given my classes in literary criticism and theory.

Exercise

Most of us who read a lot will read a spy novel if we are assured by someone we trust that it is unusually good, but some readers will read stories of this type almost without regard to their being good or not. More precisely, they are not so much concerned about their being good novels as they are about their being good *spy* novels. (Indeed, they are sometimes heard to claim that *all* spy novels are good.)

When we find that a reader has this attitude, when we find that he or she reads a very great number of spy novels and that he or she reads them with fair regularity over a long period of time, we feel justified in saying that the reader has a verbal addiction. Addictions vary in intensity and our reader of spy novels may have a very mild form of addiction—no worse, say, than an addiction to cigarettes: one may find oneself getting "hungry" for a spy novel if one hasn't read one in some time, and clutch eagerly at any opportunity to read one, but the reader won't be profoundly *disturbed* by having to go without for a long time. By contrast, those addicted to, say, the Bible may be profoundly upset if they must miss their daily reading of a chapter.

Assignment

Identify for us one of your own verbal addictions—one you have now or have lost only *very* recently—and offer a theory as to why you are addicted to this type of thing.

Alternate Assignment

If you find it too difficult (or embarassing) to deal with one of your own verbal addictions, you may find that you can write on precisely the opposite kind of phenomenon—verbal allergies. If there is a certain kind of reading—spy novels, westerns, poetry, criticism—that you *detest*, identify it for us and offer a theory as to why you are allergic to it.

Discussion Questions

1. Here is a fairly random list that might help you recognize the genres to which you are addicted:

> Western novels and films. Mystery novels: British and American styles. Science fiction and science fantasy. Poems. Plays, either read, watched, attended, or heard. Television in general. Television comedies, tragedies, or adventure. Motion pictures generally. Film comedies, film tragedies, foreign films, horror films, bikini films, or sword-and-sandal epics. Comic strips and comic books. Newspaper columnists: the personal advice, political, humorous, or medical columns. Magazines. Magazines devoted to automobiles, sports, flying, fashion, love stories, cross-word puzzles, or sex. Paperbacks. Books by a particular author (e.g., Harold Robbins) or best-sellers or books about a particular epoch—the Civil War, ancient Rome, etc. Argumentative conversations, lectures, light chatter, or narrative conversations. Popular songs, bluegrass songs, art songs, operatic arias, or folk songs. True adventure. Animal stories. Accounts of Nazi bestiality. Accounts of expected nuclear horrors. Books about stamp collecting, about cooking, about karate. History books. *Time* magazine. Movie fan magazines.

This list hardly scratches the surface. A good way to start your identification of your addictions is to examine your own bookshelves and whatever magazines you have lying around. Next, you might look through a really well-stocked magazine and paperback store and note the sections which draw your attention.

2. How long have you had this addiction? Can you remember having switched from another genre? Can you think of any reasons why the change occurred?

3. How badly addicted are you? Is it fairly regular, or is it sporadic? How much time did you give to it during the last two weeks?

4, Which features of the typical item in this genre do you find particularly satisfying: the character types, the plots, the themes, the style of writing, or the situations? Which features don't you like, or like only rarely?

5. What kind of satisfaction do you seem to get from this genre? Why is it you like more of this kind of thing than the rest of us do?

One Way to the Short Story: Newspaper Clippings as Source Material

Ken Donelson

Beverly Haley

The short story remains a favorite genre for many students. Ken Donelson of Arizona State University, Tempe, and Beverly Haley of Fort Morgan High School, Morgan, Colorado, suggest that the newspaper can be a valuable source of ideas that students might use as a basis for writing their own stories.

Authors' Comment

What's an English class without short stories? Often we begin with a short story unit because we feel comfortable with them and because we know students like them and like to talk about them. And we enjoy having students write short stories, and often, surprising to them, they even enjoy the activity. It all sounds so promising, and it may prove to be as good as we thought it might, but one major problem soon appears. Where do plots come from, what kinds of plot twists are possible, and where do workable and believable characters come from?

An often overlooked source of plots and twists and characters and motivations galore is in the daily newspaper. Short story material for our purposes doesn't come from front page headlines. Rather, it's the "little" stories that grow large with story potential, those short "fillers," ads in "personal" columns, items from "Dear Abby" or "Dear Ann," or maybe some odd sports story. Not all those items will excite you or your students, but if you keep your eyes open and your scissors handy and active, you'll find several intriguing items a week from your local paper that will appeal to you and just might appeal to your students because the items are sad or ironic or unbelievable or funny or puzzling.

Some students' imaginations mushroom from reading something like this. They're ready to start writing almost before they finish reading. But that is rare enough, and most students will need some form, some direction, some structure to proceed.

The Approach

How about playing some games with these newspaper items, games without rules, games where anything can be changed, as we changed names and dates and places and a few details in the clippings we use in class and in the ones we quote here?

For example, you might begin with this clipping about a recent sale of a Van Gogh painting for $5.2 million.

Van Gogh Oil Sells For A Record $5.2 Million

NEW YORK (AP)—A Vincent Van Gogh oil painting entitled "Garden of the Poet" was sold at auction for $5.2 million Tuesday, the highest price ever paid for an impressionist painting, according to Christie's auction house.

It was also the highest price ever paid for a painting auctioned in the United States, breaking the record set Monday when a Picasso was sold here for $3 million, and was a record for any work not done by an Old Master, Christie's said.

Sale prices for five other paintings auctioned at Christie's Tuesday night also broke records for works by each of the five artists represented, Elizabeth Shaw, a Christie's spokesman, said.

She said the 28-by-36-inch Van Gogh, painted in 1888, was sold to an anonymous telephone bidder. The previous record price for a Van Gogh had been set earlier in the evening when "Public Garden," an oil, sold for $1.9 million.

The six paintings that brought record prices were among 10 impressionist and modern paintings sold from the collection of Henry Ford II.

It might not make a particularly good story (that's a first impression, and we suspect that doing some brainstorming or musing might produce a better story than we might first feel). The clipping seems too cut and dried and dull *unless* we begin to wonder how the story might seem to (1) a millionaire who was the last person outbid for the painting, (2) a maid waiting with her rich employer, a maid who could not afford to get her husband the first-class funeral she wanted only three months ago, (3) a woman on welfare who wandered into the auction to get warm, (4) a man who had recently been turned down for credit for a house purchase because he makes $1000 less than needed, (5) the socially conscious daughter of the person who won the painting, (6) a man who knows that the painting is a forgery, and (7) a young standup comic who attended the auction to get material. We know that we're making up this material, but we're doing no more than any writer would who plays a simple but necessary game in starting fiction, "what if—." What if the maid who had not had enough money to give her husband the burial she wanted was there? What would she feel? What might she do? What might she say or think? What possible things could come out of this? What other kind of person, one you or your students could empathize with, might be there for whatever reason? What might happen? What would you like to see happen?

As we said, a story might be in that clipping (and the clipping, like all those that follow, is real. The only changes we made are basically insignificant, changes in the names and a few other minor things). The point is to get students to see that any event or object or person is perceived differently by different people; and events and people and objects hardly exist in any but the philosophical sense divorced from the context of the time and place and surroundings, events and people and motivations.

Once we get students to see that clippings can provide the start of a story, we can turn our attention to the possible variation we want them to show. For example, different ways of viewing the story, i.e., point of view. We might decide that the maid should tell her own story or a friend (I minor) should tell the story or a third person (third person omniscient or third person limited omniscient or third person objective). We would need to explore how we would go about establishing characters and their personalities and motivations. We'd need to talk about stereotypes and flat and round characters. We'd need to talk about conflict and why it arises. We'd need to talk about the best setting to get across the mode (romantic or ironic or tragic or comedic or satiric) we think appropriate and effective. We'd need to talk about the tone and plot twists and theme and anything else that seemed important to us about the short story, particularly *this* plot for *this* short story.

And all that discussion, depending upon the ability of our students to handle it, would come out of one or more newspaper clippings. We are not arguing that plots can't arise from many other sources. Of course they can, but newspaper clippings offer a starting point. Kids like them, and they like writing from them when they understand the ground rules allow them to change anything in any way they wish.

Sometimes, writing in groups can help get this moving in stimulating, enjoyable, and mutually enlightening ways. Groups of three to five students (with a mix of abilities and personalities in each group) can often go farther than they can individually, at least for the first try or two at this. Then the stories can be talked about in class and even run off on a ditto for some sort of class anthology.

We enjoyed the clippings that follow and we think you will too. So will your students who may, with your help, find ideas for stories, just as they'll find ideas in other items that you or the kids find in your newspapers.

In any case, here are some items we think are usable. Try them. We think you and your students will find them exciting to talk about *if* you play along with their ideas from the "what if—" approach to fiction.

Lottery Winner Shuns $51,282 After Gossip

TOKYO (UPI)—A Japanese office worker who won $51,282 in a year-end lottery burned his ticket and forfeited the prize to avoid hostility and envy among the people of his hometown, Japanese news media reported today.

The reports said Hiromi Kiyokawa, a 36-year-old bachelor from Kanae in central Japan, burned the ticket in the presence of his horrified office colleagues.

Officials of the Dai-Ichi Kangyo Bank, which sponsored the lottery, said such a thing was unprecedented.

Kiyokawa gained instant fame after winning the lottery and was at first delighted and planned to build a home of his own with the prize money.

But he decided to give up the money after the townspeople started to gossip about his sudden wealth and some even refused to speak to him.

Neighbors Rise, Aid A Threatened Family

TULSA, (UPI) - Aided by cheering neighbors armed with baseball bats and rakes, the police arrested a man today accused of harassing a family and breaking into their home four times in the last month.

The suspect, 28-year-old Donald Dickson of Tulsa, was seized at about 5 a.m. after he allegedly had forced his way into the Larchmont Road home of Gene Michaels, principal of Tulsa's Stanford High School. The police said they expected the arrest would end two months of harassing telephone calls, acts of vandalism and death threats that had led them to stake out the family room of the home.

When someone broke into the home today, the police fired a warning shot as the intruder bolted. Neighbors aware of the family's problem darted from their homes to aid in the chase.

"There were all kinds of people - even 70-year-old ladies - cheering for me and chasing this guy with baseball bats and rakes," said Officer Charles Williams.

"Persona" as Character in Literature

Suzanne Babcock

By working through this assignment sequence, students in Suzanne Babcock's classes are well prepared to understand the concepts of voice and audience in literature. Ms. Babcock teaches at St. Agnes School, Alexandria, Virginia.

Author's Comment

The purpose of this sequence of assignments is to introduce the idea of the speaker or "persona" to a high school English class beginning its study of eighteenth century satire. I have found that the success of this assignment sequence varied with the ability of the students and with the size of the class. Despite these two variables, I still believe that the students get much more involved with the reading, that they read much more carefully, and that they critically re-examine their initial responses to the literature when faced with the assignment's questions as well as with my reluctance to "figure it out" for them. Some of the most spirited and insightful discussions have resulted from the group analysis of Swift's "A Modest Proposal."

Procedure

Literature: Thomas Hardy's "The Man He Killed"; William Blake's "Chimney Sweeper"; Jonathan Swift's " A Modest Proposal."

Day One:

The first assignment I give my English III class in the fall is "The Voice Lesson." I ask them to write three brief, fictitious personal notes on a common topic to three different fictitious persons. The purpose of the assignment is to make them aware of the AUDIENCE to whom they write and of the VOICE that they develop to address each party. In other words, they are creating in their minds different "characters" to receive the notes as well as different "characters" for themselves. The assignment for the first day follows:

1. Write a note to your mother or father describing the kind of time you are having at St. A's as an upperclassman this year.
2. Write another note to your chief rival and/or ex-friend who is doing her junior year at another school, telling about your experiences at St. A's.
3. Write still another note to your very best friend who has had to move away; tell her about your experiences as an upperclassman at St. A's this year.

Day Two:

On the following day, each student reads three notes in class. That evening each student is asked to respond to the following questions in yet another writing assignment:

1. Describe the "character" whom you perceived in your mind's eye as your AUDIENCE. Identify as many characteristics as possible, including some suggestion of the relationship you have with this person and how it affected your note.
2. Identify the subjects you chose to discuss with each AUDIENCE.
3. Describe the VOICE you chose: the content you chose for each audience, how the content came to be described; pay particular attention to any difference in your choice of words and your sentence structure and grammar in each note.

Day Three:

On the third day, the students read their analyses of the notes, and we discuss the different VOICES which have emerged. With luck they have some idea about the instinctive creation of a role or a character in their everyday communication. At this point, we shuttle on to something more deliberate and usually more inspired: an author's creation of a "persona" in literature.

Day Four:

We continue the discussion of VOICE (now called PERSONA) with M. H. Abrams's definition of persona in *A Glossary of Literary Terms,* 3rd ed. While the definition at first may seem abstract to the student, recent experience with the student's own persona in "The Voice Lesson" should make it more tangible. At this point we read aloud Thomas Hardy's "The Man He Killed;" I ask each student to write out a brief but specific description of the character who is speaking, based on the poet's own words. Once again we listen to each student's characterization. Then

I ask them to comment on their reaction to the speaker's use of the "quaint and curious" to describe war. I ask them to speculate on whether or not Thomas Hardy intended us to agree with such a description or to think more deeply on the situation described.

Day Five:

We read aloud William Blake's "The Chimney Sweeper" and I ask them to write out their responses to the following questions:

1. Characterize the speaker; develop the characterization by observing the speaker's age, the attitude toward the father's treatment, what "harm" has come to the speaker so far in this life, and the attitude toward the situation in life.
2. What is your response to what the speaker has had to say—to him personally, his age, and to his attitude toward his situation? Does your response agree with the speaker's ? Why?

Day Six:

In class, we read and discuss the students' responses to the questions on the Blake poem. At this point, we begin talking about persona in the terms of the Abrams definition and I ask them the following:

1. Compare the degree of difference in attitude between the persona and the poet in the Hardy poem and between the persona and the poet in the Blake poem.
2. What do you think was Hardy's purpose in creating the persona in his poem?
3. What was Blake's purpose in creating a persona who was a child?
4. What message did each poet send along with his persona?
5. What would have been the difference in effect if each poet had stated his case directly, without the assistance of a persona? What does the use of a persona bring to each poem?

Day Seven:

After a brief discussion of the historical Anglo-Irish situation, I read aloud to the students Jonathan Swift's "A Modest Proposal." Without further discussion, I ask them the following:

Having just listened to a reading of Jonathan Swift's "A Modest Proposal," re-read the essay to yourself. (Several careful readings may produce more startling information.) Then tonight, prepare in writing (basically think on paper) answers to the following questions. Some of the answers will be found easily and obviously in the reading; however, for other answers you will have to rely on intuition and second-guessing. Try, in any case, to make educated guesses rather than totally absurd "sillies." Come to class tomorrow prepared to refine your answer and to continue the investigation of Swift's essay.

1. What form or genre does this writing take?
2. What is the situation that has prompted the speaker to digress?
3. What exactly is the speaker's proposal?
4. Who is the speaker? Characterize him by answering the following:
   a. how old is he?
   b. what nationality is he?
   c. what social class does he come from?
   d. is he educated?
   e. what is his profession?
   f. what is his philosophical outlook?
   g. what is his political persuasion?
   h. what is his religious preference?
   i. what are his special talents?
   j. what interests motivate him?
   k. what kind of personality does he hope to project?
   l. what is his greatest strength?
   m. what is his greatest weakness?
   n. how knowledgeable an individual is he?
   o. is he sincere?
5. To whom is the speaker speaking?
6. How does he wish to be perceived by his audience?

Day Eight:

I divide the class into groups of four students and they review their answers to the previous night's questions together. When they seem familiar with each others' responses, we discuss their findings as a reassembled class. I ask them to re-read the essay and to answer the following questions:

1. Does the speaker have preconceived notions (unconscious assumptions) about the poor people? If yes, what are they?
2. Does the speaker have preconceived notions about those who are not poor? If so, what are they?
3. How do these preconceived notions affect the speaker's feelings and ideas?
4. What is the speaker's chief interest . . . the most important to him?
5. What element is missing from the speaker's proposal?
6. What or who is Jonathan Swift satirizing (criticizing in the hope of effecting a change)?

With this final question answered, we are ready to tackle a whole new subject: satire.

Thomas Carlyle in the Survey Course

Carroll Viera

Teachers of literature classes frequently encounter students who, frustrated by the writing styles of a particular time period far removed from them, dismiss their reading as inaccessible and unrelated to their lives. Carroll Viera, using Thomas Carlyle as an example, recommends taking time before introducing a difficult author or work to engage students in a writing activity designed to bridge the gap. Ms. Viera sent this from Tennessee Technological University, Cookeville.

Author's Comment

Many students are so frustrated by Thomas Carlyle's convoluted syntax, extensive allusions, and richly symbolic language that they lay aside their texts after initial attempts to read assigned passages and return to class complaining that his writing is altogether inaccessible. Yet because Carlyle's influence on his contemporaries was so pervasive, even a cursory acquaintance with his writing equips students in survey courses with an invaluable foundation for understanding most of the other major Victorian writers.

The Approach

To take fullest advantage of the potential Carlyle's writing affords as an encapsulated version of the Victorian period, instructors must help students to identify with him. One means of establishing this identity is through a simple classroom exercise based upon the two most frequently anthologized chapters of *Sartor Resartus*—"The Everlasting No" and "The Everlasting Yea." ("The Centre of Indifference," though usually anthologized as well, can easily be omitted, since Carlyle covers the significant moments of this transition stage in the early paragraphs of "The Everlasting Yea.") This exercise, the first stage of which requires about thirty minutes, should be begun two class periods before *Sartor Resartus* is to be discussed.

Students are first asked to write down on scrap paper the names of the two most exemplary people they know personally, the two people whom they trust above all others and whom they would like to emulate. It

213

is essential that students actually record these names; otherwise, some will be tempted by the nature of the subsequent directions to substitute the names of people whom they venerate less, and the value of the assignment will be diminished. They are then asked to imagine the unimaginable—that through no fault of their own, these two people completely betray them and that no effort on their part can ever effect a reconciliation. Before proceeding, the instructor should allow the students to ponder this possibility for a few moments; the gloomy faces in the classroom indicate that most are thoughtfully considering the problem. Then, reminded that they are absolutely certain that they have done nothing to inspire the betrayal and that they are equally certain that their faith in the betrayers will never be restored, they are asked to record whatever responses they feel, not in a tightly structured essay but rather in discursive and impressionistic fashion. If this assignment is given in the latter portion of a class and if students are allowed to leave early only after completing a full page, most will have no difficulty in providing an extensive account of their feelings.

In sifting through these papers, the instructor will discover remarkable similarities not only in content but also in imagery and allusions to Carlyle's spiritual autobiography. These similarities provide the focus of the next class.

Usually at least one phrase or image can be selected from every student's paper, thus giving each student confidence in an ability to comprehend Carlyle. The phrases can be duplicated and distributed or simply read aloud in class. Here are some common responses:

> I just can't believe this happened. It must be a bad dream.
> If these people have betrayed me, how can I trust anybody?
> I wouldn't know where to turn or what to do. I would feel completely lost.
> Words can't express the depth of my feelings.
> I'd want to go away. Maybe in a new place I could pull my thoughts together.
> I would lose my faith in my fellow man and in God. I would think that if these people are evil, God must be evil too.
> I'd feel physically sick and very shaken and unsure of everything.
> Just the idea of this betrayal makes me want to throw up.
> I'd be so depressed that I'd lose confidence in myself. I'd think that I must be at fault in some way I couldn't understand.
> I'd think about suicide.
> I would feel like a lost person wandering around trying to find his way.
> I'd feel completely alone. I would feel as though the whole world had turned against me.
> I'd never be the same person again.
> I wouldn't care about anything or anybody.
> It would take years for me to get over this. Maybe someday I could learn to trust people again.

After enumerating these responses in class, the instructor can point out that these feelings are precisely those of Diogenes Teufelsdrockh after he is betrayed by Blumine, his fiancee, and Towgood, his best friend (the more complex circumstances of Diogenes's depression can be laid aside until students have read "The Everlasting No"). Students now readily apprehend the concept of the spiritual autobiography and can be introduced to the critical terms usually applied to its stages: the dark night of the soul, which designates the deepest stage of despair; the everlasting no, which designates a temptation to succumb to the despair, including a temptation to suicide; the center of indifference, which designates a transition stage; and the everlasting yea, which designates a new faith.

Students can then be given a brief outline of Diogenes's story—his betrayal, his loss of faith, and his reaffirmation of faith in his recognition of the brotherhood of man, his apprehending of the spiritual nature of the universe, and his commitment to duty. Similarities between their imagery and Carlyle's can also be stressed: the searching protagonist as a pilgrim, mental confusion as loss of physical direction, despair as physical sickness. These images, easily understood because students themselves have used them in their own hypothetical spiritual autobiographies, can then be related to recurring image clusters in *Sartor Resartus,* such as those of food, animals, and clothing. The students' own symbolic use of imagery fully prepares them to accept Carlyle's symbolism as inherent in the text rather than as imposed upon it by a symbol-hunting literature instructor.

At this point the instructor can concede that Carlyle is difficult to read and can call attention to the Able Editor's complaint as he sorts through the six paper bags: "Singular Teufelsdrockh, would thou hadst told thy singular story in plain words!" After looking at this passage, students can be reminded that just as they felt words inadequate to describe the complexity of their emotions, so Carlyle often feels that the complexity of reality must be conveyed in a corresponding complexity of form.

With this preparation and with short reading assignments, students can gain from the central chapters of *Sartor Resartus* not only an introduction to other frequently anthologized sections of spiritual autobiographies— Mill's *Autobiography, In Memoriam,* Newman's *Apologia*—but also an introduction to many major themes that dominate nineteenth-century literature—the quest for new values, the relationship between man and nature, man's continuing war against empiricism, the role of the past. Although students rarely echo the extravagant praise of Carlyle's contemporaries, they find he has much to say: they recognize his detested steam engine as our computer, the nineteenth-century fundamentalist's fear of science in the twentieth-century creationist's attack on evolution, and in the individual's unchanging need for self-knowledge.

Beowulf Redux

Susan Marrs

Susan Marrs of Seven Hills School in Cincinnati, Ohio, calls upon
students to use the elements of the mythic tale in creating their own
written account of some contemporary struggle or conflict.

Author's Comment

We sat there sweating together, my colleagues and I, that sultry August
afternoon. It was our annual preschool trial: the visit by some local
expert (a pediatrician one year, a businessman the next) designed to pull
us out of our summer lethargy and send us back to the classroom,
stimulated and invigorated. Often it only sends us back to the classroom.

But this speaker dropped a pearl that *was* stimulating and invigorating.
She announced that one generally retains very little of what one sees, a
moderate amount of what one hears, but next to all of what one does.

The Approach

And so, several weeks later when my sophomore English class had finished reading and discussing *Beowulf,* I assigned them a paper requiring
more "doing" than usual. Rather than analyze a myth devised by someone else, they were to create a contemporary heroic struggle of mythic
dimension. The assignment was to cast some current battle (in Congress,
say, or at school or in their own homes) as a mythic tale: to establish a
hero, a villain, a theme; to incorporate such Beowulfian devices as the use
of kennings and alliteration, references to lineage, and instances of super-
human powers. They were directed to write in prose, to open with an
introduction explaining the history of the conflict, to stage at least one
but no more than three battles, and to close with a suitable conclusion.
All that could be accomplished, I declared, in 400 to 600 words, due in
one week.

The papers that arrived were delightful in their range of topics, their
inventive interpretation of my instructions, and the energy and wit with

which they were constructed. Several students chose to begin with scenes from their own homes. One serious and hardworking girl presented herself in combat with a personified Despair, her struggle arising from the endless and excessive demands of homework and soccer practice.

> Listen well! For here is a song of unrest and fear, a song of bravery and triumph. . . . Fate had so far been favorable toward Janet, before [Despair] began her siege. Janet had friends, talent, energy, and a full day's work each day she faced. But life began to sour as Despair attacked. Homework began to pile up alarmingly, though school had always seemed easy before. She began to shorten her hours of rest and interrupted them in order to finish, which strained her great stores of energy. A great fatigue began to catch up to her as she stayed up all night for weeks upon weeks, trying to finish. Her work became less worthy the longer she stayed up to do it, which only made her work longer and harder, yet she was never quite finished, and it was never quite good enough.

> (Janet Goering)

Janet, you'll be relieved to know, vanquishes Despair most satisfactorily.

Another student turned old-fashioned sibling rivalry into an older-fashioned myth:

> Life in the hall of Searcy was quite peaceful until the first-born, a girl, reached the age of four. Then *he* was born and the ten-year siege began. He was the Searcy's second-born, their bouncing baby boy. His birth brought havoc to the hall. The hall was soon filled with baby-boy noises. This havoc went unnoticed by the parents, but the first-born, Erdied [Deidre spelled backwards], was terrorized. He bit and scratched her. He pulled her hair, broke her toys, and colored in her coloring books. Worst of all, he became Erdied's shadow and tagged along wherever she went. Years went by. He, known as Son by his parents, became Grendel in the eyes of Erdied. The siege continued.

> (Deidre Searcy)

One of the most amusing papers detailed the struggles of one student's father with the family dog in their daily race for the mail:

> Sir Daddy-O spends this hour before the battle in his upstairs study awaiting the arrival of his *Business Week* magazine, the warrior's indispensable guide to tactics in an evil business climate. Suddenly, he hears the roar of his formidable foe, Juno, queen of the most evil of all household demons—dogs. Juno, with her sharp, devouring, white fangs, and with her monstrous, thwacking tail, is descended from a race of malevolent New Jersey Labrador Retrievers, mighty to behold and terrifying to fight. More of this evil villainess's ancestry could be told if she had not, in her awesome anger, devoured all records of her noble lineage.

> (Liz Rosenberg)

Other papers sent heroes into battles taking place at school. One social critic pitted student against student in a short but violent war "lasting only sixth bell. . . . It began with the slashing of tongues and tearing of polo collars." Another set the Headmaster against the Dean of Students, whose chief weapon ("his evil detention list") proved no match for his superior's "magical and almighty chalk dust."

Most students, however, turned to more global affairs in selecting their topics. There were several aptly named environmentalists struggling against the exploitation of the land: John Green vs. that evil oil baron Rhett Dason; Aksala the Eskimo vs. a "huge yellow dirt-eating monster." In Iran, Darren N. Gallent came to the aid of Hrothgarian King James in a fight with the "magnetic mesmerizing of Khomeini . . . , a fearsome character with a flowing beard, beady black eyes, sleek sinister eyebrows, and a hawk-like nose. He wore flowing black garments, darker than night itself. His fierce, intense stare drove fear into the hearts of his subjects and motivated them to do evil deeds." (Dorothy Kim)

Two papers presented Poland's struggle with Russia.

> Listen, friends, to these words, for the future of mankind lies in struggles like this. Late in the twentieth century the greatest evil left in the world was the Soviet Union. Her ancestors were the wealthy few and the poverty-stricken masses. During the life of this abomination, it crushed many smaller nations into the dirt. One of those nations was a small but brave nation called Poland. Poland was born of the same parents as Russia, but matured in a far more beneficial way. In this small country's youth, Russia trampled it and bound it to herself. This is the story of Poland's breaking that bond.
>
> (Andrew Jergens)

Even Jerry Brown appeared, as Jerrinth, the leader who rose to heroism by refusing to "sprinkle the poisonous waters" over the land and people, choosing instead to summon all his strength and kill California's Med flies with "two tremendous swats." (Sally Bidlingmeyer)

Nineteen papers, no two on the same topic, but all nineteen fulfilling, to one degree or another, the dictates of myth. They were fun to read. Their authors said they were fun to write. And my teacher's soul was delighted with the evidence of my class's working understanding of so many of the structural and stylistic qualities of Old English myth.

Using Semantic Clues to Get at Meaning in *Henry IV, Part I*

Irene de La Bretonne Hays

A series of writing activities suggested by Irene de La Bretonne Hays helps students build connections between their lives and the reading they do. The model could be transferred easily to various literary studies. Ms. Hays submitted this exercise from Battelle Pacific Northwest Laboratories, Richland, Washington.

Author's Comment

Can no man tell me of my unthrifty son?
'Tis full three months since I did see him last.
If any plague hang over us, 'tis he.
I would to God, my lords, he might be found.
Inquire at London, 'mongst the taverns there,
For there, they say, he daily doth frequent,
With unrestrained loose companions.

King Richard II, Act V, Scene iii, Lines 1–7,
to which *Henry IV, Part I* is a sequel

Most everyone has been there: A teenager out of touch with father; a mother not comprehending her daughter's world; a son at cross purposes with his family. The theme abounds in literature and in life. Reading about such common, yet poignant, themes is good for something: For living. Students need to know this. Ultimately, the "how to" of living, the quality of valuing, is the chief concern of literature and the chief concern of teaching.

If we ask our students to parrot the teacher's (or critic's) response to literature, to seek the so-called author's intent, to analyze the writer's craft—at the expense of asking them to actively and personally relate to the ideas in the reading—we may be stopping so long at the inn we mistake it for home.

Shakespeare is great not because of some inherent genius in his technical skill, but because when we experience his plays we are moved—and moved to read again. Allowing students the opportunity to be moved by literature and to construct their own meanings in response to it has immeasurable value.

It is important, then, to design teaching strategies that mesh a student's life with an assigned piece of literature. The student's prior knowledge of the world, that system of built-in semantic cues, can be tapped—linked with the literature—to get at meaning. Exploiting these cues within students can help even the most reluctant readers among them gain access to meaning in a reading selection.

Writing in Response to Reading *Henry IV, Part I*

A way to mesh life with literature is to write, not "about" a piece of literature, but in response to reading it. The following sequence of writing exercises may be assigned in response to reading Shakespeare's *Henry IV, Part I*. The model applies generally to any piece of literature, once a central theme is identified. The material for the writing comes from the student's background of experience, knowledge, and attitudes in response to a theme in the literature.

The writing exercises presented here are sequenced to correspond to stages in the writing process, beginning with prewriting serving an expressive function. The written responses occur both before reading the play and after reading certain passages, and are collected as private writing. After reading the entire play, the teacher guides students to locate and extract significant ideas from this seedbed of accumulated expressive responses. Students then expand these seed ideas into public writing— transactional or poetic. This final stage in the process allows the teacher to have students revise carefully and pay attention to audience.

Before reading *Henry IV, Part I*, students write freely in response to a theme or conflict that is a central concern of the play and is also a problem or issue encountered in the experience of living. In this case, the theme "generation gap" from *Henry IV, Part I* illustrates the sequence of writing assignments that lead from private expressive response to public communication. The misunderstanding and alienation are between father and son; between Henry Bolingbroke and Prince Hal, his son, in *Henry IV, Part I*. Thus prepared, the students respond to the same issue or conflict as it appears in reading the play.

Writing before Reading the Play

I. A taped stimulus for writing on the theme "generation gap."
   "She's Leaving Home"   The Beatles, *Sergeant Pepper*
   "Father and Son"   Cat Stevens, *Tea for the Tillerman*
   "Cat's in the Cradle"   Harry Chapin

A. Play the taped stimulus for the students. It is designed to create cognitive dissonance about the topic. Provide a handout of the lyrics for them to follow.
B. Immediately following the taped stimulus, have the students respond in a ten-minute nonstop writing. (The pen keeps moving; the writing is free and associative.)

Writing after Reading Selected Passages of *Henry IV, Part I*

As the students progress through the play, they will come upon certain passages that develop the theme "generation gap." The following three passages from it, with exercises, lead the students first to analyze and discuss what is actually happening in the passage between King Henry and Prince Hal, and then through a series of questions or specially designed activities, to relate to the play actively and personally.

II. Why Aren't You More Like Your Cousin?

King Henry: Yea, there thou mak'st me sad, and mak'st me sin
In envy that my Lord Northumberland
Should be the father to so blest a son,
A son who is the theme of honor's tongue,
Amongst a grove the very straightest plant,
Who is sweet Fortune's minion and her pride;
Whilst I, by looking on the praise of him,
See riot and dishonor stain the brow
Of my young Harry. O that it could be proved
That some night-tripping fairy had exchanged
In cradle clothes our children where they lay,
And called mine Percy, his Plantagenet!
Then would I have his Harry, and he mine.

Act I, Scene i, Lines 78–90

A. Analyze and discuss the meaning of the passage with the class.
B. Relate the theme to the students' experience by discussing the following:
Brainstorm ways in which parents compare sons or daughters with siblings or other relatives. Are comparisons fair? What are examples of unfair comparisons? Discuss situations in which you feel you have been compared unfairly.
C. Beginning with the words "How can you be so unfair . . .", have the students respond to the discussion in a ten-minute nonstop writing; again, associative and free flowing.

III. Someday I'll Surprise You All . . .

    Prince Hal: I know you all, and will awhile uphold
                        The unyoked humor of your idleness,
                        Yet herein will I imitate the sun,
                        Who doth permit the base contagious clouds
                        To smother up his beauty from the world,
                        That, when he please again to be himself,
                        Being wanted, he may be more wondered at
                        By breaking through the foul and ugly mists
                        Of vapors that did seem to strangle him.
                        If all the year were playing holidays,
                        To sport would be as tedious as to work;
                        But when they seldom come, they wished-for come,
                        And nothing pleaseth but rare accidents.
                        So, when this loose behavior I throw off
                        And pay the debt I never promised,
                        By how much better than my word I am,
                        By so much shall I falsify men's hopes
                        And like bright metal on a sullen ground,
                        My reformation, glitt'ring o'er my fault,
                        Shall show more goodly and attract more eyes
                        Than that which hath no foil to set it off.
                        I'll so offend, to make offense a skill,
                        Redeeming time when men think least I will.

                                  Act I, Scene ii, Lines 168–190

   A. Have students paraphrase Prince Hal's soliloquy, making it clear, direct, and modern. (This activity could occur in groups.) Read several of the paraphrases aloud to the class.

   B. Discuss with the class:
       What is Hal up to? What if his father had over-
       heard this speech? What if Falstaff or his friends
       had overheard?

   C. Relate the theme to the students' experience by asking them to discuss situations that cause them to feel as Hal must have felt.

   D. Have students mentally visualize an audience (parent, friend) and write to that audience for ten minutes, nonstop, beginning with the words "Someday I'll surprise (show) you all. . . ."

IV. Oh, What Did I Do to Deserve This? (father) and
    I Promise I'll Do Better! (son)

    Have students read Act III, Scene ii, Lines 1–161, from which the following passages are extracted.

    King Henry: I know not whether God will have it so
                        For some displeasing service I have done,

> That, in his secret doom, out of my blood
> He'll breed revengement and a scourge for me;
> But thou dost, in thy passages of life,
> Make me believe that thou are only mark'd
> For the hot vengeance and the rod of heaven
> To punish my mistreadings. Tell me else,
> Could such inordinate and low desires,
> Such poor, such bare, such lewd, such mean attempts,
> Such barren pleasures, rude society,
> As thou art march'd withal and grafted to,
> Accompany the greatness of thy blood,
> And hold their level with thy princely heart?

> Act III, Scene ii, Lines 5–18

Prince Hal: I shall hereafter, my thrice-gracious lord,
                 Be more myself.

> Act III, Scene ii, Lines 92–93

A. Have students write a precis of this dialogue between the father and son, grasping the central thought and expressing it succinctly.
B. Have students read precis to response groups (3–5 in each group); then select two members of each group and prepare to stage an ad-lib dialogue between Henry and Hal; feel free to update the material and the language; include strong feelings and current topics.
C. Have students respond to the staged dialogues in a ten-minute nonstop writing.

Finding the Seed Idea

After students have completed reading the play and have accumulated expressive responses to the theme, have them read through their seedbed of writings, jotting in the margin, underlining, or circling significant ideas or images. These are seed ideas that they may use for further writing. Have the students then focus on one such idea or image and, using it as the stimulus, write a ten-minute nonstop in response to it. The topics thus will be elaborated, explored, or expanded in preparation for the next stage of the writing process.

Expanding the Seed Idea from Private to Public Writing

To guide students to expand the seed idea into a public writing, have them first select or discover an appropriate form or mode for it. Following is a "Mode Array" presenting possible ways students can expand the theme, "generation gap."

Mode Array

Personal Writing

Write a letter to a younger member of your family explaining how to get along with your parents.

Write a letter to your parents explaining yourself on an especially difficult issue.

Write a dialogue or an essay comparing and contrasting your parents' expectations, behavior, and attitudes as a teenager with your own.

Re-create a scene from your own experience (as participant or observer) of a conflict or misunderstanding between parent and child.

Literary/Poetic/Imaginative

Write a poem or song lyrics about the "generation gap."

Imagine yourself as the parent of a "wayward" teenager.

Write a week of diary entries in the life of a parent whose teenager has run away.

Write Henry Bolingbroke's response to overhearing Hal's "I know you all . . ." speech.

Write a letter from Prince Hal explaining his motives to one of his brothers or to Falstaff.

Write a conversation between Falstaff and Poins after overhearing Hal's "I know you all . . ." speech.

Explanatory/Informative

Research and describe the psychological aspects of sibling rivalry and comparison.

Write a newspaper or magazine article describing the behavior and activities of young Prince Hal in *Henry IV, Part I.*

Research the whereabouts of the top five students in the high school class of a generation ago; the bottom five. Write an interpretation of your findings.

Focus on a cause of misunderstanding between the generations and attempt to find a solution. Write a report on your solution.

Persuasive

Analyze and evaluate discrimination against teenagers in the media or another area of society.

Write a letter to the editor of the local newspaper about a change that is needed in parent-child community service.

Write an ad, commercial, or short vignette for public television promoting better understanding between parent and teenager.

Write an essay about a topic on which you and your parents or family have recently disagreed. Persuade your audience that your point of view is valid.

Note that a teacher could create a "Mode Array" for each theme encountered in various pieces of literature. However, it is not necessary to do so. In time, students internalize the mode categories and invent their own specific public (transactional or poetic) writings.

Expanding the private response to a public writing requires that students be guided through the stages of drafting, revising, and editing. Response or editing groups, read-alouds, and specially designed editing sheets should all be a part of the process—a process that can lead to a synthesis of reading and writing not often found in a literature class.

Starting Where They Are

Too often the activity in a literature class is a deadly, alienating task of learning "about" a piece of literature, rather than a lively, authentic process of responding to it. If, in our reading assignments, the end goal is the literal translation of meaning from the printed page, I propose we may have difficulty getting even that from students. But, if we motivate the reader to make some sense of the literature by relating it to the students' reality outside the classroom or inside their minds, the rest of the learning "about" literature may well be facilitated. If, on the other hand, we do not thus motivate students—that is, start where they are—we run the risk, once again, of training them to be tolerant of nonsense.

Astro Poetry:
Students Working as Poets

William Rakauskas

What decisions does a writer have to make in creating a poem? This activity shows students the importance of selectivity in word choice, the role of metaphor, and the impact of compression in the writing of poetry. Mr. Rakauskas contributed this exercise from the University of Scranton, Pennsylvania.

Author's Comment

Poets must have experience, direct or vicarious. They must be openly susceptible, and willing to observe closely. They must be selective, choosing only those impressions, observations, details, or gleanings which fit the impression they intend to convey, deleting those which add nothing. Poets write from abundance, yet they are economical, stripping their writing of excess—no fat allowed. Their purpose is to amuse, to instruct, to embellish truth, or to vitalize dull reality. Poets compress, using the minimum number of words to gain the maximum effect, yoking seemingly disparate ideas into metaphors, creating poetic shock, leading the reader to expect one idea, and then offering the reader another.

The Approach

One approach I have employed successfully in making students aware of these qualities of the poet is a strategy I call "Astro Poetry." Students are asked to clip the "Astrological Forecast" from the evening or morning newspaper and to bring the forecast to their next class. Or, I clip the morning forecast, duplicate copies, and distribute them to the class.

In class, we first discuss the four types of meaning in a poem, as identified by I. A. Richards in *Practical Criticism:* Sense, Feeling, Tone, and Intention. "Sense" refers to the literal meaning of the lines, the plain sense of what is said. "Feeling" is the attitude of the poet toward the subject. "Tone" is the poet's attitude toward the audience, and "Intention" is the aim the poet attempts to achieve. I shuffle these "types" to produce an acronym—FIST, the clout of a poem.

Then, students, working individually with their Astro Graph, read their forecast to get the literal "sense" of the message. What they must do next is to generate the first draft of what eventually will be their Astro poem by translating the sense of the astro message into poetic form. To do this, they must capture the "intention" of the original message and transform it into the aim of their poem. Also, they must establish the "feeling" of their poem—serious, humorous, ironic, satiric, didactic. The students know they will be asked to read their finished creation to us, so determining "tone" is not too difficult. Their finished poem must have clout—FIST.

The poem's structure is prescribed. The words of the poem must string out in sequence the letters of the student's sign in coherent-sounding connections. One student produced the following Astro poem:

"Aries"

Amorous reunion

Increases

Enthusiastic sex.

Another wrote:

"Libra"

Loose-tongued idiots
Bellow

Ridiculous

Accusations.

What should be evident from the above examples is that the strings of consecutive words not only must be coherent, precise, and unified but also must be so shaped that they look like a poem—a special arrangement of words on paper.

Here is a poem produced by a student in my advanced composition class. Note, of course, the longer signs require more work, but students enjoy the process so much that those with longer signs actually have more fun searching, deleting, adding, sequencing, and shaping their poems.

"Capricorn"

Complete all projects.
Rearrange itinerary carefully;
Or,
Regret negligence.

Given the opportunity to generate language themselves, to string a few words coherently together, to discover connections among the developing intentions, and to arrange and shape the strings, students learn to approach poetry with a nurtured appreciation for what other poets have done. Students' own creative attempts serve as transitions for reading poetry better, more emphatically, and with greater pleasure.

Language Can Do What We Want It to Do

Helen J. Throckmorton

When students discover meaning in literature for themselves, they seem to enjoy their reading more. Helen J. Throckmorton of Wichita State University in Kansas offers a series of steps that provide an opportunity for students to discover their own meanings in a poem.

Author's Comment

In my experience, students most enjoy learning, and learn best, when they feel they are discovering something for themselves. Whatever its limitations, such learning is at least authentic. This is especially true when students study what for them are unpopular or difficult subjects or concepts. Poetry is one of these.

These exercises were originally designed for students in a freshman English composition course, most of whom frankly admitted that they seldom understood and therefore almost never read, let alone enjoyed, poetry. Moreover, they did not see any particular reason why writers would choose to write poetry instead of prose to say what they wished to say, or why any reader would choose to read poetry instead of prose when to them poetry seems more to obscure than to clarify communication.

Yet one major purpose of the course was to examine ways that language works, and to examine ways that language works in poems was an integral part of that purpose. As I saw it, my task was to help students (1) realize that the language of poetry differs from the language of prose in kind, of course, but also in degree; (2) develop confidence through competence in reading and talking about poems; and (3) learn to recognize and to do some of the things that "good" writers do, to achieve writing that works.

It was not intended that we study "elements" of poetry. However, we found it convenient to use some terms commonly associated with concepts of poetry. Students remembered some terms they thought they had forgotten, others they thought they had never learned, and used them with increasing facility to describe qualities in words and sentences that accounted for what was happening, what was working.

Nor was it intended that we study "definitions" of poetry, although more than one classroom comment began, "This is poetry, because . . ." or "This is not poetry, because . . .," an acknowledgment that poetry is characterized, or perceived to be characterized, by certain definable attributes. Certainly it was altogether unexpected when one student proposed an operational definition that no one challenged: "Poetry is what poetry does."

At most, these exercises may have led to "an heightened prizing." At the very least, they led to greater awareness that those "imaginary gardens with real toads in them"[1] that Marianne Moore describes may be worth inspection, after all.

Exercise 1

1. Using the overhead projector, I presented the following assignment:

> Imagine that you are traveling swiftly from east to west, across Kansas, as a passenger in a bus, a car, or train. As you travel, you are looking at Kansas—and thinking about the mountains that lie ahead.
>
> In one sentence describe Kansas as you see it.

2. When students finished writing, I asked them to read their sentences, then select what they considered to be key words and phrases. These I listed on the chalkboard in the order given. With all students responding, and few duplications, a list emerged:

flatland	quiet
dry land	barnyard
rolling flat plains	flat
hot	warm-dry
dusty	endless blank plains
unpicturesque	no contrast
buffalo	no color
sod	monotonous
rolling plains	vast prairieland
level	grassland
miserable	many wide open spaces
hot-dry	golden wheat

dust	grassland
sand	wheatfields
flat barrenness	old tattered patchwork quilt
sun-dazed farmers	sun beating down
unmerciful sun	lonely
tawny yellow desert	rough patches
treeless	no end, no purpose
hot	drab
windy	scattered trees

3. In an effort to open, but not direct, discussion, I asked: "What do these words and phrases reveal?"

Comment

Students expressed surprise at the length of the list and at the variety and diversity of words and phrases. They went on to observe that most were uncomplimentary, a few relatively neutral, and relatively few positive. Not all agreed about which was which, though. Is the phrase "many wide open spaces" neutral? Positive? Is the phrase "old tattered patchwork quilt" neutral? Positive? Or even uncomplimentary, pejorative? What did the writer intend? How did the reader or listener perceive? Are intentions and responses congruent? In what ways do the writer's experiences or perceptions affect the choice of words? In what ways do the listener's or reader's experiences or perceptions affect their responses?

In considering these and related questions, students applied, and frequently stopped to clarify their understanding of, the following terms: *denotation* and *connotation, concrete* and *abstract, literal* and *figurative, nouns* and *verbs* and *adjectives*. Students especially liked the phrases that "suggest more than they say" and that "help us see." *State, suggest, infer,* and *imply* were recurring terms.

Exercise 2

1. Again using the overhead projector, I presented the next assignment:

In your imagination you conjured up a fairly graphic picture of Kansas. The sentence you wrote conveyed that picture. As you were looking at Kansas, you were asked to think about the mountains that lie ahead.

In a second sentence, describe the mountains either as you "see" or "perceive" them.

2. Again, students read their sentences, then selected key words and phrases. Again, all students responded, with few duplications, and we had this list:

coolness	cool large
running streams	rocks
high green blue timberline	nature's haven
tower endlessly	stately majestic
snow in August	adventure
haze of purple	cooler
ground squirrels	fear
rugged	terrifying mountains
steep slopes	trees
deep valleys	snow
blue peaks	shade
crystal blue sky	pine
cool respite	picturesque
adventures	exhilarating

3. Again I asked the question, "What do these words and phrases reveal?"

Comment

As before, students remarked on the effect of certain words and phrases, noting the predominance of expressions evoking positive, pleasant, even euphoric responses. Someone questioned the kind of experiences underlying the choice of "fear" and "terrifying mountains." Another observed the use of abstractions: "nature's haven" and "cool respite." Some of the terms used earlier were used again, most notably *concrete* and *suggest*. So, for the first time, were the terms *image* and *metaphor*.

Exercise 3

1. I distributed the following take-home assignment:

Here are three sentences written by someone who is as familiar with western Kansas, and the mountains that lie beyond, as you are. In the first sentence, the writer gives us his perception of western Kansas. In the third sentence, he gives us his perception of the mountains beyond. Compare your first sentence with this writer's first sentence, and your second sentence with his third.

> *The telephone poles have been holding their arms out a long time now to birds that will not settle there but pass with strange cawings westward to where dark trees gather about a waterhole. This is Kansas. The mountains start here just behind the closed eyes of a farmer's sons asleep in their work clothes.*

2. All students completed the assignment, and I duplicated and distributed excerpts from their papers, with this request:

> As we read each one of these aloud, let's see if we can discover precisely what it is that the writer is trying to tell us about the way that the language of the sentences being compared seems to work and with what effect.

These are some of the excerpts we examined:

> The feeling of "farminess" and of "wide-open-spaces" comes across in both passages, but both passages leave unanswered the question of whether or not the people really like Kansas.

> Two main differences show the basic weakness of my sentences. First, the paragraph brings Kansas to life by conveying the idea that people really live in the state. My sentence mentions scenery alone. Second, my terms are ones that everyone generally uses when speaking of Kansas and mountains, but the paragraph uses unconventional terms to convey similar ideas. For example, the telephone poles standing with arms outstretched suggested to me the picture of a flat, seemingly endless highway lined by telephone poles, and this, in turn, suggested great expanse.

> Obviously it is the wording that makes one better than the other for words are all we have and if one is better than the other it must be because the words are more informative or more conveying of a feeling. The most significant difference that I can see is that I just describe an area but in that writer's sentence the words make lifelike objects alive and real. An example is "the telephone poles have been holding their arms out." This suggests a very real feeling that the poles are alive. Also, "dark trees gather about a waterhole" suggests live animals which are capable of moving around.

> I was thinking of Kansas as a whole without the details that make that whole. Mine was a statement that could be said of any time and place. The other writer implies the monotony of watching a countryside by how that person has picked a detail that doesn't change each quickly passing mile. He has stared at those telephone poles for so long that he knows the birds that light there, stay for just a moment and then gather at some other place.

> With mountains behind the closed eyes, that writer can make them anything he wants. The sentences in this passage set the imagination flying.

The writer's sentences are more open to investigation and interpretation than my sentences, which are definitely very clear-cut.

The similarities between the students' and that writer's sentences seem great to me. The essential part is in being able to interpret his sentences to understand the inner meaning.

I tried to explain how Kansas and the mountains actually looked to me. The unknown author, however, gives a skeletal framework which forces the reader to fall back on his experiences and take these experiences to the skeleton to form the flesh. My sentences are purely descriptive. One reads my sentences and that is it. They stand still. The unknown author's sentences, though, move and work.

I, through a rather unskillful manipulation of thoughts, managed to scratch out nearly fifty words which communicate nothing other than exactly what the words say.

It is interesting to me that such a short passage as the one presented can say so much for being so short. It gives just as much detail as mine did in about a fifth as much time.

Comment

Discussion revealed students' belief that language used to suggest, connote, compare, or personify worked with particular effectiveness. They were unusually attentive to, and admiring of, those uses of language that either stimulated, allowed, or required "interpretation" and "imaginative play" (or as one wryly put it, "imaginative *work*"). A number felt that they themselves had achieved these effects with some degree of success; even they, however, found more differences than similarities between their sentences and "the writer's" sentences. Finally, they demanded to know "the writer" and the source of those sentences before taking one more step or taking on one more "assignment." Nothing for it, then, but to present the original text.

Crossing Kansas by Train[2]
The telephone poles
have been holding their
arms out
a long time now
to birds
that will not
settle there
but pass with
strange cawings
westward to
where dark trees

> gather about
> a waterhole. This
> is Kansas. The
> mountains start here
> just behind
> the closed eyes
> of a farmer's
> sons asleep
> in their work clothes.
> —Donald Justice

Reactions to the poem were immediate, intense, and diverse, reflecting outright glee, discovery, satisfaction—or dismay.

"Aha! I knew it was a poem!"

"Well. So that is a poem. But it made good prose, too. Only, well, subtle. And the way the poem looks might make it more difficult to read but doesn't necessarily have to, if we pay attention to the fact that the lines are parts of sentences."

"That wasn't too hard to understand. But why didn't Mr. Justice just write it the way *you* did? I can read sentences!"

"You expected us to compete with a true poet? Not fair!"

We considered the effect of the arrangement of words on the page, not just the words in relation to one another but, as one student succinctly put it, "in relation to the reader." Nothing for it, then, but to present my "arrangement" of two students' sentences paired in sequence.

> 1
> The flatlands
> of Kansas
> with its dry lands
> one can s e e f o r m i l e s
> 2
> I sure do wish we'd
> hurryandgetoutof Kan-
> sas!

Click! Typography—space, shape, and distribution—not only works for poets but can be *made* to work for us. Further, in these arrangements one student heard rhythm, another rhyme. "They were there all the time, but I missed them before!"

It was time to go fishing. Behind the eyes of those farmer's sons, of course.

Notes

1. Marianne Moore, "Poetry," in *A Little Treasury of Modern Poetry,* ed. Oscar Williams (New York: Charles Scribner's Sons, 1946), p. 311.

2. "Crossing Kansas by Train" by Donald Justice from *Selected Poems.* Copyrighted © 1961, 1962, 1963, 1964, 1965, 1967 by Donald Justice. Used by permission of Atheneum Publishers.

Disintegration

Peggy Ann Knapp

What happens when students are asked to destroy something they have created? Peggy Ann Knapp outlines a procedure that helps students develop critical observations about how an author creates a fictional world. Ms. Knapp sent this exercise from Carnegie-Mellon University, Pittsburgh, Pennsylvania.

Author's Comment

Those of us who teach freshman writing courses and are serious about it are always looking for assignments that will really create a link between the professional writing we discuss in class and the student writing we expect to improve during the term. The last thing to occur to freshmen is that they themselves can do something the novelist we are studying has done. I owe an exercise which addresses this problem to an art professor at Carnegie-Mellon University, where I teach. I think it might prove useful for others.

The Disintegration Exercise

Professor Herb Olds described process, disintegration, or metamorphosis series drawings in our faculty newspaper *Focus*. The idea of a disintegration series is to draw a simple object representationally and then to distort it in successive drawings according to some natural or mechanical process (e.g., wind, growth, erosion, etc.). Professor Olds says that if you tell students to create something, they think about the thing to be created, but if you tell them to destroy something, they think about the process. A pedagogical aim behind this assignment is to place process and not product at the center of the student's activity, although the product may, in fact, be very beautiful.

When I saw Professor Olds's discussion, I thought of a writing exercise to be designed for my current, rather talented, class of freshmen in a course called The Literary Imagination. We were reading Bernard

Malamud's novel *The Tenants,* in which direct, "realistic" writing is interspersed with some very ingenious fantasy sequences. Further, *The Tenants* is a book about writing a book, and the course is about writing and interpreting writing. The novel concerns Harry Lesser, the sole inhabitant of a fast-decaying tenement in New York, who has been working for nine years on his third novel when Willie Spearmint, who is black and also writing a book, sets up his "office" in one of the abandoned flats in his building. In an opening that is subdued and straightforward, and at the same time rich and arresting, Lesser "wakes to finish his book."

I asked my students, after they had read the novel completely, to write a paragraph which described *Willie* waking in *his* office/pad to write *his* book. Then I asked them to disintegrate their objective descriptions through three or four stages, until they saw the waking as a bizarre or fantastic event.

In making the assignment, I was hoping that the students would develop some critical observations about Malamud's fictional world and assess what sorts of actions and surroundings would harmonize with his vision. I wanted them, as well, to experiment with writing until they saw something of how they could convey the tone and style of Malamud's narrative. To this point the assignment was an exercise in literary analysis and stylistic imitation. But I also wanted them to feel and enjoy the process of destroying the neat, "realistic" description they had written. I wanted them to find out (and I wanted to find out myself) how the description of a fantastic or fantasized experience differs from an informational description. I wanted to give them a taste of the omnipotence a writer exerts over the universe he is creating in his fiction.

These critical objectives were served admirably. Every student's work demonstrated a clear insight into some facet of Malamud's world, and many descriptions were strikingly like his style (even the element of wordplay, so strong in *The Tenants,* but so difficult for younger students, was present in many). The process of disintegration, though, was even more interesting. Pulling an event out of its ordinary shape presupposes a theoretical or psychological principle beyond disinterested observation. Many students made use of the undercurrent of aggression, violence, and pressure in a closed system—New York, modern civilization, the dilapidated flat—which is apparent even in Malamud's quiet scenes. Others chose the sexual ambiance of *The Tenants* or of fantasy itself, as the principle of distortion. I would not want to suggest that such a principle was always consciously chosen, only that there was a direction, in each case, which could be readily isolated and discussed.

The assignment also produced some "sweet surprises" (Lesser's term). Although I had hoped that a general appreciation for Malamud's techniques would be developed, I was not ready for the sophistication with which students picked up his way of making metaphors and weighting them with significance. In one disintegration series the white daylight which woke Willie up burned through the haze and soot of New York, gently at first, and then more fiercely, until it became a flame destroying the obstacles to Willie's hopes. In another, the light stabbed Willie's eyes, at first the way it does everybody's in the morning, and gradually became a white hand stabbing with a white blade. The blanket became a metaphor of protection for some students, of escape for others. The typewriter gleamed at Willie more and more brightly in one student's series, inviting him to renew his true vocation and promising soon-to-be-acknowledged greatness. In another it moved closer and closer until it sat on Willie's stomach, constricting his breathing and keeping him prisoner. I was impressed with the grasp the students showed for the metaphoric way of creating meaning; one's assignments on interpreting Marlowe's or Yeats's images often elicit latter-day student allegory, or complete bewilderment.

Moving within Malamud's world, as it were, seemed to free my students from certain inhibitions in the use of language. A young woman who had been extremely shy in class and over-orderly in papers, unreservedly used blasphemy and scatology in imitation of Malamud's characters, thus freeing her language and expanding her range.

This class was about equally divided between black and white students, each group trying to be cautious and deferential toward the other. Our early discussions of *The Tenants,* an explosive novel, had expressed rather distantly the social issues and structural qualities of the book. The disintegration exercise allowed students to encode their own strong feelings in a seemingly oblique way and therefore gave many of them a means of expression they might not otherwise have found. There was, for example, a good deal of sympathy for Willie's point of view (which black students, especially, might not have wanted to express in their own voices), and a good deal of hostility toward Lesser and writing itself (which many probably thought would offend *me* if stated directly). These personal emotions were able to come out in the disintegration series because it was a fiction, and even to some extent *someone else's* fiction.

Malamud's book was a particularly good basis for using the disintegration series, but any novel which contains dream or fantasy sequences would do. (Or one might experiment with the technique when studying a particularly straightforward novel; my feeling was that Malamud's fantasies provided a kind of model.) The insights students achieve into the writer's world, his style of creating events, characters, and metaphors is only one strength of the exercise. The disintegration series also lets them use their own feelings to create something of their own, without demanding that they undertake the working-out of a whole fiction. They can see for themselves, with much less of the gloomy isolation that Lesser and Willie had to endure, what it is like to be a writer.

Willie Waking

The sun, knifing its way through one torn shade over the window, catches Willie momentarily in the eyes as he tries to gather the sparse blankets in the heatless tenement. No use. His morning breath vaporizes perfectly with the soot caught by the intruding sun. The Black, his eyes tumid, beats his head against Lesser's wall, as the writer, not without pleasure, looks on.

The Black, his eyes tumid, beats his head against Lesser's wall. The plaster cracks and portions fall to pieces on the floor. Lesser, with pleasure, looks on.

The Black beats his head fiercely against the wall as more plaster falls to the floor. His head and face are covered by white dust as Lesser looks on with pleasure. Willie is now completely covered by the white. He is white. Lesser, no longer laughing, realizes that Willie is white; he may write the novel Lesser could not.

The white White, his eyes tumid, red hair aflame, beats his head against his wall. As the writer, Willie, looks on, not without pleasure.

James Fletcher

Using *Working* to Teach Writing

Robert C. Rosen

In Studs Terkel's *Working,* real people talk about their professions and their attitudes toward work. Robert C. Rosen suggests that the text offers a multitude of possible writing assignments that relate closely to students' interests and needs, as well as to the traditional goals of composition and literature classes. Mr. Rosen teaches at William Patterson College, Wayne, New Jersey.

Author's Comment

I want to recommend Studs Terkel's *Working* as a reader in composition courses, especially with students who work while going to school. In the book, well over one hundred people—including, even, an English teacher—talk about their jobs; and their stories are vivid, moving, and often very funny. You should be able to find interviews in here to interest almost any group of students, and since the issues raised (money, authority, boredom, freedom, social mobility, sex roles, etc.) are central to most students' lives, you can count on lively class discussions and even some enthusiastic writing.

Approaches

Working provides ample material for the usual sorts of composition assignments. Pairing—to take but one example of many—Eric Nesterenko, the hockey player who loved the game as a boy but now hates it as a pro, with George Allen, the fanatically competitive pro football coach, makes for pointed comparison/contrast papers, on values and sports. For an exercise in generalizing, students can discuss five female workers Terkel groups together—a stewardess, airline reservationist, model, executive secretary, and hooker—and decide what things their work tends to have in common; the answers reveal much about the jobs and roles traditionally available to women. In another cluster of interviews, various workers—from spot welder to plant manager—describe the same workplace, an automobile plant, very differently; and this can be the basis of a lesson on fact vs. opinion and point of view (how the selection of facts shapes and is shaped by it), as well as of argument papers in which students defend the perspective of one of the employees.

Writing assignments can also draw directly on the students' own experience in working, whether full time, part time, summers, babysitting, around the home, or even just imagined (for the rare student who has never worked). The focus of a writing assignment on "the worst (or best) job I ever had" can be descriptive (what the experience was like), narrative (a typical day at work), or expository (how that workplace functioned). Students can also interview a parent, friend, or stranger about his or her job or, as a class, in a sort of press conference, interview one member of the class, a "volunteer." In either case, turning interview notes (or a tape) into a finished essay will provide practice in selection, organization, and the development of a thesis.

Except for Terkel's introduction, *Working* does not, of course, present students with models of excellent prose to learn from and imitate. For that you would need an additional book. *Working,* basically, is speech, transcribed and somewhat edited. But this itself can be very useful to help show students (and many do not really know it) how writing differs from speech. For a good exercise in revising, you can ask them to rewrite one of the interviews—focusing on organization as well as sentence structure—into a finished essay.

These are only a few of the ways to use *Working* in a composition course; reading through it will suggest many others. It is a very flexible book, in part simply because there are so many interviews to choose from. And the theme of work is a rich and interesting one (provided you don't overdo it). The teacher given to social criticism can ask students what the many unpleasant and unsatisfying jobs have in common; how much of that is inevitable and how much the result of the particular organization of American society; and finally how work (and society) might be restructured to make work more often a genuine pleasure (as it is for the stonemason, piano tuner, English teacher, and some others interviewed) and less often a meaningless, debilitating experience. You might bring in articles describing employee-owned and controlled workplaces (some do exist) and ask students to imagine how places they have worked might be run more democratically. The teacher eager to discuss literature can easily find poems, stories, and novels about work. And the teacher who wants to, or must, teach the research paper (where coming up with a topic is often the biggest problem for students) can ask the class as a group to define and focus problems as they come up in class discussions in order to create a list of possible topics. But whatever your approach, organizing a composition course at least partly around a theme, such as work, will enable students to see the need for increasingly complex forms of writing to express their increasingly complex understanding of what they write about.

Responding to Literature via Inquiry

Jerry L. Sullivan

Students often encounter difficulty in trying to phrase questions about the literature they read. Jerry L. Sullivan offers an intuitive/inquiry approach that fosters class discussion of literature, as well as the development of more meaningful written responses. Mr. Sullivan contributed this exercise from California State University in Long Beach.

Author's Comment

For the past few years I have been exclaiming that the question is more important than the answer—that if teachers work at teaching students how to pose the right questions about a piece of literature, they will elicit eager response from young readers, particularly adolescents. Teachers need to design questions that lead students to understanding and enjoying not only the poem or story itself but also questions that help them relate personally to the work being read and discussed.

The possibilities are endless and unpredictable, but that is what is so thrilling about literature. The thrill and excitement, however, may never arise if the questions posed in the attempt to teach literary appreciation do not probe the hearts and minds of readers, helping them realize that they and their problems are not new or unique. Young readers need to find out where they stand with others, with those they love and those who love them. In short, they need to learn where they fit in the immense design of things and literature teaches that. Very simply, by discussing stories and poems, listening and responding to peers, they begin to realize they are not alone in their joys, sorrows, hopes, and frustrations.

In a recently published textbook on teaching literature inductively [Jerry L. Sullivan and John Hurley, *Teaching Literature Inductively* (Anaheim, Calif.: Canterbury Press, 1982)], another writer and I outline a simple inquiry schema that deals with ways to design questions which lead to interpretation of a work under discussion (interpretive inquiry), ways to design questions that relate what is in the work to students in their own world (intellectual inquiry), and suggested activities (improvisational inquiry) that provide for creative entry to and/or creative exit from the study of a poem or a story—dramatic, role-playing activities, for the most part. In it we ask teachers to use the schema as a guide in preparing a poem or story for class discussion. The objective of the schema is to provide a general focus for teachers to consider in an effort to arrive at specific questions about the work that leap out at them in their analysis. This intuitive/inquiry approach is designed to trigger the kinds of questions that prompt instant, spontaneous response to the particular work. This method works very well for teachers, and teachers do indeed develop the kinds of questions which provoke eager response from young people in junior and senior high schools, even students in introductory literature courses in college.

Admittedly, getting young people to respond to literature is a difficult task, but responsive discussions are crucial to involve them deeply in reading. Response is the heart of the matter, so it is where teachers must begin. I decided to practice what I preach to teachers about the question being more enlightening than the answer and proceed to try the same idea on my students.

The Approach

In one group activity, students work together on an assigned poem, using only interpretive inquiry as a guide to help them arrive at specific questions they feel the poem yields:

Interpretive Inquiry

1. What questions of character does the work pose (archetypes, stereotypes, believable, unbelievable)?
2. What questions of setting does the work pose (realistic, fantastic, absurd)?
3. What technical questions does the work pose, i.e.
   A. Structure and form?
   B. Image and symbol?
   C. Theme?
   D. Language?

These interpretive questions are designed to arouse curiosity by moving the reader gradually from a simple to a complex discussion of meaning, or from a discussion of one meaning to a discussion of many. The questions serve as a starting point for reader immersion into the work, "gut" questions, if you will, that entice the reader to react at the physical level as well as the intellectual: What do you find in the work that moves you, puzzles you, turns you on or off? What does it say to you personally? Which technical questions seemingly apply—any, a few, all? What do they add up to? What does it all mean?

The group work, then, sets the stage for a short paper in which they study a poem, using as their guide these interpretive questions. I ask them to frame those questions which they feel will lead a fellow reader (perhaps an adolescent) to an acceptable interpretation of the poem. I then review their questions to see where they are going, sometimes suggesting revisions, additions, or deletions. Then I return the questions and ask them to write an interpretation, *answering their questions only,* in a tight, one-two page explication (the answer).

As you probably suspect by now, this assignment has turned out to be a fruitful one. For the most part, it works with a majority of the students, and they actually enjoy their own discoveries, pleased, in fact, that they can indeed work through the maze of a poem on their own and arrive at quite acceptable interpretations. But, even better, some papers challenge the more sophisticated, literary critics themselves, proving to me, at least, that we literature teachers do too much answering and interpreting in the classroom, doing what is legitimately the students' work. And we do it, I suppose, because we feel the students cannot. But in the process we impose upon the piece of literature too often our own narrow interpretations, our own answers, implying (students must take notes) that our version is the only interpretation.

Our task should be one in which we lead students to their own interpretations if we think we are ever going to instill a genuine inquisitiveness in them, something to serve them on their own when they leave the confines of our classrooms. We need only to set into operation the thrill of discovery in reading literary art and that thrill will manifest itself into acceptable interpretations that will result and grow with further reading. After all, our tasks should be ones in which we instill or arouse or implant curiosity about life and the human condition in hopes of setting into operation a kind of reading interest that generates its own momentum and serves the students once they leave our classrooms to enter their engineering, accounting, or nursing careers. I was amused by one student who closed her paper with this comment:

> By the way, I didn't know what the hell E.E. Cummings was talking about in "In-Just" until I finished answering all my questions.

Sample Paper

I wish to conclude with one example, a short paper written by a college freshman who is not majoring in a discipline offered by the School of Humanities. The poem is the well-known "Reflections on a Gift of Watermelon Pickle Received from a Friend Called Felicity" by John Tobias, and is quite available and commonly used with high school students. The paper has been slightly edited for style and grammar/mechanics purposes, but the content comprises the student's original work. One can quibble with various points of interpretation, I suppose, but one must admit that the questions are leading the student toward a relevant, viable meaning.

Poem: "Reflections on a Gift of Watermelon Pickle Received from a Friend Called Felicity" by John Tobias.

—Linda L. Shaheen,
Fall 1980

Questions

1. What does "When unicorns were still possible" mean?
2. What is meant by "the purpose of knees was to be skinned"?
3. What is "green lizard silence"?
4. What is meant by "the softening effects of civilization"?
5. What does the author mean in the second stanza and in the second line of the last stanza when he says that the summer maybe never was? Do you think that the summer he described actually took place? If not, what does it mean or symbolize?
6. What does the watermelon symbolize in the poem? What is the significance in the change in form from fresh watermelon to watermelon pickle?
7. What is the significance of the name, Felicity, the friend who gave the gift of watermelon pickle?
8. Why are the bites fewer now, each one "savored lingeringly, swallowed reluctantly"? What is meant by the contrast between limitless bites and careless gorging, and fewer bites?

9. What phases of life does this poem describe?

10. What imagery does this author use that creates vivid pictures or sensations for you? Do you think these are universal?

11. What form of verse does this poem take?

Answer

This poem seems to be a comment about childhood from the point of view of an adult who remembers the idealistic summer side of childhood. He reminisces about the time when unicorns were still possible, meaning a time when he could believe in magic. Essentially, it was an ideal world, a world in which dreams come true. The practical side of life—skinned knees, and hungers quickly felt and quickly forgotten—was taken for granted. It was a time when he lived a wild, enchanted life, like a lizard, hiding from the interference of parents and those who, misunderstanding the wild nature, try to tame and domesticate him or prepare him for their adult world.

By suggesting that the summer maybe never was, I think that the author is trying to say that the particular summer being talked about is only metaphorical. Though there could have been a summer like that— indeed there could have been many summers like that—it really is the idea of it, the mood of it that the author is reminded of. In fact, summer is a symbol of childhood. The watermelon symbolizes the abundance of time and leisure in childhood. The name of the friend, Felicity, also gives a clue about the nature of the gift of watermelon pickle. It is a gift of happy memories. The change from fresh watermelon to watermelon pickle represents the change from that real, exhilarating experience of childhood to the preserved form of the experience, the memories. Whereas once the bites were limitless, symbolizing, perhaps, the seeming eternity of life one faces as a child, now one takes fewer bites and savors them lingeringly, meaning that time is more precious now and one has to plan it wisely to get the most out of life. The reluctance to swallow symbolizes his reluctance to see the passage of each year.

Tobias uses a lot of imagery in the poem to create very clear pictures, even sensations for the reader. For example, "green lizard silence" and "straddling thick branches far above and away from the softening effects of civilization" create for me the image and mood of sitting hidden away up in a tree and being able to watch and do whatever I want without being observed. Also, I think just about everyone could practically taste the watermelon and feel it on their tongue when Tobias uses the description, "Thick pink . . . melting frigidly on sun-parched tongues dribbling from chins."

Tobias's use of free verse serves to convey the freeness of the mood. A more structured form of poetry might have detracted somewhat from the unbound sense of childhood.

Student Writing in the Foreground of a Literature Class

Eugene Smith

One problem that teachers in large literature classes share is finding ways to have students write frequently without overburdening the instructor with papers. To address this problem, Eugene Smith of the University of Washington in Seattle outlines a classroom management procedure calling for collaborative writing and peer review that can occur concurrently with the reading of literature.

Author's Comment

"Every English class is a writing class." So it has often been said, yet how many literature classes really bring student writing into the foreground, making it prominent throughout the quarter or semester and drawing on it frequently for classroom discussion?

Isn't it tempting for instructors, the de facto experts in literary matters, to grab the spotlight and precede students' writing with their own remarks? Don't students often feel that whatever they say about a literary work had better correspond fairly closely with what the instructor thinks? Doesn't writing that occurs after classroom discussion of a literary text has concluded seem not to be an intrinsic part of the brew of interpretation? Why should writing be left only for the late stages, presented primarily for evaluation and read only by the instructor?

In the many years that I have taught literature classes, I have felt an increasing disparity between the teaching of writing I was doing in "writing" courses and what I was accomplishing with students' writing when our focus was principally literary. The tug of precedent was strong to design the conventional end-of-quarter term paper and to have a mid-quarter and a final exam, but that precedent seems hard to defend.

Though journals, for students who were willing to commit themselves to them, did supplement those standard writing assignments, they have drawbacks for any explicit teaching of writing skills. Assigning more frequent short essays ("opinion papers," I once called them) seemed a possible solution. They allowed more frequent writing, at least, and probably seemed to students more like an invitation to state their own opinions about literary interpretation than does the conventional documented term paper. In classes of forty or more students, that many essays coming in three or four times during a quarter becomes an overwhelming task for careful reading and response.

Since I have now found a solution that comes close to being ideal, I offer it to high school and college English teachers who want to achieve the following:

> demonstrate to students that their ideas about literature will be taken seriously;
>
> integrate students' opinions about literary works with the instructor's and with those of other critics;
>
> engage students in frequent writing and revising;
>
> actively and explicitly teach skills of writing throughout the term;
>
> develop a classroom tone in which cooperation in literary inquiry is genuinely felt, where the instructor is guide rather than lecturer and holder of the last word;
>
> establish criteria and procedures for evaluation of student work that are perceptibly and genuinely related to students' performance in the course.

This plan will probably work best in a literature course based on the premises of what has come to be known as "reader-response criticism." These premises make each reader the formulator of responses that have potential validity and that deserve a hearing in class. They permit the inclusion of feelings about literature as well as the cerebration associated with *explication de texte*. They encourage variety in response, though they also require reasoned support for response.

My students found these premises, as they were later worked out in practice, to be almost opposite those they had experienced in many previous literature classes. Several found the new premises difficult to apply, suspecting a trap or simply being unable to shift away from the conventional "objective" literary analysis. And a few over-extended the seeming freedom implied by the premises, writing journal-like responses of dubious relevance, particularly to other readers. However, the prominence given to the importance of each reader's response seems critical to fully incorporating student writing into a course with a literature title.

The Approach

The plan needs to be introduced in the first two or three days of the course so that it quickly becomes an established part of class routine.

Fortunately, the procedural elements can be explained quickly, and students can readily understand what is expected of them. Only later do they realize the potential depth of their engagement with the literary texts and with their formulation of responses to them.

This is the essence of the scheme:

> The class (in my case, up to fifty students) will be divided into groups of about six each, the groups to be stable in membership throughout the quarter.
>
> One person in each group will write a two- to three-page response to the literary work assigned for study each week.
>
> All students in the class will write two such "mid-quarter responses."
>
> On a designated day, announced two or more weeks in advance, the students will read their responses to others in the group.
>
> The small group will use a guide sheet (Appendix 1) to focus its responses to the essay.
>
> The version read to the group is to be considered an early draft which will be revised, sometimes so extensively as to constitute a rewriting, after discussion by the small group.
>
> A more polished version, preferably typed, will be submitted to the instructor before class time of the day following the small-group reading and discussion.
>
> The instructor will read all the essays (only eight per week in a class of about fifty students) quickly before the next class session and will select one or more for discussion.
>
> The instructor will write extensive comments on each essay (preferably using an evaluation sheet containing class-developed criteria and evaluation scales, Appendix 2; for my explanation of this procedure, see "Evaluation of Writing with Semantic Differential Scales," ERIC 222 900), many of which deal with qualities of writing and will encourage revision before resubmission and reevaluation.

It is also important to know that these mid-quarter responses are written before any classroom discussion has begun about the literary text under study. They are therefore "uncontaminated" by opinions uttered in class (though small-group discussion may lead to productive shifts in a writer's initial literary interpretation).

By distributing a reading schedule, subject to minor revision, I establish the expectation that students will have completed the first reading of a book or story two or three days before discussion is to start. (Assuming that the amount of reading involved seems reasonable—up to about 150 pages of fiction a week—most students seem to stick to the schedule.)

Students must also know the importance placed on these mid-quarter responses in relation to overall evaluation of their performance. I state that the final grades will be determined according to these proportions: mid-quarter responses (grades based on final revisions), 40%; discussion participation (estimated both quantitatively and qualitatively), 20%; final examination (two questions calling for essay responses, to be written at home over approximately five days), 40%.

I offer now a more detailed explanation of the elements in this teaching plan.

Having a classroom with movable chairs is essential, both to make the small-group meetings (which occur usually once a week) physically possible and to allow a semicircular configuration on other days when I am the discussion leader. (Getting students to discuss in a productive way, with most people actively participating, when they see only one another's backs, is nearly impossible.) It is also important that students attend regularly since there will be few lecture notes to be transmitted. I tell them that regular attendance is a minimum requirement for credit in the course, explaining that I do not have arbitrary or punitive intentions but that they will not feel genuinely involved in the course unless they are there most of the time.

Dividing the class into groups *can* be arbitrary; however, I ask students on a questionnaire, distributed early in the course, whether they have preferences of certain literary texts scheduled for reading for their written responses. Where they do express such preferences, I form the groups so that they can be accommodated. Then, when class membership has stabilized after the first week or so, I make the assignments of texts and student writers for the rest of the quarter. Each student therefore knows several weeks in advance what text he or she will be writing about and when the first version of the response is due for small-group discussion.

By limiting the mid-quarter responses to two or three pages, I signal to students that they are not expected to produce full-blown term or research essays. They may use secondary critical sources if they wish, though I emphasize that the focus of the response must be their own original thought and feeling. They should not hesitate to use the word *I,* and they may include direct reference to their own experiences outside of but relevant to the literary text. What we want is a concise essay, sometimes in narrative form, that informs us how and why they responded to the text as they did. "This is the heart of the matter: You, as a unique reader of this text, have a unique response. What is it? Why is that response valid for you? What specific elements of the text and of your own experience give rise to that response?"

These preliminary instructions for formulating written responses become particularized and the variety they allow is revealed as we discuss students' essays. Typically, I duplicate all or parts of two or three essays during the first couple of weeks (with oral and written variations on this procedure later in the quarter) so that both ideas and writing techniques can be discussed with the whole class. My selections of essays to duplicate, usually anonymously, are based largely on a concern for demonstrating an array of possible interpretations and not so much on interpretations that seem fully worked out or that correspond to mine. Later in the quarter, after we have established a tone of trust and openness, I ask some students to read their essays orally, with discussion to follow.

At the first presentation of each written response in the small groups, I urge at least two readings, using my duplicated "Questions for Reader-Based Feedback to Mid-Quarter Responses" (Appendix 1) as a guide. These questions give some direction to the discussion and encourage more varied reactions than students typically give. The writers of each essay are sometimes directly engaged in the discussion but are often listeners rather than overt reactors. Their time for reaction comes after the full period of discussion when they set about revising their ideas and manner of expression in light of usually vigorous and often conflicting reactions. I consider this one of the crucial times for students' reflection on the effectiveness of what they have written. They can seldom avoid taking their peers' comments seriously. The potential strengths and the large and small flaws become matters for strenuous rewriting as they prepare the essay for sharing with the instructor and potentially with the whole class.

By asking that the next, more polished, version reach me at least two hours before the time of the next class, I have time to read each of the eight essays (or less, depending on class enrollment) and to select those that seem most useful for extending discussion. I look for ideas that I know will stimulate disagreement or that seem only partially thought through. Sometimes I even select the bland, conventional essay that seems very unexciting. In any case, I explain that the examples I present are not intended as models for the correct way to respond but as discussion starters. Usually, I can find at least a phrase in one of the essays that connects with one of my interpretations of the text. My purpose, after all, is not to efface myself or to pretend that I don't have ideas about the texts; it is to integrate those ideas as gracefully as possible with students' ideas, building a community of interpretation, not a consensus.

While class discussions led by me proceed, I respond in writing to each essay. Because I don't have essays from all the students, I do not feel the pressure of quantity. My comments, therefore, are quite detailed. I give suggestions for revision of content as well as technical matters, such as word choice, punctuation, and spelling. While I have not insisted on revision, I have announced a grading policy that allows for raising the grade if the essay is revised and improved. My returning the essays within a day or two, while we are still discussing the book about which students wrote, seems to preserve the momentum of desire to revise. As a consequence, many students have seized the opportunity, turning in a revised essay that is often more fully developed, more coherent, and freer of surface technical errors than was the earlier draft.

Involvement of students as a result of these procedures is perceptibly great. Nearly everyone in the class contributes orally, at least during small-group meetings. On any given class day when I am discussion leader, oral comments from fifty percent or more of the class are common. Such a high level of participation, when students perceive that it arises out of their own thoughtful written responses and when it often goes beyond what they originally wrote, gives the class an exuberance and a momentum that stimulates still further involvement. Many students have expressed to me their intense desire to continue revising their mid-quarter responses as they continuously raise their expectations about quality. Time to do the revising, rather than desire, seems to be the chief limiting factor for most.

When the end of the quarter comes and I read the take-home final examination responses, I have little cause to doubt the efficacy of the writing experiences that preceded. Because the questions offer latitude for varied response and invite imaginative approaches, I have no trouble in sustaining my attention to them. Some students are still plodding; some still write laboriously or irrelevantly. But on the whole, there is a level of engagement with literature and their reactions to it that seems to grow naturally out of the previous class work. Writing has become a satisfying way of shaping response to literature.

Appendix 1

Questions for Reader-Based Feedback to
Mid-Quarter Responses

(Adapted from Peter Elbow, *Writing with Power,*
Oxford University Press, 1981)

I. What was happening to you, moment by moment, as you were
reading/hearing the piece of writing?
   A. (after one or two paragraphs of the first reading)
      What was happening to you as you read this opening passage?
      Tell which words or phrases stuck out most or had resonance.
      What has this section just said? What do you now expect the
      whole piece to say?
      The writer has just been introduced to you. How was the intro-
      duction made? Formally? Casually? Intimately? Did the writer
      thrust out a hand for you to shake?
      At this early stage, are you more *with* or *against* the writer?
      Dragging your feet or helping pedal?
   B. (after the completed first reading)
      What is happening to you now? Changes in reaction or loyalty?
      What's the most important thing about the piece?
      Describe the way the writer ended the piece. As though the writer
      were ending a letter, saying good-bye, ending a telephone conver-
      sation? Did the writer hang up abruptly? Stand around on the
      porch unable to say good-bye? End with a sudden gush of warmth?
      Which aspect of *you* does the piece bring out? Your motherly or
      fatherly helpfulness?
      What kind of person has the writer turned out to be? How did
      the writer turn out differently from what you had first suspected?
      What do you like about the piece at this point?
II. Summarize the writing: give your understanding of what it says or
    what happened. (after a complete second reading)
      Summarize it. If you have difficulty, pretend you have only thirty
      seconds to tell a friend what this piece is saying. Tell the friend
      quickly and informally. Let the writer hear you fumbling to find
      the center of gravity.
      Then summarize it in one sentence.
      Then summarize it in one word, first one from the piece itself,
      then a word not in the piece.
      Summarize what you feel the writer is trying but not quite man-

aging to say. Where is the writing trying to go, perhaps against the writer's will?

Summarize what you *wish* it were saying.

III. Make up some images for the writing and the transaction it creates with readers. (after the summarizing responses)

What other pieces of writing does it remind you of? What *forms* of writing does it remind you of: a love letter? a federal inter-departmental memo? a late night diary entry?

Make up an image for the relationship between the writer and the reader. Does the writer seem to have an arm draped familiarly over your shoulder? Is the writer shouting from a cliff to a crowd below? Reading to you from a stage? Shaking a fist at you?

Describe the writer's relationship to the reader in terms of distance. Close? At arm's length? Distant? Describe changes that occur (e.g., "backing off toward the end").

Find words or metaphors for the voice or tone in the writing. Intimate? Shouting? Coy? Tight-lipped? Describe the voice in metaphors of color or of weather.

Look especially for changes in the voice. Perhaps it starts out stiff and loosens up. Where do you detect that change?

What images of the writer come to mind? Hunched over a desk? Sprawled on a couch? Sitting on a beach?

Who does the writing seem to address? Strangers? An old friend? Dumbbells? Tough guys? Is the writer talking *up* or *down*?

Appendix 2

Evaluation of Mid-Quarter Response Essay

Writer _____ Evaluator _____

Criteria	*Evaluative Scales*

FOCUS
Provides a focus on literary
interpretation

!____!____!____!____!
clear   ambiguous

SUPPORT
Develops support for assertions

!____!____!____!____!
specific   vague

!____!____!____!____!
convincing   unconvincing

!____!____!____!____!
thorough   absent

ORGANIZATION
Has pattern of organization

!____!____!____!____!
orderly   random

Flows through pattern

!____!____!____!____!
coherent   haphazard

VOICE
Maintains a consistent voice

!____!____!____!____!
distinctive   confused

Achieves harmony between
voice and message

!____!____!____!____!
congruent   conflicting

AUDIENCE
Addresses target audience

!____!____!____!____!
identifiable   obscure

FORMAT
Follows reasonable college
essay conventions

!____!____!____!____!
appropriate   distracting
conducive to
  ease of reading

COMMENTS:

V Language, Mechanics, and Style

Writers need a sensitivity to the words they use, the constructions they build, and the manner in which they arrange these things to bring meaning to readers. Word choice, denotation and connotation, the development of effective introductions and conclusions, the role of sentence structure and punctuation, the importance of tone—articles in this section provide ideas about how to engage students in writing activities that will highlight many of these areas.

Precision in Language Usage

Bruce W. Speck

Language must be used accurately if communication is to work effectively. By drawing upon analogies with other subject fields and by using inductive reasoning, Bruce W. Speck of the University of Nebraska, Lincoln, helps his students obtain a clearer sense of why precision in language usage is so helpful.

Author's Comment

How can the teacher of English impress upon students the need for precision in language usage? One could begin this endeavor with an appeal to rules about language. However, I have found it helpful to approach this issue by attempting to show students (1) that precision in language usage is not unique to the English classroom (most disciplines utilize a symbolic system that must be used accurately if one intends to communicate) and (2) that the richness of English vocabulary is not antithetical to a minimization of ambiguity. Thus, precision in language usage entails at least two essential elements: "correctness" or the grammatical relationship between words, and diction or the level of language acquisition one possesses.

The Approach

There are a number of allied fields that can be used to compare language to other symbol systems. I will cite three that have been helpful to my students. These are mathematics, music, and computer science. First, I turn to mathematics.

I put an equation on the board that looks something like this: $f(x) = 4b + 7y (9.6 + 3^2$. Then I ask the students if this is an acceptable equation. They generally find fault with my use of a single parenthesis. We don't know if the equation should read $(9.6) = 3^2$ or $(9.6 + 3^2)$ or $(9.6 + 3)^2$. We admit that this is ambiguous. I then point out the ambiguity in a sentence like: Leaping across the road we saw two deer. Point:

We need to be precise in language usage just as a mathematician needs to be precise in manipulating mathematical symbols.

Next, I turn to music, and draw this on the board:

The Problem

Is this the key signature for A-flat major, and thus a misprint, or is the C-flat an accidental? The first measure of music might answer the accidental question; however, it is important to note that if the C-flat is a misprint, the problem of reliability is at stake. What else is misprinted in this piece of music? The player (or the reader) is put in an awkward position when attempting to interpret such a score (piece of writing). The meaning of a string of symbols can be changed dramatically by the addition or deletion of a job or title. "Let's eat grandmother" is measurably different from "Let's eat, grandmother."

Computer science also offers an example of language precision. If you say to the computer the following:

Y = 1
X = 2
Z = Y + X
P = Z − M
PRINT P

the computer will not be able to ascribe a value to P because M has not been defined. This program will not run. Likewise, if you write, "The instructor showed us a seashell and explained how they live in them" what value do we assign to *they*? Have we been given a value for *they*?

After I have laid this groundwork for talking about "correctness," the next step is to show that precision is not merely a matter of observing grammatical relationship, but also consists of knowing the words that are available to accurately describe and classify the experiences and concepts one wants to communicate. Thus, the notion of grammatical precision is logically followed by a discussion of diction. And I am particularly focusing on the aspect of diction that pertains to the choices a writer or speaker makes when faced with a range of seemingly synonymous terms. How can these ideas be conveyed to the students?

A basic mental block students often have about diction goes under the rubric BIG Words. Whether one teaches writing or literature, it is not uncommon to hear students say, "Why does this author use such BIG Words?" or "Is it OK if I use BIG Words in my essay?" This view of vocabulary hinders the student from looking at words as possibilities, tools, for accurately constructing what the student wants to build in terms of communication. The problem, therefore, is that this whole notion of a BIG Word is used as a subterfuge that hides a need to become more proficient with language.

One way to approach this issue is to ask for a definition of a BIG Word. I do this in a back-door fashion, using the following approach: (1) I write ten words on the board and ask the students to define them. These words are: *antipodes, argot, clamber, hiatus, pique, aegis, lodestar, anima, penury, melee.* (2) I then ask how many defined all ten words. There is usually a ripple of laughter over such a question. A few students define one or two of the words per the dictionary. (3) I leave that exercise for a moment and ask the class to give me a definition of a BIG Word. How will I know one when I see it? I write their responses on the board. The responses usually go something like this: (a) a word used in a technical sense, (b) a word that is multisyllabic (three or more syllables), (c) a word that is not frequently used, etc. (4) I then take the list and apply it to the ten words the students attempted to define. Three of the ten words are three syllables long, but no word is over three syllables in length. True, some of the words (*argot, aegis, antipodes,* for instance) can be traced historically to demonstrate a technical base, but they are not generally used as technical terms today. Foreign words are considered BIG Words by some, but only those words that are not familiar to the individual are BIG Words. Is sombrero a BIG Word? Not if a person knows the word, but melee might be an unfamiliar word to many. (By the way, the whole notion of "common" words is only viable if one can use the scientific method to construct a list of words common to a particular population.) In short, most of the ten words don't meet the criteria established by the class. (5) What is a BIG Word? I suggest that a BIG Word is a word a person doesn't know. Once a word is integrated into one's vocabulary, the word is familiar. Certainly, we may use words to impress people because we are aware that by using these words we can have an influence on the way people view us. But the word used is not BIG to the one using it.

This approach to the concept of BIG Words is startling for some, but it helps students investigate a label that they may be using to keep them from admitting a need to learn more about language and increase their facility with language. Once this label is examined it is a relatively simple step to show that one reason an author chooses to use certain words is because some words are more precise than other words (given a certain context) even though these terms may be unfamiliar to the author's audience. For instance, red is a primary color with a particular brightness, hue, and saturation. We often use the word *red* to describe colors that may be more or less red, when we actually mean carmine or vermilion or ocher or madder or crimson or scarlet. We ought to say and write what we mean and we can only do so if we recognize that ambiguity unduly expands our meaning while our grasp of the language's vocabulary can narrow the meaning and give our speaking and writing more precision.

A final note. The second half of this exercise makes the teacher look pretty smart and can make the students feel inferior. Therefore, the teacher should make the students aware of the fact that we all know words that others don't know. If the teacher allows the students to write down five words that will be used to play Stump the Teacher, this exercise can also be an image builder for the students.

Using Astrology to Teach Connotation and Bias

Theresa Ammirati

Ellen Strenski

By selecting material for which most students share some common interest, Theresa Ammirati and Ellen Strenski have prepared a classroom exercise that develops students' ability to recognize the effects of connotation in writing. Ms. Ammirati and Ms. Strenski submitted this exercise from Mohegan Community College in Norwich, Connecticut.

Authors' Comment

Practice in recognizing bias is obviously an important part of any composition course. Recognizing bias in turn depends on the skill of recognizing the connotations of words, and identifying them within some range of alternatives. Such recognition does not happen automatically; it is developed with practice exercises. We need not labor the point that these are survival skills. But how to teach them without raising distracting issues of belief embedded in the examples under discussion? At the same time we need to find material for practice exercises that does interest everyone. One answer—astrology. This subject also lends itself well to reviewing other aspects of language use such as levels of generality, levels of diction, vocabulary, and outlining. Students are required to bring a dictionary.

Whether or not students believe the system doesn't matter. According to a recent Gallup Poll, nine out of ten people know their zodiacal signs. Everyone is amused by thinking about his or her personal traits, and most astrological signs provide a quantity of description to work with, beginning with adjectives, the easiest, and leading straightforwardly to sentences making claims.

The Approach

Begin by listing on the blackboard the traits of a particular sign. For instance, here is a description of Gemini's traits taken from *The Compleat Astrologer* (by Derk and Julia Parker, McGraw-Hill Book Co., 1971):

264

What kind of person is a Gemini?

adaptable

witty

versatile

intellectual

logical

busy

spontaneous

lively

talkative

amusing

curious

These traits obviously have good connotations. Now ask students to suggest as many equivalents as they can. For example:

adaptable	spineless, fickle, resilient, flexible
witty	flippant, sarcastic, sharp-tongued
versatile	superficial, wishy-washy, undependable
intellectual	egg-headed, brainy
logical	picky, nit-picking, analytical
busy	restless, scattered, workaholic, compulsive
spontaneous	off-the-wall, unpredictable, unstable
lively	frantic, manic
talkative	gossipy, a blabbermouth, a good conversationalist
amusing	funny, ridiculous, silly, laughable
curious	prying, cunning, snooping, inquisitive

You can use this list to define and demonstrate connotative meaning. The discussion can then include levels of generality by soliciting from students concrete examples to illustrate each abstract quality. At this point you can combine this lesson on connotation with instruction on levels of diction (slang, informal, formal, colloquial, etc.), asking students how they would choose among these synonyms volunteered by the class.

You can also review outlining by asking them to classify these traits (emotional, intellectual).

The next step is to give students handouts containing two or three clearly positive characteristics of each sign (which can be easily excerpted from a source like *Linda Goodman's Sun Signs,* Bantam Books, 1979) and ask them to come up with one neutral and one negative equivalent for each characteristic.

After examining connotations of single words, the next step is to examine their collective effect in sentences. Bring in the daily newspaper, and write up the astrological forecast for one of the signs, for example:

Get busy at duties that will clear the path to greater advancement.

Students will agree that this sounds good. Show them how to change the effect by replacing these words with alternatives having the same denotation but different connotations. "Get busy at duties" can become "Knuckle down to chores." "Take care of your health" turns into "Pamper your hypochondria." On a blackboard you can fill in columns under individual words or phrases:

Be loyal to	a friend	who has done favors
Stick up for	an associate	delivered pay-offs
Testify on behalf of	a colleague	gone out of his way
Give a reference for	a pal	stuck up
Tell lies for	a buddy	benefited
Defend	one of the gang	thrown business your way

With this preparation, students are now ready to practice these procedures in small groups, working on another handout with one day's complete astrological forecast. This step generates useful alternatives for class discussion. For homework, you can assign students a comparable exercise; that is, to consult the next daily papers for their own astrological forecast and to create as many variants with different connotations, in column form, to hand in, as they can. Or you can expand this lesson and the following assignment to include levels of generality (general to specific; abstract vs. concrete) and work with the forecasts (which are always general and abstract) to make them specific and concrete. "Figure out a way to have added income in the future" could be anything from "Learn

how to crack a bank safe" to "Take an evening course in accounting."
"Take care not to irk those who dwell with you" could be "Remember to
clean up your room as you promised your mother."

This lesson sequence moves easily on to a number of possible topics,
among them: propaganda analysis (especially "Glittering Generalities"),
public doublespeak in ads, or even literary imagery.

Writing on a User-Friendly Topic: Language

Chris Hall

Drawing upon basic linguistic principles, Chris Hall involves his students in activities which provide opportunities for genuine investigation of language and result in a variety of written responses. Mr. Hall teaches at the University of New Mexico, Albuquerque.

Author's Comment

Many composition programs have turned to everyday language as a general subject for writing because it is immediately accessible to students. Unfortunately, I have discovered that, for many students, language is viewed as an enemy to be conquered and subjugated to pass a writing class and not as a subject that they know intimately. Students, therefore, need to be instilled with a sense of authority about their language. One way of addressing this problem is helping students realize that they possess a body of information about everyday language interesting to other people, and that they are capable of evaluating that information. Coming from a linguistic background, I subsequently have concocted two methods for eliciting written responses from students that have them genuinely investigating their language and generating topics for which they are knowledgeable authorities.

In the first method, students become aware of the unique vocabulary of speech communities. They collect and analyze words from their own peer groups or other groups of speakers. From this initial exercise, they write extended definitions for an outside audience. While teaching them to use a valuable writing strategy is one important feature of this method, there is an even more important benefit—they are writing from an authoritative position about the subject of language. This offers them the challenge of presenting their topics in such a way that an unknowledgeable audience can understand them. In a sense, real communication is the object of this approach. The second method is suggested from William Morris's "The Making of a Dictionary" (In *Words and the Writer,* Michael J. Hogan, editor, Scott, Foresman and Company, 1983). Morris describes

268

the *American Heritage Dictionary's* Usage Panel (composed of eminent writers, editors, and public figures) which provides guidelines for word usage. As he comments, "Not surprisingly, there is nothing like unanimity in the replies of the panelists" (p. 45). Since these authorities on words often cannot agree on the proper and improper usages of words, I thought it might be interesting to see how students would respond if they were called upon to be usage panelists and then have them write up their conclusions in reports.

Method 1

The first exercise and writing assignment needs to be introduced carefully so that students realize that they, like other groups of people, represent a unique group with interesting language characteristics. I usually start out by giving them examples of slang, argot, or cant from groups of people they know of or are familiar with. For instance, I have used groups of words from American Yiddish culled from Leo Rosten's *The Joys of Yiddish.* Many students have heard words like *shlep, shtik, chutzpa,* or the taboo word *shmuck,* but they do not always associate them with a particular group of people. Some of them are surprised to learn that these words come originally from the Yiddish-speaking Jewish communities and have since become an integral part of American English vocabulary. This gets them thinking about the origins of words and the groups that use them.

Each group of words is presented by explaining the group that uses them, the derivative forms and meanings, and by illustrating their uses. The goal of this introduction is to get students thinking about what makes words interesting to study, what makes them unique.

Finding useful examples is not usually a problem. There are many dictionaries and books on the subjects of slang and argot. I have used words from the *Dictionary of American Slang,* edited by Harold Wentworth and Stuart B. Flexner; *The Underground Dictionary* by Eugene E. Lindy; *The Totally Awesome Val Guide* by Jodie Ann Posserello; *Buzzwords: The Official MBA Dictionary* by Jim Fisk and Robert Barron; and the delightful *Poplollies and Bellibones: A Celebration of Lost Words* by Susan Katz Sperling.

After this introduction, I ask them to collect words and phrases from their own peer groups or other groups of speakers. They are instructed to collect about five examples and analyze them using these questions:

1. What does the word mean? What are its denotative and connotative meanings?

2. Which group of speakers uses this word? Is it used in a special part of the country?
3. What derivative forms does it have? Can it be used as a noun, verb, etc.?
4. How would one use this word in a conversation? Can you give an illustration?

After they have collected their data, we discuss their findings. Often, when discussing the connotative meanings of their words, they discover that their words need careful usage. I therefore introduce the purpose of extended definition to clarify an unfamiliar concept embodied in a word. I then discuss several techniques of definition—by negation, classification, illustration, or synonym. At this point I usually give them an extended definition model, constructed from one of my earlier example words. Next, I ask them to select one of their own words and write an extended definition, usually giving them several days to compose their papers. Before they turn in their papers, however, I have them break into groups and have their peers evaluate the content of the definitions and suggest ways of improving the paper's presentation. These peer groups use the original questions for collecting the words as guidelines for the evaluation. Finally, after the papers are handed in, I select certain papers to be typed and distributed to the entire class as examples of effective definitions for an unknowledgeable audience.

Method 2

The next exercise and writing assignment gives students a chance to critically evaluate the ways words are used in their language. In my class I have the students read William Morris's article (mentioned before). However, reading the article is not absolutely necessary. What is important, though, is explaining the purpose of *AHD*'s Usage Panel and giving examples of the comments of panelists taken from the article. Many of the comments that Morris has collected demonstrate a wide range of attitudes about word usage. During the discussion of these comments, students realize that even people who know how to use words effectively can be irreverent, petty, and pompous about what is proper usage.

> *Myself,* as in "He invited Mary and myself" and "Neither Mr. Jones nor myself is in favor of this."—Panel Verdict: Yes 5%, No 95%.
> "No, no—a genteelism."—Malcolm Cowley
> "Prissy evasion of me and I."—Gilbert Highet
> "Unforgivable. Myself is the refuge of idiots taught early that me is a dirty word."—Walter W. [Red] Smith (from William Morris's "The Making of a Dictionary," p. 46)

After the discussion, I tell the students that they are going to be usage panelists. I break them into small groups and give them a list of words and examples of their usage. I try to organize this list around certain types of words. For example, I might give them noun phrases that have been turned into verb phrases:

> Neutron Bomb, as in "The European Braces Conglomerate recently neutron bombed the American suspenders industry, leaving the factories intact, but destroying the companies' presidents and boards of trustees."

> Apple Polish, as in "Albert Shleger apple polished the teacher so much he got an 'A' for Health Science."

Other types of lists might include examples from the argot of computer specialists:

> Interface, as in "Hey, before you punch my headlights out, let's interface on this problem between us."

> User Friendly, as in "I hope that new Algebra teacher is user friendly."

After the list is handed out, the groups of panelists are instructed to vote on the appropriateness or inappropriateness of each illustration and to write comments, similar to the example comments. From each group's findings, several writing assignments can be constructed. The one I favor requires each group of panelists to write a collaborative report on the findings, using the votes and comments as supporting details. Some teachers may want each student to write an individual report. The reports are then collected. I usually type example reports for distribution to the entire class. These reports make interesting topics of discussion because, as Morris has already pointed out, not everyone is going to agree with the findings.

Conclusion

Both these methods represent a way of stimulating students to think and write about language. The writing assignments that evolve from the introductory exercise are definitely goal oriented towards specific writing needs. In the first method, students come to appreciate the relation between an audience and a subject when writing extended definitions; in the second method, they learn the value of supportive details for making conclusions. Of even greater benefit, though, is the realization students make that they have at their disposal a body of information on language that can be turned into interesting writing topics.

An Action-Learning Approach to Reading, Grammar, and Punctuation

R. Baird Shuman

Students who do not read well often have difficulty with basic concepts of sentence structure and punctuation in their writing. R. Baird Shuman suggests a visual and active way of helping students discover some basic principles underlying such concepts. Mr. Shuman contributed this exercise from the University of Illinois at Urbana-Champaign.

Author's Comment

The teacher working with youngsters who have reading disabilities generally finds that these students have problems as well with grammar—in this case defined as the function and structure of language—and punctuation. Many students with reading problems have short attention spans and are easily bored by any activity which involves their sitting and reacting passively within the learning situation. Discipline problems are common in such groups of students, and these problems are often of such magnitude that more time is spent dealing with them than is spent teaching.

In working with hundreds of such students, I have found that cogent lessons in reading can be taught in a very active and interesting way. I have found as well that valuable lessons in grammar and punctuation are spin-offs of the activity.

Since I often work in demonstration situations with groups of students I have not seen before, I usually devise materials drawn from textbooks that those students are using in their content area classes. I begin with easy sentences and work toward more complicated ones. Using cardboard placards, I write each word in a given sentence on a separate card, using a magic marker. I also place such punctuation marks as periods, question marks, commas, and semicolons on separate cards, generally using different colors for each. On other cards, I write words like "however," "moreover," "nevertheless," and "therefore." All of these words are written in the same color but in a color different from that used in writing the basic words of the sentence. On still another set of cards, I write words like "did," "does," and "will." These cards are done in the same color ink used for the question mark.

Working recently with a group of tenth graders who were studying forestry, I turned to their textbook, *Manual of Southern Forestry* by Howard E. Weaver and David A. Anderson. I had made cards for the following words: *considerable, of, involves, production, the, timber, time.* I announced, "I need seven students to make a sentence." Students, although they did not know me well, volunteered immediately. I gave each one a placard and said, "Okay, make yourselves into a sentence."

The students scrambled around trying to find mates. The simple determiner *the* latched onto *timber,* then onto *time,* and finally onto *production.* Students in their seats cheered and gave all sorts of advice. Someone said, "The sentence probably begins with *the,*" a rather astute observation. I had purposely lettered the cards wholly in capital letters so that no clues would be given about the placement of any word at the beginning of the sentence. One student perceived that *production of timber* probably had to go together. I vounteered, "If you really think so, *production* and *timber* had better grab *of* so that she won't get away."

In about three or four minutes of very intense languaging, participated in by the entire class, some severely handicapped readers were able to construct the sentence, "The production of timber involves considerable time," which appeared on page 147 of their forestry textbook. I then asked who wanted to be a mark of punctuation and if so, which mark of punctuation the student wanted to be. A hulking football player volunteered to be a period and to put himself at the end of the sentence.

Then I handed *moreover* to a girl in the back of the class and said, "Break into the sentence whenever you can." She positioned herself at the very beginning; and I invited someone to become a punctuation mark. A five-foot-seven comma inserted himself between *moreover* and *the.* Then someone asked, "Can't *moreover* go between *timber* and *involves?*" I let the class discuss this and the decision was that *moreover* could go either there, provided another comma were inserted, or at the end of the sentence. This led to a discussion of style. The class, with no goading from me, concluded that if *moreover* comes at the beginning of a sentence, it must be connecting the sentence with some meaning that has come before.

At this point, I asked for a definition of *moreover* and found that no one could define the word explicitly, so we looked it up in the dictionary. Denis Rodgers ("Which Connectives? Signals to Enhance Comprehension," *Journal of Reading,* 17 [1974]) has presented convincing evidence that students who do not understand the meaning and uses of connectives are likely to find this an impediment to their reading, so we emphasized quite fully the definition and variety of uses of each connective we used in building our sentences.

I then asked the punctuation marks and the *moreover* to sit down and I gave one student *does* and another student a question mark of the same color. The students soon found that the transformation from an affirmative statement to a question in a sentence like this is a fairly simple matter, but that the sentence will not work unless *involves* holds his hand over the final letter.

Students wanted this activity to last the whole period every day. I had virtually 100% participation, much of it from students who had been officially designated non-readers. I usually limited the activity to twenty minutes, drawing upon it at some point in the class hour during which attention seemed to be flagging.

As the week wore on, we worked toward progressively more difficult sentences taken from the textbook. One sentence presented a unique challenge, but the students unraveled the stylistic mystery it presented and reproduced the sentence, which actually appeared on page 22 of their textbook. The words composing the sentence were *and, are, beneficial, both, forest, in, influences, nature, physical, social.* The sentence, arrived at after much discussion and negotiation, was "Beneficial forest influences are both physical and social in nature."

One day, in order to teach yet another concept and to involve the students in a writing activity, I printed words like "after," "when," and "if" on cards. Working with the base sentence, "Chemicals are relatively new in farming," we tried to impose a subordinating conjunction upon the sentence. Students were surprised to find that what had been a perfectly acceptable and understandable English sentence became, with the addition of one small word and without the omission of a single word, a non-sentence. I asked the class why the word group "If chemicals are relatively new in farming" did not constitute a sentence? One student said, "Because it doesn't go anywhere." I asked what she meant. She paused and another student volunteered, "Well, it just kinda hangs there." I asked, "How can you make it a sentence?" She responded, "Get rid of the *if*." I retorted, "That's the coward's way. Who can give me the hero's way?" Another student said, "You need to say something more, to give more facts." I agreed and said, "Let's each write at least five endings to 'If chemicals are relatively new in farming' so that we have five good solid sentences." Although I had never mentioned the word *subordination* or the term *subordinating conjunction,* every student in the class had imbibed the essence of this concept which many English teachers find very difficult to teach. We later made some complex sentences, color coding the subordinate and independent clauses and imposing the necessary comma upon each one. Through this exercise the youngsters learned that the subordinating conjunction, which I still had not identified by name, can turn any independent clause (we termed it, "complete sentence") into a subordinate clause (we termed it, "A group of words that needs to be completed").

The students involved in this activity began to forget and overcome many of their language disabilities and inhibitions. They began to react to language in a positive way which involved them physically as well as mentally. Many of the students turned this activity into a game that they played at home. Perhaps the best homework is that which is not assigned. It appears that many of the most important language skills as well as many of the more complicated aspects of transformational grammar can be taught by involving students actively and physically in the construction of a broad variety of sentences.

Grammar Recharted: Sentence Analysis for Writing

Anne J. Herrington

To show students that knowing grammatical patterns is helpful in writing, Anne J. Herrington has devised an approach that heightens students' awareness of syntax. Ms. Herrington submitted this assignment while at Johnson State College in Vermont.

Author's Comment

Most of the students I teach have no sense of syntax; they write fragments, run-ons, and awkwardly phrased sentences. They do not perceive that words in a sentence function together in certain predictable ways. To them, grammar means arbitrarily prescribed rules and endless exercises. This is in part because grammar instruction has been separated from writing instruction. These students must be shown that grammar is a helpful tool for describing the way sentences work, and that knowledge of grammatical patterns is useful when writing. To develop this understanding to the point where students apply it in their writing, the teacher has certain options. Rules can be prescribed (many of which the students can already parrot verbatim). Grammar exercises can be assigned. Or, the teacher can try to individualize grammar instruction by commenting on the specific errors of each student as they arise. The latter approach seemed best to me, but I soon became aware that it was not enough. Although it corrected specific errors, it did not encourage an awareness of syntax and the functioning parts of a sentence. To achieve this end, one needs an approach which does not become an end in itself, but which supplements writing and can be used to describe each student's writing. (See Chart 1.)

Grammar Charted

The five-column sentence pattern chart was the means I chose to give students this awareness of syntax. Although it was originally designed to analyze style, it is also useful for grammar instruction.[1]

Chart 1

Preceding Subject (1)	Subject (2)	Between Subject and Verb (3)	Verb (4)	Following Verb (5)
Although it was originally designed to analyze style,	it		is	also useful for grammar instruction.

It does not require students to learn all of the jargon associated with most grammar instruction. It is linear; the sentence is charted in exactly the same sequence in which it was written. It is an analytical tool which shows the way words, phrases, and clauses function in a sentence. Using it, the teacher can illustrate various sentence models, and the students can analyze the way their own sentences are patterned.

Before I present the chart to the class, I try to get them to develop working criteria for a sentence. By comparing the following word strings, they quickly agree that a sentence is an ordered string of words:

> to went the concert man the
> the man went to the concert

Someone will add that the sentence must have a subject and a verb. Another may add that it must be a complete thought. At this point, I leave these three catch-all terms undefined. I put "pigs eat" on the board and ask if it is a sentence. Most agree that it is and that it fits the criteria. I then add the word "when" to form "when pigs eat" and ask if this is a sentence. Most sense that it is not, but agree that it does meet the criteria of being an ordered string with a subject and verb. This gives me the chance to introduce the added sentence criterion of the independent clause. The addition of "when" creates a dependence which the students sense as the thought not being complete. It is not enough to have a subject and verb; the two must exist free from dependency words.

At this point, I introduce the chart to the class as an alternate way of explaining the functioning of sentences. I have the class work out how to chart "Pigs eat." I then make the stipulation that only the subject and verb of independent clauses can be charted in columns 2 and 4. Thus, one has:

Chart 2

Preceding Subject (1)	Subject (2)	Between Subject and Verb (3)	Verb (4)	Following Verb (5)
	Pigs		eat.	
When pigs eat,	they		snort.	

Using the simple sentence "Pigs eat," I gradually lay on modifiers, all the while stressing that it is just the combination of the two words "pigs eat" that makes the string a sentence:

Chart 3

Preceding Subject (1)	Subject (2)	Between Subject and Verb (3)	Verb (4)	Following Verb (5)
	Pigs		eat	garbage.
	The fat, dirty pigs		eat	ravenously the garbage.
After they wallow in the mud,	the fat, dirty pigs	who are being fattened for market	eat	ravenously the greasy garbage.

In the seeming complexity, there is simplicity once one can begin to see the pattern. The independent clause, subject and verb, the sentence core, remain unchanged.

The above expansion shows how dependent clauses, such as subordinate and relative clauses, are charted in their entirety in columns 1, 3, and 5, the modifier columns. Subordinate conjunctions like "after" and "when" and relative clauses like "that" and "who" tie together clusters of words with a single function. This is one of the most difficult concepts for my students to grasp because they have been conditioned to think in terms of labels for isolated words such as subject, verb, and preposition. They have little sense of words functioning together in phrases. Thus, "after they wallow in the mud" can be a sentence since it has a subject and verb. Once they begin to see the way "after" affects the entire cluster, they will begin to manipulate syntax more successfully. Since the chart does not break up dependent clauses and does not chart them across the columns, it visually underscores the differences between dependent and independent clauses.

The chart also graphically shows the way simple sentences are combined to form compound or complex sentences. In *Ways of Writing,* William Irmscher uses the following two sentences:

> He followed the directions carelessly.
> He ended up far from his destination.

to illustrate how compounding and subordinating show different causal relationships.[2] I give these two sentences to the students and ask them to combine the two into one sentence at least eight different ways. After they have done this, I ask them to chart each variation. This gives me the opportunity to see whether the students understand the principle of dependency and whether they recognize the subject and verb of independent clauses.

In class, we discuss the variations, the different emphasis each conveys, and the way each functions as a sentence. In Chart 4, I have charted some of the variations. The compound sentence is the simplest. I ask for at least one sentence using "followed" as the verb of the independent clause (D). I also ask the class to create at least one sentence which uses a relative clause in column 3—Between Subject and Verb (G). Variation H introduces a new verb.

The chart is also a useful tool to analyze non-grammatical sentences. Most student writings are dittoed and discussed in class. Whenever a student questions the syntax of a sentence or I question it, I put the five columns on the board and ask someone to analyze the sentence by telling me how to chart it. It is the class's responsibility to decide how; I just write and erase at their direction.

In Chart 4 examples I–L, I have charted a few sentences from my students which are representative of common sentence errors.

When trying to explain the first sentence (I), most students can easily see that "calmness" is the subject. But someone may try to put "that" in column 3 and "is" in the verb column. If so, I will question the class as to the function of "that." With some prodding, I will get them to see that "that" introduces a dependent clause with "is" as the verb of the clause. Once this dependent clause is charted correctly, it becomes clear that there is no verb for "calmness," and thus no sentence.

The second example (J) represents a common pattern. Many will want to chart "clouds" as the subject because it is what the sentence is about. In their mind, "there" cannot function in the subject slot because it is not

Chart 4

Preceding Subject (1)	Subject (2)	Between Subject and Verb (3)	Verb (4)	Following Verb (5)
A therefore,	He he		followed ended up	the directions carelessly; far from his destination.
B	He		followed ended up	the directions carelessly and far from his destination.
C	He		ended up	far from his destination because he followed the directions carelessly.
D	He		followed	the directions carelessly which made him end up far from his destination.
E After he followed the directions carelessly,	he		ended up	far from his destination.
F Following the directions carelessly,	he		ended up	far from his destination.

G	He	who followed the directions carelessly	ended up	far from his destination.
H	Following the directions	carelessly	brought	him far from his destination.
I	*The calmness	that is not disturbing.		
J	There		are	dark clouds beginning to gather overhead. *Bringing the smell of rain.
K	*Heavy gray clouds		covering	the sky like a blanket.
L *Revision*	Heavy gray clouds	covering the sky like a blanket	warn	of rain.

a person, place, or thing. The chart encourages the students to recognize that "there" is functioning as the subject since "there are" has no function alone in column 1. Once the first sentence has been charted correctly, it is easier to see that *"Bringing the smell of rain." functions just like "beginning to gather overhead." Both are modifiers which belong in column 5. Using the chart, I have yet to have a student find a satisfactory way to explain a fragment like *"Bringing the smell of rain."

It is also common for my students to try to use participles as verbs. They will try to chart the third example (K) with "covering" as the verb. To challenge this, I use the "I swimming" example. They can hear that "swimming" does not function as a verb. They would not say *"I swimming." but would say "I swim" or "I am swimming." Likewise, one says "I cover" or "I am covering." Once "covering" is rejected as the verb, the class can be led to see that the phrase "covering the sky like a blanket" described "clouds." It functions in column 3, and an independent clause verb needs to be added (L Revision). Someone may also suggest that another way to revise the sentence is to change "covering" to "cover" so that it functions as the verb.

The chart helps explain the formation of participles. If one has two sentences with common subjects, they can then be combined as in Chart 5.

Chart 5

Preceding Subject (1)	Subject (2)	Between Subject and Verb (3)	Verb (4)	Following Verb (5)
A	I		glanced	out the window.
B	I		could see	the mountains creep up from the valleys.
Glancing out the window,	I		could see	the mountains creep up from the valleys.

If there is not a common subject, the two sentences cannot be combined in this manner since the result would be nonsense. Thus, the student sentence "Glancing out the window, the mountains seemed to creep up from the valleys," can be broken apart to show that one is saying:

Chart 6

Preceding Subject (1)	Subject (2)	Between Subject and Verb (3)	Verb (4)	Following Verb (5)
	The mountains		seemed	to creep up from the valleys.
	*The mountains		glanced	out the window.

The five-column chart can also be used to complement style imitations. In the November 1973 *College English*, Phyllis Brooks suggests *persona paraphrase* as a way to understand sentence patterns and the effect of these patterns on the reader.[3] We have adopted her method, using a paragraph of simple sentences from Hemingway's *A Farewell to Arms*, a Twain passage from *Life on the Mississippi* which uses more compound and complex sentences, and a Faulkner passage with many column 3 intrusions between subject and verb. The student is to try to imitate the style of each—phrase by phrase. The chart aids in this imitation by graphically showing the pattern of each passage and the differences between patterns.

Chart 7 shows the first sentence of each passage with a student imitation. The first Hemingway imitation fails to imitate the three-verb pattern of the original. In the Twain imitation, the student had to discern the implied verb in the second clause in order to imitate the sentence correctly. When imitating this passage, most students sense the way Twain varies rhythm by his choice of balanced clauses and long and short word strings. Almost everyone recoils against the Faulkner passage, which is the tortuous beginning to "Barn Burning." Once the first sentence is charted in comparison with a Hemingway or Twain sentence, students can articulate the difference their ears heard. Faulkner rudely intrudes long phrases between the subject and verb. The imitation, using a shorter phrase, mimics this pattern accurately. The imitations are useful because they introduce various models to the students. By trying to imitate each, the student has a heightened consciousness of style and his or her own style.

Chart 7

Preceding Subject (1)	Subject (2)	Between Subject and Verb (3)	Verb (4)	Following Verb (5)
Hemingway	He		had	gray moustaches,
			wore	a doorman's cap, and
			was	in his shirt sleeves.
Imitation	*He		wore	a black beard, with a sailor's hat, and
			was	in his dirty trousers.
				—Ann King

(Chart 7 continued)

Preceding Subject (1)	Subject (2)	Between Subject and Verb (3)	Verb (4)	Following Verb (5)
	He		had wore was	a blond beard, a blue suit, and in a winter coat. —Steve Long
Twain Once a day, and	a cheap, gaudy packet another		arrived ( )	upward from St. Louis downward from Keokuk.
Imitation Once a week and	a shiny, large space ship another		arrived ( )	down from Venus, up from earth. —Ann King
Faulkner	The store	in which the Justice of the Peace's court was sitting	smelled	of cheese.
Imitation	The jetty	on which the seagulls roosted	smelled	of dead fish. —Wanda Guptill

The logical step after this is for the students to analyze their own style in a few passages. Chart 8 illustrates passages from two students. Written as a prose passage, the first sounded very descriptive to most students. When the author charted it, however, she discovered a string of weak core subjects and verbs: there was, it was, there was. In contrast, the second passage shows more interesting verbs and more variation in sentence pattern. In each case, the chart revealed the patterns to the student so that she could analyze them, draw some conclusions, and revise for style if she chose. At this point, it is not necessarily a matter of right or wrong; it is a matter of choice, the writer's choice.

The preceding is just a sampling of the various ways in which this simple chart can be used. The more I use the chart, the more satisfied I become with it. My students find it a fresh, logical way of explaining written language. A junior math major who is in my class this semester told me that this is the first time that grammar has made sense to him.

My students do not get the charted examples included in this article. All they get is a blank chart on the chalkboard and, I admit, a slightly heavy-handed discussion leader. It is their job to fill in the chart, to make the decisions, to discern the patterns. These students are the products of tree diagrams which distort syntax and of definitions of two kinds of words out of any context: nouns and verbs. These definitions can be recited upon demand, but they really have little use to a person when

Chart 8

Student Samples

> And as I sat in the small room, there was only the single light of one burning candle. Although the room was dark, it was warm. All around there was absolute silence. Only the moaning of the gentle breeze and the roaring of the distant furnaces broke the quietness.
>
> Barbara Judd

> Looking like a rounded egg and waddling slowly towards her desk, the librarian lifts her weight carefully and deposits it into a small chair. For a moment, her attention is averted to a student asking for a book. In reply her words slowly but nasally flow out of her mouth as her delayed gestures attempt to make a point.
>
> Kathy McLelland

Preceding Subject (1)	Subject (2)	Between Subject and Verb (3)	Verb (4)	Following Verb (5)
And as I sat in the small room,	there		was	only the single light of the burning candle.

(Chart 8 continued)

Preceding Subject (1)	Subject (2)	Between Subject and Verb (3)	Verb (4)	Following Verb (5)
Although the room was dark,	it		was	warm.
All around	there		was	absolute silence.
Only	the moaning of the gentle breeze and the roaring of the distant furnaces		broke	the quietness.
Looking like a rounded egg and waddling slowly towards her desk,	the librarian		lifts deposits	her weight carefully and it into a small chair.
For a moment,	her attention		is averted	to a student asking for a book.
In reply	her words	slowly but nasally	flow	out of her mouth as her delayed gestures attempt to make a point.

writing. It becomes the class's responsibility to develop new working criteria which apply to the way their sentences function. The five-column chart reveals how sentences work so they can begin inductively to generate these criteria. Most students then have the tools to understand the pattern of their sentences and to manipulate the syntax as they choose. For many, grammar is then no longer just right or wrong; it involves choices which reflect one's personal style.

Notes

1. Virginia P. Clark, "The Syntax of John Berryman's *Homage to Mistress Bradstreet,*" Diss. University of Connecticut, 1968. The grammar instruction methods explained in this aticle were developed by the author and her Johnson colleagues, Peter Eddy, Joyce Hundley, and Ann Turkle.

2. William Irmscher, *Ways of Writing* (New York: McGraw-Hill Book Co., 1969), p. 154.

3. Phyllis Brooks, "Mimesis: Grammar and the Echoing Voice," *College English,* 35 (1973), pp. 161–168.

Make Your Students See Red:
A Lesson on the Topic Sentence

Tahita Fulkerson

Students often forget the function of a topic sentence. Tahita Fulkerson describes a classroom technique she uses to help students rediscover that function. Ms. Fulkerson is at Tarrant County Junior College, Northwest Campus, Fort Worth, Texas.

Author's Comment

To highlight a lesson on the function of the topic sentence, I made my basic writing students see red; the technique was so successful that it became a code of special, clear communication between the class and me. More important, it taught them in an unforgettable way the purpose and value of a topic sentence.

The Topic Sentence Lesson

Quite honestly, the technique evolved because of poor communication between teacher and class. As I struggled one day to make the class understand the importance of the topic sentence for helping them achieve unity in their paragraphs, I realized that they were faking attention, if not actually sleeping. I needed something dramatic and immediate to involve them in the lesson. Suddenly, I asked them to clear their minds of all I had said so that they could take part in a simple experiment. For ninety seconds they were to look around the classroom, mentally noting every red item they saw. The group fell eagerly into this eccentric break in routine. At the end of the time limit, when I asked them to close their eyes and list aloud the red items they had seen, they named everything: red pencils, red dictionaries, red stripes in a navy skirt, red fingernails, red dots on the clock, tiny red words on cabinet labels, even red blood-shot eyes.

Of course, I praised them extravagantly for their keen observation and their enthusiastic response to the experiment. Then I told them the next experimental step: they were to close their eyes again, and this time name all the *blue* they had seen while they were looking for red. Dismay transformed their proud faces. Not having concentrated on blue, they seemed almost stunned; and only a few could name the bright blue chairs on which they were seated, my blue blouse, and their own blue jeans. When I told them to open their eyes, they looked around rather sheepishly, realizing that the classroom actually had more blue than red in it.

As we analyzed the activity, they saw that when they were concentrating only on red, they overlooked the distractions of blue and green and all the other colors of the setting. Rephrasing their discovery in terms of the objectives of my aborted lesson, I explained again the purpose of the topic sentence: to limit the subject and to control the details of the paragraph. The topic sentence helps them see only red; that is, it allows them to focus only on the subject of the paragraph.

Bold with success, we applied our experiment further. We named the requisite key or controlling word of the topic sentence the "red word." In our sample topic sentence—"The experiment in red was startling"—*startling* was the key word, our red word, which controlled the details that could be used in the narrative paragraphs composed about the activity. Finally, this simple experiment was our reference point for one other important lesson in writing. I told them that just as focusing on red had caused them to exclude other colors from their view, so settling on a topic too soon could cause them to overlook many approaches to their subjects. Because they had seen for themselves the truth of that lesson, they needed little urging to spend more time in generation, more time in probing their topics, before deciding on their topic and (later) their thesis sentences.

This gimmick helped both my students and me through (dare I confess it?) a boring lesson. Fortunately, the gimmick worked. But then any teaching technique is effective when it makes the students active participants. Students understand and remember lessons that they themselves have illustrated. (Edward de Bono and Michael de Saint-Arnaud have used a parallel technique as an essential first step in clearer thinking. See *The Learn-to-Think Coursebook,* New York, 1982.)

Generating Paragraphs in a Four-Part Formula

John H. Clarke

When all else fails in teaching paragraph structure, John H. Clarke suggests resorting to basics. Using four questions, his students practice the development of focused paragraphs. Mr. Clarke sent this exercise from the University of Vermont in Burlington.

Author's Comment

I used to ask my students to write a paragraph and dread the results. Some would turn out one sentence in three lines. Some would hand in three sentences, each neatly indented, on six lines. Others spun out yards of tortuous detail, textured here and there by random abstractions. Some wrote nothing but abstractions. Others wrote nothing. They didn't know what I meant by the word "paragraph" and I couldn't give them a definition that they actually could use in their writing. We needed a vocabulary to use in talking about paragraphs and a process to use in turning them out.

The Paragraph Formula

The "ideal" paragraph emerged from an understanding of my own ignorance. My ignorance seemed to reflect the ignorance of all readers and enlighten the task of all writers. Before my students began to write, and often after they had written, I didn't know:

1. what they believed to be true and important;
2. why they believed or how they believed;
3. when or where their belief was shown to be true in real instances;
4. what those instances meant.

If my writers could answer four questions in four rudimentary sentences, they might have a formula for writing paragraphs which could diminish the proportions of my ignorance.

The "ideal" paragraph consisted of four distinct elements, each at least one sentence in length, each sentence generating from a question. The elements were a statement of conceptual truth, a clarification of that statement, an example of the clarified truth, and an interpretation of the example. I dubbed these elements:

> The Leader—answering, "What's true?"
>
> The Qualifier—answering, "Why is it true?"
>
> The Example—answering, "Where or when, with details."
>
> The Interpretation—answering, "So what?"

Working together, those elements compose a little domain of thought that we could call a paragraph.

Having assumed dictatorial control over such domains, I proceeded to banish, like tyrants in other realms, all other contenders for control. I outlawed one-sentence paragraphs, and their demented cousins, the exclamatories. Description went. Convoluted generalization vanished without a trace. As a precaution against resurgence, I banished the word *is,* its relatives in other tenses and its attendants, the passives. I proclaimed that all verbs would take active, energetic forms. Like any despot trying to confirm a recent coup, I promised that democratic forms of expression could return when order had been assured.

The paragraphs that began to assemble all looked the same, but said different things. The word "marijuana," for example, inspired as many belief statements as there were students in the room. All belief statements can generate a paragraph. One example follows:

> Leader—Marijuana remains an antidote for frustration among the young. Smoking dope
>
> Qualifier—allows high school and college students to change their feelings about experience without struggling to improve the experience
>
> Example—itself. If classes bore, conversation lags, parents nag or confidence sags, the dope high will substitute cloudy
>
> Interpretation—mirth for disenchantment. This estrangement from one's own condition may represent the sources of severe disability among heavy marijuana smokers.

Virtually all of my students could write formulaic paragraphs of this kind if they used the questioning technique.

The paragraph process and the reign of uniformity produced immediate and positive results. The writers gained confidence in their ability to translate one thought into a comprehensible paragraph. Later, they learned that the paragraph formula was not visible to their other instructors, who tended to grade formulaic paragraphs beneficently. At the end of the semester most students were able to produce acceptable research papers simply by gathering up some important examples in a topic area, developing a thesis—then writing out leaders, qualifiers, and interpretations in the established sequence. If they could write in a pattern that reflects the interaction of abstraction and specifics, presumably they could also think in that pattern—a form central to academic discourse.

As the writers gained skill with ideal paragraphs, despotic rule disappeared. They discovered that doubling any element would increase the power of lucidity or the paragraph. By doubling the qualifier, they gained clarity of intent. By doubling the example, they developed persuasive power. By doubling the interpretation, they produced more cogent evaluation or deeper analysis. Their paragraphs grew to greater length without losing focus.

Soon the banished forms returned from exile, enlivened by their temporary rejection and reintegration. The more dominant and durable forms received names recognizable from traditional writing instruction.

Persuasion	*Definition*	*Induction*	*Comparison*
Leader	Leader	Example	Leader
Example	Qualifier	Example	Example
Example	Qualifier	Example	Example
Example	Qualifier	Interpretation	Interpretation

Each of the variations retains the order of the ideal form, but some elements drop out, replaced by a double of the element following. Each writer must decide, for each paragraph, whether the ignorance of the reader will succumb most easily to emphasis on qualification, example, or interpretation.

I have used the paragraph formula in teaching sixth graders, high school students, college freshmen, and graduate students. Some cling to its steps for extended periods. Some try and then revise it to their own ends. Some see, understand, and then reject it. I, myself, use it all the time, preferring its gentle tyranny to the terrible ignorance of not knowing what comes next in writing.

Piecing Together Bertrand Russell's "What I Have Lived For": An Exercise for Students Studying the Five-Paragraph Theme

Doyle W. Walls

Wrestling with the concept of organization, students in Doyle W. Walls's classes reconstruct a passage by Bertrand Russell. In the process, they learn the significance of a clear thesis statement, the power of word choice, and the options available to a writer when putting together ideas. Mr. Walls teaches at the University of Wisconsin-Madison.

Author's Comment

I have found the following exercise helpful in teaching the sense of sentences and their place in the larger fabric of paragraphs which one can weave into organized papers, specifically the five-paragraph theme. After having presented the idea of the five-paragraph theme, I like to hand the students the following assignment, a scrambled version of Bertrand Russell's "What I Have Lived For," his prologue to *The Autobiography of Bertrand Russell, 1872-1914.*

Exercise

Use what you have learned about the construction of a five-paragraph theme to determine the proper order of the following sentences which should be grouped in five paragraphs.

1. With equal passion I have sought knowledge.
2. I have sought love, first, because it brings ecstasy—ecstasy so great that I would often have sacrificed all the rest of life for a few hours of this joy.
3. A little of this, but not much, I have achieved.
4. But always pity brought me back to earth.
5. This has been my life.

6. I have sought it, finally, because in the union of love I have seen, in a mystic miniature, the prefiguring vision of the heaven that saints and poets have imagined.

7. Three passions, simple but overwhelmingly strong, have governed my life: the longing for love, the search for knowledge, and unbearable pity for the suffering of mankind.

8. I have sought it, next, because it relieves loneliness—that terrible loneliness in which one shivering consciousness looks over the rim of the world into the cold unfathomable lifeless abyss.

9. I have wished to understand the hearts of men.

10. Love and knowledge, so far as they were possible, led upward toward the heavens.

11. I have wished to know why the stars shine.

12. I have found it worth living, and would gladly live it again if the chance were offered me.

13. These passions, like great winds, have blown me hither and thither, in a wayward course, over a deep ocean of anguish, reaching to the very verge of despair.

14. And I have tried to apprehend the Pythagorean power by which number holds sway above the flux.

15. I long to alleviate the evil, but I cannot, and I too suffer.

16. This is what I sought, and though it might seem too good for human life, this is what—at last—I have found.

17. Echoes of cries of pain reverberate in my heart.

18. Children in famine, victims tortured by oppressors, helpless old people a hated burden to their sons, and the whole world of loneliness, poverty, and pain make a mockery of what human life should be.

Introduction: _____

Body Paragraph One: _____

Body Paragraph Two: _____

Body Paragraph Three: _____

Conclusion: _____

Summation

The scrambled version of Russell's essay presented above challenges students to read and think about writing in a way they seldom do when given the regular reading assignment. Delighting in the puzzle, they pay more attention than usual to key words on which sentences and paragraphs turn: "equal," "first," "finally," "next," and the number "three." However, the students realize that their first priority is to find a more powerful structural element than such words as "equal" and "finally." For example, "first," "next," and "finally" do not signify body paragraphs one, two, and three. The students—working individually—usually find Russell's thesis statement and, in the process, realize the value of a clear thesis statement. They appreciate Russell's clarity; they understand that it was Russell's effectiveness—not their own magical powers—which helped some of them find the proper order for the sentences. A few students, invariably, will determine the correct order!

Here is the proper ordering for the sentences of "What I Have Lived For":

Introduction: 7-13.

Body Paragraph One: 2-8-6-16.

Body Paragraph Two: 1-9-11-14-3.

Body Paragraph Three: 10-4-17-18-15.

Conclusion: 5-12.

Prologue

What I Have Lived For

Three passions, simple but overwhelmingly strong, have governed my life: the longing for love, the search for knowledge, and unbearable pity for the suffering of mankind. These passions, like great winds, have blown me hither and thither, in a wayward course, over a deep ocean of anguish, reaching to the very verge of despair.

I have sought love, first, because it brings ecstasy—ecstasy so great that I would often have sacrificed all the rest of life for a few hours of this joy. I have sought it, next, because it relieves loneliness—that terrible loneliness in which one shivering consciousness looks over the rim of the world into the cold unfathomable lifeless abyss. I have sought it, finally, because in the union of love I have seen, in a mystic miniature, the prefiguring vision of the heaven that saints and poets have imagined. This is what I sought, and though it might seem too good for human life, this is what—at last—I have found.

With equal passion I have sought knowledge. I have wished to understand the hearts of men. I have wished to know why the stars shine. And I have tried to apprehend the Pythagorean power by which number holds sway above the flux. A little of this, but not much, I have achieved.

Love and knowledge, so far as they were possible, led upward toward the heavens. But always pity brought me back to earth. Echoes of cries of pain reverberate in my heart. Children in famine, victims tortured by oppressors, helpless old people a hated burden to their sons, and the whole world of loneliness, poverty, and pain make a mockery of what human life should be. I long to alleviate the evil, but I cannot, and I too suffer.

This has been my life. I have found it worth living, and would gladly live it again if the chance were offered me.

—Bertrand Russell, "What I Have Lived For," in *The Autobiography of Bertrand Russell, 1872-1914* (London: George Allen and Unwin Ltd., 1967). p. 13.

A Switch in Point of View

Lynne Shackelford

On occasion, teachers need exercises that help students focus on a particular concept in writing. Lynne Shackelford suggests two such exercises for helping students grasp the importance of point of view. Ms. Shackelford contributed this exercise from the University of North Carolina, Chapel Hill.

Author's Comment

Both in their writing and their reading my students demonstrate little understanding of the concept of point of view. They seem unaware that selecting a point of view is an important decision for a writer, because it controls the relationship between the writer, the reader, and the characters in a narrative. To make the concept of point of view very clear to my students, I help them to assume a different angle of vision from their own with two exercises.

Exercise I

I ask my students to help me stage a tableau of a typical, or rather stereotyped, English class. Each student selects a role—the paper rustler, the pencil dropper, the snoozer, Mr. Big Mouth, the whisperer, the giggler, the note passer, the daydreamer, the doodler, the paper airplane thrower, the flirt, the egghead, the gum popper, etc. At my signal they all begin their characteristic actions. Then alone or in small groups (depending upon the class size) I let each student come up to the front of the class, stand behind the podium, and pretend to be the teacher. I encourage them to get into the mindset of the teacher, to try to feel as the teacher would in facing such a class. Once every student has become "the teacher" for a moment or two, I ask them to write a description of the class from the teacher's viewpoint. They are free to choose any method they wish. Students can use a stream-of-consciousness technique and actually present the teacher's flow of thoughts. They can record a conversation between the teacher and another instructor. They can pretend they are the teacher writing a letter to a friend. They can write the teacher's diary entry. Any method is valid. The only requirement is that the students drop the student's view and try to perceive the class as if they were the teacher.

Exercise II

To give my students further practice in thinking of point of view, I divide them into five groups. Then I give them a set of facts about a particular situation; for example, a football game. One group describes the game from the perspective of the quarterback who made the winning touchdown, another from the viewpoint of the coach of the losing team, a third from the point of view of a cheerleader for the home team, a fourth from the perspective of an alumnus who's come back to see how things have changed since the days when he was a football hero, the fifth from the viewpoint of Howard Cosell. After each group has made a presentation to the class of its particular perspective, we discuss how point of view can affect the basic facts of a situation—how some points of view are more objective than others, how point of view can reveal character traits.

Evaluation

I have found these two exercises to be very beneficial. First of all, they generate much enthusiasm in the class. Students appreciate a change in the class routine and participate eagerly in both the acting situation and the discussion of the different points of view. Second, the written descriptions of the class from the teacher's viewpoint are far more imaginative than the usual compositions, often employing such sophisticated literary tools as dialogue, irony, figurative language, humor, and interior monologue. Finally, these exercises enable me to establish the proper atmosphere for a presentation on literary point of view. After the exercises, we read and discuss several short stories with intriguing points of view. Henry James's "The Turn of the Screw" is a classic example and fascinates the students by raising the question of the reliability of the narrator. The results of these two exercises extend throughout the semester. After using them, I find my students attempting further experiments with point of view in their journals. I also find that they become more perceptive readers, as they begin to analyze the significance of how the storyteller chooses to tell a story.

Unwriting the Pros

Kathleen Lampert

Much attention has been given to the effects of sentence-combining activities on students' writing skills. Kathleen Lampert of Wayland High School in Massachusetts offers two samples of how to begin with excerpts of writing by professional authors and "unwrite" them in an effort to see how and why they are constructed as they are.

Author's Comment

During the past ten years much of our attention as English teachers has been directed toward using rhetorical principles to understand the writing process more fully and to teach it more effectively. For many of us, our developing understanding of the writing process has led to a parallel development in the way we understand literature and teach literary interpretation.

One rhetorical principle I have found equally useful in teaching reading and writing is voice: the complex interaction among a writer's attitudes toward self, subject, and audience which gives a work its individuality and which can establish much of its meaning. A writer must, consciously or unconsciously, develop a voice appropriate to a rhetorical situation as he or she perceives it; a reader must be able to respond to the writer's voice to interpret effectively. A reader's ability to respond to an author's voice depends largely on sensitivity to a writer's choices of diction and syntax, a sensitivity which can reveal levels of meaning not apparent from examining content alone. When, for example, E. B. White begins "Walden": "Miss Nims: take a letter to Henry David Thoreau. Dear Henry: I thought of you the other afternoon as I was approaching Concord doing fifty on Route 62," his casual diction and conversational syntax are clues to a subtle criticism of Thoreau's impersonality that White develops in the essay. A reader, to fully understand this complex, delightful essay, must recognize that White's voice qualifies his explicit admiration for Thoreau.

Classroom Activity

Not surprisingly, most of my students don't come naturally to this necessary awareness of voice and its role in shaping meaning. One strategy I've developed to give students a concrete approach to syntax, which they find particularly difficult to discuss, is "unwriting the pros." The procedure is a relatively simple one. First take a more or less complex series of sentences from a work in which voice is particularly important in conveying meaning and return those sentences to their kernel state (reverse the sentence combining process). Give the kernels to students and discuss any clues to voice offered by diction and content; then ask them to recombine the kernels, using syntax trying to suggest the voice discussed. Finally, mimeograph their versions and the original and compare all versions, discussing the various syntactic choices made and their effects.

Consider, for example, the following excerpt from Dickens:

> It was Miss Murdstone, and a gloomy looking lady she was, dark like her brother, and with very heavy eyebrows, nearly meeting over her large nose. She brought with her two uncompromising hard black boxes, with her initials on the lids in hard brass nails.

I give my students the following list of kernels:

1. We had a visitor.
2. The visitor was Miss Murdstone.
3. Miss Murdstone was a lady.
4. Miss Murdstone looked gloomy.
5. Miss Murdstone was dark.
6. Her darkness was like her brother's.
7. Miss Murdstone had eyebrows.
8. The eyebrows nearly met.
9. The meeting was over her nose.
10. Her nose was large.
11. Miss Murdstone brought something with her.
12. The things were two boxes.
13. The boxes were uncompromising.
14. The boxes were hard.
15. The boxes were black.
16. The boxes had her initials.
17. The initials were on the lids.

18. The initials were in nails.
19. The nails were hard.
20. The nails were brass.

Our preliminary discussion focuses on the way Dickens suggests Miss Murdstone's physical and psychological hardness. Students then attempt to build a passage from the kernels which emphasize those qualities. In the discussion which follows, we look at his use of *and* as a coordinator in the first sentence, the placement of the adjective phrase "dark like her brother," and the repetition of *hard* in the second sentence, all syntactic choices which place emphasis on negative qualities. At the end of our discussion we've begun to see how Dickens's syntactic choices help communicate his attitude toward character and to influence our own responses to her. In some cases, it may be appropriate to give students material which precedes the unwritten passage to help them hear the writer's voice. For example, when we work with *Time*'s account of a gangland murder, they receive:

> From *Time* magazine, April 1972: "Death of a Maverick Mafioso"
> The scene could have been lifted right out of that movie. First, a night of champagne and laughter at Manhattan's Copacabana as mobster Joey ("Crazy Joe") Gallo, one of New York's most feared Mafiosi, celebrated his 43rd birthday. Then on to a predawn Italian breakfast at a gleaming new restaurant in the city's Little Italy area. Seated at his left at a rear table in Umberto's Clam House was his brawny bodyguard, Pete ("The Greek") Diopioulis; at Gallo's right, his sister Carmela. Across the table sat Gallo's darkly attractive bride of just three weeks, Sina, 29, and her daughter, Lisa, 10. Quietly, a lone gunman stepped through a rear door and strode toward the table.

Kernels:

1. Gallo was facing the wall.
2. Diopioulis was facing the wall.
3. Gallo was not facing the door.
4. Diopioulis was not facing the door.
5. Gallo was careless.
6. Diopioulis was careless.
7. The triggerman opened fire.
8. He fired with a revolver.
9. The revolver was a .38 caliber.
10. Women screamed.

11. Joey was hit instantly.

12. Pete was hit instantly.

13. The Greek drew a gun.

14. The gun was his own.

15. The Greek began shooting back.

16. One Gallo ally began shooting back.

17. The ally was seated at a bar.

18. The bar was for clams.

19. The bar was at the front.

After we've discussed *Time*'s characteristic breathless news narration and they've had a chance to write their own versions, we compare them with the original.
Original:

> Both Gallo and Diopioulis were carelessly facing the wall instead of the door. The triggerman opened fire with a .38-caliber revolver. Women screamed. Joey and Pete were hit instantly. The Greek drew his own gun, began shooting back. So did one Gallo ally, seated at the front clam bar. Within 90 seconds, 20 shots ripped through the restaurant. Tables crashed over, hurling hot sauce and ketchup across the blue-tiled floor to mix with the blood of the wounded. The gunman whirled, ran out the same rear door and into a waiting car.

Students may notice the use of short sentences and ellipses (". . . his own gun, began shooting . . .") to create a dramatic "you are there" quality. We may also discuss the connection between *Time*'s voice and the "objective" voice we usually associate with news reporting.

Additional Comments

The approach described can easily be adapted to any course content whose interpretation attention is to voice. So far I've worked only with narrative and descriptive material because kernels in these modes are related spatially or temporally; expository passages seem to require excessive annotation to indicate more abstract logical relationships. I've begun to explore unwriting students' writing; reducing their material to kernels reveals focus and coherence problems clearly and demonstrates to them concretely that as writers they can make real choices which control voice and meaning.

A similar approach can also be used with film sequences: treat individual shots as the "kernels" and discuss alternative arrangements and the way shot selection and arrangement shapes one's understanding of the sequence. Sequences from Truffaut's "400 Blows" present some particularly interesting voice material.

Most of the students I worked with had little systematic exposure to formal sentence combining, although they had done some exercises in other classes. If they have had no such work, a few practice exercises might make them more comfortable with the idea of sentence combining before they work with voice oriented exercises; some formal stylistic terminology *might* be useful for increasingly sophisticated syntactic analyses. However, my experience with these exercises indicates that students can develop their understanding of syntax and voice without a great deal of preliminary work and that specific attention to small syntactic elements leads them closer to subtleties of meaning that they might otherwise easily miss.

A Question of Style

Peggy Jolly

Teaching style is an elusive art according to Peggy Jolly. She suggests that even though it may be difficult to teach, students can learn to recognize, analyze, and initiate it. Ms. Jolly teaches at the University of Alabama in Birmingham.

No. 1
Now that she had said it, she was angry with herself for not having said it the night before, so that they would have had time to be finished with their weeping and their arguments. She had not trusted herself to withstand the night before; but now there was almost no time left. The center of her mind was filled with the image of the great clock at the railway station.

James Baldwin

No. 2
Not knowing what to do, she slowly pulled the covers over her face, so that the robber could do whatever he had to do without her seeing. She did not know what would happen while being blinded; but it was all over. She did not have a picture of the insane man who scared her so badly.

James Baldwin

Author's Comment

Which is the forgery, and which is the published work? This is an example of the exercise and question I put before my students when beginning a lesson in stylistics. Teaching style, as opposed to dwelling on mechanical and grammatical conformity, is an elusive art, elusive because the word itself escapes exact definition. Perhaps Ella Fitzgerald's definition is adequate: "It ain't what you do, it's the way howdya do it."[1] At any rate, composition teachers generally recognize and appreciate grace in writing. Their own writing may contain this quality, and they certainly appreciate its appearance in students' compositions. But teaching or learning that grace is difficult at best. Perhaps style cannot easily be taught, but it can be recognized, analyzed, and imitated.

Imitating good writing has long been accepted as an excellent method of improving one's own style. This sentiment, expressed in Lewis Mumford's words on the subject, "The imitation of other artists is one of the means by which a person enriches and finally establishes his own individuality, and on the whole such imitation is more promising than an icing of originality that hardens too quickly," is echoed by others, including Ralph Waldo Emerson, Dean Howells, Robert Louis Stevenson, and Somerset Maugham.[2] But championing imitation for its own sake is worthless; only when the imitation enables the imitator to appreciate the intricacies of good writing and transfer some of these literary devices into his or her own work does the exercise become worthwhile. The individual's experiences, knowledge, and opinions ultimately color the work, allowing the reader to see the author as much as the prose. Imitation then is but one device to hasten the acquisition of an individual's style, another tool to add to the writer's repertoire.

The Approach

The forgery exercise is but one form of imitation. The form of the exercise is variable, the rules brief, the results astounding. First, a student is asked to copy verbatim a passage of published prose from a magazine such as *Harpers, Esquire,* or *Time.* Full documentation, including the author's name, the magazine title, volume, and date follow the passage.

Next, students are asked to imitate the original passage with a sample of their own writing. The forgery may or may not be on the same topic. The students' writing should, however, include the same number of sentences and approximately the same number of words as the original sample. Documentation of the students' writing will be presented exactly as that of the published sample to ensure the students' anonymity. Both pieces of writing are then submitted to the teacher and classmates who attempt to distinguish the published writing from the students' writing, generally an easy task even for unsophisticated readers and writers.

Once the original and forgery have been identified, an analysis of the two pieces of work can begin. Questions about how the identity was made often solicit comments about obvious non-standard usages that may appear in the forgery such as pronoun or verb agreement errors, verb tense shifts, misused words, or peculiar mechanical or punctuation usages. The value of this immediate response to the class as a whole and to the student writer in particular is that importance to conformity of standard usage and careful editing is stressed. The students can see exactly why one piece of writing is not as effective as another.

More adept students recognize the subtleties that begin to reach the core of stylistics: sentence variety and length, sentence types (balanced, cumulative, periodic), use of free modifiers, the reliance on concrete rather than abstract words, tone, balance, and effect. Although the students may not know the technical names of the structures, they recognize their effectiveness. This recognition, then, is the beginning of an awareness of style. From the recognition that style affects the reader's perception of the quality of writing comes the foundation for analyzing style. Teaching sentence patterns and their appropriate uses gives the writer additional control over the composition. Identifying compact, effective use of verbals and free modifiers eliminates the static voice of immature writing that plagues many beginning writers. Other elements of style, tricks of the trade, can be identified that will then be at the disposal of the improving writer.

Evaluation

Students' abilities often are underestimated by teachers who receive a set of compositions and read them with increasing despair. But I believe the students' ineptitudes and the teacher's despair can be overcome through imitative practices such as the forgery exercise. The results I have had with this exercise have been remarkably positive. Not only does the students' writing improve, but also their proof-reading ability. The one disadvantage this exercise can have is that the students may become so proficient in imitating styles that the exercise of "find the forgery" can well become one of "trick the teacher."[3]

Notes

1. James C. Raymond, *Writing (Is an Unnatural Act),* (New York: Harper and Row, 1980), p. 163.

2. Frank J. D'Angelo, *Process and Thought in Composition* (Cambridge, Massachusetts: Winthrop, 1977), p. 301.

3. Number two in the sample is the forgery.

VI Revising, Responding, and Evaluating

How do students grasp the importance of revision in their writing? How can students work effectively as peer editors and engage in collaborative learning? What options does the instructor have when the time comes to measure the level of student achievement in writing and to assign grades? Articles in this section offer some practical suggestions about ways to answer these questions.

Magazine Advertisement Analysis:
A Group Approach to Rewriting

William Rogalski

By engaging students in collaborative writing tasks, William Rogalski reinforces the importance of audience and purpose along with revision. Mr. Rogalski submitted this exercise from the University of Vermont in Burlington.

Author's Comment

As a teacher who approaches composition as a four-part process—prewriting, writing, rewriting, and editing—I find describing rewriting to my students to be a great obstacle. Too often they see it as preliminary editing—changing punctuation marks and correcting grammatical errors. The point of this exercise is to demonstrate that rewriting often encompasses such major changes as radical shifts in focus, addition and deletion of information, and reordering of paragraphs.

I teach writing by rhetorical modes and find that analysis is well suited for the group assignment. I begin by explaining the basic types of analysis—functional, structural, causal, and process—and apply each to a simple object, a desk or chair for example. I then ask the class to apply these analytical methods to other simple objects, and once I am sure they have the feel for the process, I have them form groups of three. I specify that they should be analyzing magazine advertisements and give them a few suggested topics: sex or nature as themes in advertisement, stereotypes, class values, verbal trickery, use of photographs or headlines. I point out that these are only starting points and encourage them to pursue any project within the basic limit of advertisement analysis. What I stress is that they should examine a broad variety of ads and consider the patterns they can find. My students tend to approach each paper as an argument with a thesis to present and support. You must emphasize that they shouldn't begin with a thesis and then look for documentation for it in the ads but that they should instead be looking for recurring patterns in whatever area it is they are examining. I also allow a great deal of freedom in the choice of that area. The approaches they take to the analysis are usually far more interesting than anything I could suggest. I shall describe the exercise according to the schedule I follow, using four seventy-five-minute classes over a two-week period.

Rewriting Activity

First Class

After the introduction to analysis, the class breaks into groups of three. Each group decides on a basic approach to the assignment and on what magazines each member should examine. The assignment for the next class asks students to collect and briefly analyze (according to the approach the group has decided on) five ads. They should write fifty- to seventy-five-word notes on each ad.

Second Class

In this class each group produces a joint prewriting sheet from the ads it has collected. The group elects a secretary to take down in triplicate the prewriting information. The basic structure of the paper should be decided on now, and each student is asked to write a first draft of 500 words for the next class from the prewriting material. Students should be reminded to bring in three copies of their first drafts.

Third Class

Students meet in their groups, exchange and examine drafts, and comment on the effectiveness of each. At this point I have them concentrate on the large issues—structure, ideas, continuity, logic—and not merely on grammatical correctness or stylistic subtleties. Each group decides which of the three drafts is best and how it can be improved. Each student is asked to rewrite the group's best draft for the next class.

Fourth Class

Students meet in their groups and decide how to produce a final draft from the second drafts they have at hand. Some groups will probably choose the best draft one member has produced and discuss how to improve it, while other groups will probably decide that their final draft should incorporate the best parts of all second drafts. Each group should elect someone to be responsible for shaping the final draft, again of 500 words, into final form for submission.

Aside from showing students that radical changes in drafts often bring radical changes in quality, the exercise has other benefits: students are motivated when they know that someone other than the teacher will read their drafts; students find it easy to be objective about the quality of writing when a paper is a group effort; students see that an abundance of prewriting material—much of which will be discarded—is necessary for a good paper; and students get to know each other well through writing together.

Revision Revisited

Elizabeth F. Penfield

On occasion student writers seem to be "tone deaf." That is, they seem not to realize the possibilities inherent in different sentence constructions. Elizabeth F. Penfield of the University of New Orleans, Louisiana, provides some suggestions of how to help students discover ways to revise their sentences in order to make them more varied and interesting.

Author's Comment

I am a firm believer in revision, but frequently students do not see how a draft can be improved and simply copy it over and turn it in. The final papers often suffer from a lack of sentence variety, and although they may be grammatically and mechanically correct, the papers' style is flat, unemphatic, ineffective—the texture of gruel and the taste as well. For lack of a better term, such writing is at best tone-deaf, and work on ways of developing the students' interest in language is essential if they are to interact with what they are writing, allowing their words and syntax to develop their thoughts as well as vice versa.

A Revision Exercise

To build sentences with muscle, I ditto five to ten examples that are syntactically interesting. Sentences are double-spaced and followed by a version that provides blanks for most of the nouns, verbs, adverbs, and adjectives.

1. The Religion that is afraid of science dishonors God and commits suicide.

   Ralph Waldo Emerson, *Journal*

   The _____ that _____ _____ of _____

   _____ _____ and _____ _____.

2. Some books are undeservedly forgotten; none are undeservedly remembered.

W. H. Auden, *Apothegms*

Some _____ _____ _____ _____;

none _____ _____ _____.

3. A definition is the enclosing of a wilderness of ideas within a wall of words.

Samuel Butler, *Notebooks*

A _____ _____ the _____ a _____ of

_____ within a _____ of _____.

Each student receives a copy of the sentences, and I explain that the point is to keep the same sentence structure in each case while changing the meaning. Choosing an example that is fairly simple, I work on it with the class as a whole [William F. Irmscher describes this kind of imitation in his "What Do You Do to Teach Composition?" the teacher's manual for *The Holt Guide to English* (New York: Holt, Rinehart, and Winston, 1972).] There is an excellent one by Truman Capote: "I live in Brooklyn. By choice." Starting with a verb to replace "live," the class finds that one choice generates another and that the overall impact, the rhetorical effect, lies in the syntactical structure. One student volunteers "write," another "prose," and a third caps the statement, ending up with "I write in prose. By default." Every frustrated poet in the class cheers.

It's possible to play with the variations on one sentence for fifty minutes without the class becoming bored, for the discussion zeroes in on what works and what doesn't and why. Alliteration, juxtaposition, diction—all sorts of rhetorical effects come alive and provide springboards for discussion. The class creates one variation after another, and even the most reticent of students is apt to participate, tossing a word into the air for the other students to bat about.

Once the class understands how to manipulate the sentences, they write up the other examples as an out-of-class assignment due the next class meeting. When the papers come in, many erased to transparency, I pick the best of the lot, culling at least one from each paper, dittoing them to use as the basis of another class discussion. By this time, most of the students view a sentence as something that can be worth wrestling with, and many of them are amazed at the sheer power that syntax can add to thought.

I carry the idea one step further by asking the students to find at least three examples from their own reading, setting them up like the others, and rewriting them, again preserving the basic structure. I extend the assignment because of a hunch: frequently students are so accustomed to reading for information that style goes unnoticed. Ferreting out sentences sharpens the ability of the class to read not just with the eye, but with the ear as well, not only looking for *what* is written, but also hearing *how* it is written.

Imitation, of course, is a technique that has a venerable tradition in classical rhetoric. The exercises that I have described simply use a small unit, the sentence, to illustrate the rhetorical effect of syntax. Perhaps just as important is that students enjoy the project, this providing some living proof to the point Richard Lanham makes in *Style: An Anti-Textbook* (New Haven: Yale, 1974); Lanham maintains that good style is "a pleasure, a grace, a joy, a delight" (p. 20). That it is also hard work students already know.

After students have gone through the kind of exercise I have described, I ask them to pay particular attention to at least one sentence in each paragraph of their rough drafts, revising to provide structural emphasis. At that point, students are not going to search out a model to plug in, but they are able to play with the sentences and to try structures freshmen would not normally attempt. Occasionally this sort of revision has caused the revision of the entire paper because, accompanied by all the requisite "eurekas," the language created a new idea. At the end of all these sentence shenanigans the students who revise may not have perfect pitch, but they are no longer tone-deaf.

Structured Revision Tasks

Joyce Hicks

Do students revise automatically on their own? Joyce Hicks thinks not. Instead, she suggests introducing the idea of revising based on particular concepts that may be the subject of study at a particular time in a course. Ms. Hicks contributed this assignment from Valparaiso University in Indiana.

Author's Comment

Students have difficulty revising papers because they lack experience in making changes in tone, style, and focus which produce polished writing. Too often students merely exchange a few *ands* and *buts* and think the job is done. I have found that structured group or individual revision tasks can be very helpful in showing students just how to go about the process of revision.

The Task

I present students with a list of changes that they must make on sample dittoed passages or on their own writing. The kind of changes I call for depend, of course, on what we are studying that week. The pedagogical advantage of such revision tasks is that I can adapt principles of affective small-group work to the revision process. Group work should foster either cooperation or competition between small groups who produce a product within a given time period.

Examples of specific tasks follow:

Situation:	Students write and bring to class a descriptive paragraph. Groups of four read each paper, choose a good one, and perform these operations.
Task:	1. Add a line of dialogue.
	2. Add a detail that appeals to the sense of touch.

3. Delete two unnecessary adjectives.

4. Substitute a stronger verb for a to-be verb.

Situation: Give students copies of a student-written descriptive narrative. After dividing the class into groups, assign each group one of the paragraphs to modify. The task is cooperative because all work to improve the whole. The results are read aloud by each group leader. An interesting dimension can be added by assigning two groups the same paragraph.

Task: 1. Delete a sentence, phrase, or clause.

2. Add a sentence, word, or clause.

3. Write a new title.

Situation: Give each group the same sentence. Tell the groups to do the following:

Task: 1. Rewrite the sentence in as many ways as possible, but each sentence must be an example of good writing. Since changes in punctuation change the form and meaning of the sentence, each altered version can be counted. This task is competitive because each group seeks to perform the same operation.

2. Assign a particular sentence pattern to each group. One group must begin the sentence with a participial phrase; another must produce a compound version; another must write a compound-complex version. Here the task becomes cooperative rather than competitive.

Situation: Each student must revise the last graded paper in this manner:

Task: 1. Change the voice of the paper from third person to first or second person and make changes in word choice and style that such a change necessitates.

or

2. Shorten the paper by four sentences, omitting superfluous material. Eliminate the subject-verb combination *there is/are* and *it is* from the paper.

A Peer Review Process for Developmental Writers

Lynne Spigelmire

Using peer review groups in the writing class has become a popular method for making students more responsible for evaluation of their own work. Lynne Spigelmire outlines one procedure for organizing and implementing the peer review process. Ms. Spigelmire is at Boston University in Massachusetts.

Author's Comment

Developmental or beginning writers characteristically have a very vague sense of audience, and therefore find it difficult to distance themselves from the "texts" they have written, and then to criticize these texts as part of preparation for revision. Because beginning writers need to become "naive readers," or critics of their own written work, they need guidance not only in getting started (that is, in learning how to use invention procedures fruitfully), but also in examining one another's work through a structured peer review process. After repeatedly applying critical standards to first versions written by their peers, students are able to judge their own first versions, using the same criteria as they did in peer review. Thus, in a developmental writing course, peer review is a necessary prelude to teaching revision. The rationale for peer review is this: if students can learn to recognize weaknesses and strengths in their writing, then they are ready to devise successful strategies for revision.

Exercise

The peer review process I use in my two-semester freshman composition course requires each student to prepare one original and two copies of a first draft on the assigned topic. The drafts may be handwritten or typed, but must be double-spaced. At the beginning of the first semester, my explanation of the peer review protocol usually elicits a mixed response from students. Those who have been introduced to peer review in the past and have found it helpful accept the process as a normal part of a writing course. However, these students are usually a small minority. Some students balk, out of shyness or skepticism about the critical skills of their classmates. Nevertheless, on the first day of peer review, most students appear with copies of their essays. Except for three or four students in each section of 25 to 30, students generally continue to participate fully in the peer review sessions during both semesters, producing a total of eight peer evaluations over 28 weeks of instruction.

Before preparing the final version of each essay assigned during the course, students go through the following steps: completion of various heuristic procedures, discussion of writing plans with the instructor, preparation of the first version, peer review, and optional conference with the instructor. Students are asked to complete specific heuristic procedures for each assignment, and to hand them in. Then, they receive assignment sheets listing the essay's topic, prescribed length (usually 500 words), and due dates for first and final versions.

Sample Assignment

Paper No. 1: Description/Narration

Topic: An important relationship in your life which contains (or contained) dissonance for you

Recommended length: two pages, typed, double-spaced

First version due: September 24, by class time (Make two copies for peer review)

Final version due: October 1, 4:00 p.m.

The assignment sheet also reminds students that each essay should have an introductory paragraph with audience appeal and orientation, functional paragraphs, each with a clear organizing idea or topic sentence, and a conclusion or appropriate closure. In addition, the assignment sheet reminds students to review the two checklists for conventions and mechanics on our departmental Theme Analysis Blank, which must be submitted along with each final version.

Establishing Peer Review Groups

In September, I establish year-long peer review groups, randomly dividing each class into clusters of three or four students. After the second round of peer reviews, I make minor changes in those groups which contain more than one "no show" (often students whose writing anxiety prevents them from producing a first version on time, or who are dogmatically opposed to the notion of peer review). Each group decides whether writers will read first versions aloud, or whether peer critics will read copies of the draft silently before completing the required Peer Review Analysis Form.

The Peer Review Analysis Form is useful because it provides a list of relatively objective criteria. Students who are just beginning to learn about audience appeal and the importance of unified, coherent paragraphs often regress when they are called upon to write an extended discourse. Early in the semester, Peer Review Analysis Forms are rather simple and straightforward like this one, asking student-critics to focus on the beginning and concluding paragraphs of the essay, and to locate specific details which appeal to the senses. Each peer review process requires critics to give authors specific guidelines for revision, since students have a full week between completion of peer review and due date for the final version of the essay.

Each peer review process takes two fifty-minute class sessions. If students are unable to complete their peer reviews within the allotted class time, they must make arrangements to meet outside class, or to exchange papers overnight or over a weekend; this arrangement evolved out of student-initiated meetings outside class time, and has proven acceptable to most students. As the Sample Peer Review Analysis Form illustrates, student critics are required to check for the presence of various components of the essay, and to cite specific features such as descriptions. Student critics also are asked to give an overall evaluation of the essay, citing the author's successes and making suggestions for revision.

During the first peer review session, I review the ground rules briefly, then have student groups begin reading one another's essays. I sit in with each group for ten minutes or so, sometimes participating in the review process to insure that everyone understands the procedure. For the entire first semester, I avoid asking critics to point out cosmetic or mechanical errors, since I believe this leads to an erroneous perception of peer review as "just editing" or "correcting the spelling." Late in the second semester, however, one entire peer review session is given over to proofreading and copy editing.

Once students have completed their reviews of first versions and have filled out the Peer Review Analysis Form in duplicate, using carbon paper, critics return one copy of the form to the essay's author, and one form to me. Student critics receive an evaluation from me for their critical work, according to a pass/high pass/fail system. Before authors revise their first versions and submit them for a grade, each author reads the three Analysis Forms, confers individually with me if necessary, then makes final revisions and prepares the typescript of the final version.

Peer Review Analysis Form

Assignment No. 1: Description/Narration of an Important Relationship

Author of Essay _____ Peer Critic _____

Title of Essay _____

I. Introductory Paragraph (s)	Satisfactory	Suggestions for Revision
Audience Appeal Step		
Orientation of Audience		
II. Body Does each paragraph have a topic or organizing idea?		
Are there enough specific examples? Cite one description which appeals to reader's sense of sight: _____ _____		
Cite one description which appeals to reader's sense of hearing or touch: _____ _____		
Are transitions clear?		
Does time sequence make sense to you?		
Are you aware of writer's sense of dissonance in this relationship? State the dissonance: _____		
III. Conclusion Is the dissonance resolved? Do you have a clear sense of an ending?		

IV. Peer critic's summary:

Write a paragraph in which you give your suggestions for revision. Also mention what you like about the essay—what the author should *keep*.

This form should be filled out in duplicate. Use carbon paper. Return one copy to author, the other to your instructor.

By the end of the second semester, student response to peer review continues to be somewhat mixed, but in a final series of memos and self-assessments of writing progress, the majority of students acknowledge the usefulness of peer response, as a prelude to the instructor's evaluation of the final versions, and as the first step in learning about revision. In addition, students gradually learn that their peers can be competent readers and critics. Thus, they begin to have a sharper sense of actual readers in the real world, and the difficulties those readers can and do encounter.

The *Viking Portable* . . .

Alan S. Cohen

Students often display remarkably good sense when it comes to evaluating their own progress as writers. Alan S. Cohen describes an assignment that permits students to display their understanding of their progress. Mr. Cohen is at the University of Vermont in Burlington.

Author's Comment

All composition teachers want their students to leave the semester with a sense of accomplishment and an idea of how they stand as writers. All too often, the semester concludes with many students walking out of the classroom saying something like: "Whew, I'm glad that's over." For me, this "I'm glad this is over—I wonder what the purpose of this course was" attitude can be the most frustrating aspect of teaching composition.

What I am proposing is not a successful formula for all writing classes, but rather, a final exercise that gives students a better sense of how they have grown as writers during the course of the semester. Instead of finishing the term with a "What I wanted out of this course" or "open topic" type of paper—I am especially against ending a semester with a traditional "research paper"—what I have found to have some lasting value (and something that is fun), is to have my students review, edit, and make conclusions on their "selected works." The folder that they prepare looks very much like a manuscript version of a Viking Portable edition. Their observations pertain to writing style and content, work habits, particular prejudices toward certain papers or modes of discourse, and suggestions for continued growth.

The introspective and professional nature of this assignment directs students toward leaving the semester with a more encompassing sense of how they stand as writers and what avenues of improvement need further exploration. This assignment is valuable inasmuch as the instructor helps the students put these folders together. Frequent conferences and in-class workshops, like the editor session at a publishing house, are suggested. In preparing this selection of their work and reviewing it honestly and

321

thoughtfully, students become better editors and critics of their own writing, an important goal of any writing class.

The Approach

Midway through the semester, or whenever you believe that your students have done a substantial amount of writing, introduce this assignment. For the last few weeks of the semester (I usually delegate the last three) they will write no new papers but collect what they believe best represents their writing and present it in a special folder edition. Have them go to the library or bring in a few Viking Portable editions (e.g., Joyce, Lawrence, Stein) so they can get a grasp of how this is handled professionally. Note: You should remind them that they are preparing a manuscript for publication; the aesthetic of economy can not be stressed too often and too fervently. This is a *selected* rather than *collected* edition of their work.

Form

1. The format of the Viking edition provides an excellent role model. Students may develop their own format (e.g., add a conclusion after the text or offer two versions of a representative piece of work).
2. Following the Viking format, the folder should begin with the 5–6 page introduction/critical survey of their writing.
3. This is to be followed by the selected works. Any piece of writing done over the course of the semester is fair game. Remember the aesthetic of economy.
4. A chronological pattern is, of course, advised.

Suggestions to Students

1. Avoid the "stockpile" approach. Why are certain pieces omitted?
2. Discuss both strengths and weaknesses of papers included.
3. Use thoughtful, honest, and concise remarks.
4. Refer to material enclosed (quote yourself) and be careful of random comments.
5. Review the growth of the writing style.
6. Discuss the merits of any final revisions prepared solely for this edition.

7. Designate ways to watch out for certain recurring problems and provide ways to combat them.

8. Have conferences all through the process. Share your work with others and get feedback.

9. Avoid mentioning a letter grade. If you insist on pandering a final grade, be extremely subtle. The tone is to be, at all times, objective and professional.

An Adaptable Exam for Use in Composition Courses

Thom Seymour

Sally Seymour

Do you want to know whether or not your students have learned how to distinguish between effective and ineffective writing? Thom and Sally Seymour of Harvard University, Cambridge, and the Social Science Research Institute, Boston, Massachusetts, have designed an examination for that purpose.

Authors' Comment

In a composition course, testing can be a problem. Any sort of "objective" exam, such as a multiple choice test, violates the whole purpose of a composition course: the teaching and learning of good *writing*. But since composition courses don't have content in the same way that, say, history or philosophy courses do, what sort of exam question can you ask that doesn't require "outside" knowledge to answer and that tests whatever it is that composition courses teach? The following exercise is one solution to this problem. It is an exercise that asks a student to choose between two pieces of writing, one good and one bad.

The Exam for Composition Courses

The easiest way to set up the exercise is to begin with the good passage and rewrite (or, more accurately, *de*write) it to the level of badness you want. The content of the two passages should be as close to identical as possible; only the compositional elements should be recomposed. For example, here is a passage from E. B. White's essay "Here Is New York" and a rewrite of that passage:

> There are roughly three New Yorks. There is, first, the New York of the man or woman who was born here, who takes the city for granted and accepts its turbulence as natural and inevitable. Second, there is the New York of the commuter—the city that is devoured by locusts

each day and spat out each night. Third, there is the New York of the person who was born somewhere else and came to New York in quest of something. Of these three trembling cities the greatest is the last—the city of final destination, the city that is a goal. It is this third city that accounts for New York's high-strung disposition, its poetical deportment, its dedication to the arts, and its incomparable achievements. Commuters give the city its tidal restlessness, natives give it solidity and continuity, but the settlers give it passion.

Rewritten, this becomes:

In New York City there are three kinds of people who each contribute something different to the atmosphere. I will first describe these three kinds of people and then relate how they affect my perception of the city. First, there is the commuter, who prefers to live outside the city, coming in only to work. Second, there are the natives, who were born there and more or less take everything about the place for granted. Finally, there is the sort who were born somewhere else and has moved to New York City. The first kind makes the city seem jumpy (because they are always coming and going.) The second kind makes the city seem very old and ordinary and settled because they've been there forever and are pretty settled. The third kind are here because they think the city will be the answer to its dreams. After all, they left they're native homes to come here. Sometimes they are disappointed and sometimes not, but they usually attribute these feelings to the city, and that makes the city seem more or less exciting. They also give more to the city artswise and businesswise than the commuters who come to New York only to work and the natives who just take everything for granted.

These two passages would be given to the students, who would be asked to write a short essay (*not* a list) in which they would choose one passage over the other and defend that choice.

That is the basic model of the exercise. But you can also tinker with it in specific ways to test specific knowledge. Suppose that you want to test the students on their ability to recognize a certain writing problem—sentence fragments, comma splices, and run ons, for example. You could rewrite the original passage so that it was loaded with these errors but few or no others:

There are roughly three New Yorks, there is, first, the New York of the man or woman who was born here, who takes the city for granted and accepts its size and its turbulence as natural and inevitable and second, there is the New York of the commuter—the city that is devoured by locusts each day. And spat out each night. (Etc.)

Or, with more advanced students, you might want to test just their "feel" for written English. Your rewrite then might contain not a single error but, because of word choice, still be noticeably inferior to the original. For example, the last two sentences of the White passage could be rewritten as:

> It is this third city that accounts for New York's sophistication and glamor. Commuters make the city seem busy, natives give it a sense of tradition, but settlers give it a sense of excitement.

However you modify the passage, you have an exercise that, for any level of competence, tests both the students' knowledge of what distinguishes good writing from bad (the "content" of a composition course) and their ability to write a short piece communicating that knowledge (the goal of a composition course).

A Writing Course Final Exam

Thomas Brownell

Designing a final examination in a writing course can be difficult; Thomas Brownell, however, offers an idea for how such an examination can incorporate all the elements of the composing process. Mr. Brownell contributed this exercise from Zanesville, Ohio.

Author's Comment

The semester was drawing to a close. I had taught writing for 16 weeks and my students were asking what types of questions they could expect on the final exam. Their apprehension was legitimate. I wondered too. My curriculum for "Writing Techniques," a junior year, high-level course geared to college bound students, was new. For grammar drill interspersed with 500-word essays, I had substituted a writing process approach that emphasized student conferencing and required each paper to be revised through a series of drafts. Writing Techniques exams had typically consisted of sentence diagramming and questions that tested a student's ability to recognize and correct errors in punctuation, parallel structure, pronoun agreement, and the standard list of grammatical constructions. Since the old course had culminated in writing a research paper, a block of the final exam listed random reference sources and required the students to structure the material in proper footnote and bibliography form. A series of vocabulary questions was also standard fare.

Since I had designed the new "Writing Techniques" course to stress that sound writing evolves from information, I hadn't taught grammar specifically. Instead, when a student reached the editing stage and still was making serious grammatical errors, I would spend parts of several classes in mini-lessons on trouble areas using examples from student writing to teach the principle involved.

In planning the exam, I knew I couldn't ask the old set of questions. The students felt relieved when I explained that this year's exam would reflect the altered course format, but they seemed baffled that I could compose an exam that would test the skills they had learned. My advice, while I searched for effective questions, was that they simply relax on the exam issue and finish their last project, writing a paper they would submit for publication.

The purpose of a final exam, as I see it, is to give students the opportunity to review the course content in hopes that they grasp the structure and significance of materials that they received in bits and pieces. My major goal in "Writing Techniques" had been to convince my students that they could write well, provided they worked from a topic that drew on their expertise. I also had felt they should understand that clear, forceful writing rarely flows from an inspired pen. Each writing assignment had been revised in a substantial way. Student conferences had given audience contact to stimulate that revision. I had assigned a research paper, but instead of laboring over footnote and bibliography form, I had explained the purpose of referencing sources and provided copies of Kate Turabian's style manual for them to use as they documented their research. In one class I distributed copies of several different style sheets to show that even though authorities differ on footnote and bibliography format, all required the same information.

The Approach

As I wrote the exam, I tried to make it mirror the course. The major segment, roughly three-quarters of the two-hour time slot, I devoted to an exercise in writing using the process approach. That question asked the students to brainstorm a topic, write a first draft, revise the draft, edit the revision, and produce a final copy. The pace would be tight, I knew, because although I had advised the class that the exam would test the writing approach they had practiced in class, I did not divulge the specific nature of this question. Even so, the students sensed what they would be asked to do and I knew that during final exam week, no student would be lacking in information for a fresh topic. I divided the balance of the exam into five rather straightforward short-answer questions on topics such as the purpose of bibliography and footnotes, and the use of different styles of reference.

Evaluation

Both from student attitudes during the exam and from the response to the questions, I felt the new exam format had accomplished its purpose. One student cleverly summarized the last assignment of the course, writing for publication, as his exam topic. In parts of several classes Kevin had studied the manuscript preparation chapters of *Writer's Market* and when he mailed his sci/fi story, "Idiot—Savant" to *Omni* magazine, it was packaged with a professional's attention to detail.

Kevin approached the exam exercise by listing the elements he considered to be essential for effective writing. From his list he extracted a three-word outline: imagination, information, determination. These key words would serve as the framework for his essay. Having gathered his fuel and organized his thoughts, Kevin began writing. The lead paragraph appeared in the first draft, emerging in nearly final form. The first draft also contained all essential information, drawn from his "brainstorming" list, along with a description of free writing and instructions for marketing a manuscript.

In his revision, Kevin concentrated on adding details, like an observation that it isn't necessary to seclude yourself in a cabin to write. By fleshing out his essay with picturesque description, Kevin was able to avoid the trap of lengthy explanations and quicken the pace of his writing.

Though he produced an exemplary essay, Kevin wasn't the last student to finish the exam. As a group, the Writing Techniques students approached this exam with a greater sense of purpose and worked more intently than any previous class. Nearly all students used the entire exam period to revise and edit their writing.

Like Kevin, the students typically began their exam essay by brainstorming to gather information, then they ordered their thoughts and wrote a rough draft. As the writing process stresses, they spent the major share of their effort on revision. Topics ranged with student interests. I graded the essays by evaluating the writer's skill following the steps of the writing process. All students achieved the goal of generating topics and refining rough copy. As an added bonus the exams were interesting and enjoyable to read.

The final draft of Kevin's exercise in the writing process follows, illustrating the fact that the writing process, from brainstorming to editing, can be compressed into an exam period.

"The Secret to Writing a Story"

by

Kevin Kennedy

Many dream about it, yet few ever attempt it. What I'm talking about is, of course, writing a story. All it takes is three simple tools—imagination, information, and determination. All of these tools are easy to come by, and once you've begun to master them, a whole new world of expression is yours.

Think of it, in a few weeks or months you could be a published writer, in a few years, an established author. And don't think it's too late. Every writer had to start somewhere, and few began their careers in one magnificent burst of talent. They started out like you: a student, factory worker, housewife, whatever your occupation.

To begin the writing process, you need the first tool—imagination. Everybody has an imagination and all are unique, so everyone has something to share in print with others. To use it, find a quiet spot somewhere with a pen and paper and free-write. Free-writing is simply doodling with words—putting down your own personal thoughts in no particular order and with the only purpose being to let your imagination run wild. Enjoy it and follow any random ideas that may come to you. After awhile, bring your thoughts into focus on a specific subject, especially something you can claim to be an expert on, or know a lot about. Science fiction, baseball, politics, cooking; all are interesting topics when expressed with the right words. This is brainstorming, and here is where information comes in. Take your topic and outline what you know and what to say about it. With this accomplished, and, keeping it in mind, start writing.

This is only the first draft, so grammar and sentence structure don't matter, only ideas. Write until you have nothing more to say. Don't get stuck in a particular place like the conclusion or introduction, pass over it and fix it later.

Once done with the first draft, read through it and see if you've gotten across what you want to say. Have a friend (maybe a fellow writer or even an English teacher) read it and critique it, telling you its strong points and weak points. Next, bring the paper through successive drafts, correcting the weak spots (if you think they are weak) and capitalizing on the good points.

By the way, don't feel you have to lock yourself up in a cabin in Alaska just to write. Once the first draft is complete and you know what you have to say, take your time revising. Some writers prefer absolute seclusion until a story or book is complete, while others are more easygoing in this respect. This is your story, you decide.

Once a final draft is complete (which could be draft number two or ten) start to look for a possible publisher. In most cases, if you've written a short story or article, this would be in the form of a magazine. The perfect source for magazines and what they look for is the *Writer's Market*. This listing can be found or ordered in book stores or probably found in many libraries. In it, magazines will be listed under their specialized interest. This way, the article can be matched with the magazine. The book will also give excellent information on exactly how to type a story and write a cover letter.

If you can't find this book, look through magazines at your local library until you've found one that seems to cover your topic. Write an interesting, personal, concise cover letter to the editor telling him generally about your article (type it) and send it with the story (typed) with a self-addressed stamped envelope. Expect to wait three or four weeks for a reply. Good luck.

A Grading Contract That Works

Walter H. Beale

Don W. King

The prickly question of grading always seems to arise in writing classes. This exercise describes a qualitative grading system that emphasizes revision. Mr. Beale contributed this from the University of North Carolina at Greensboro and Mr. King from Montreat-Anderson College, Montreat, North Carolina.

Authors' Comment

"Is this essay a B– or C+? Let's see . . . the student got a C+ on the last essay, and this one does seem to be an improvement, if only slightly. I guess a B– is about right, besides, it will encourage the student." Almost every composition teacher has agonized in this way during a long session of grading essays. The business of assigning letter grades to essays is clearly frustrating for teachers and very often debilitating for students, frequently to the point of undermining the goals of a course in composition. On the other hand, most attempts at ungraded or pass/fail composition courses that we know about have been considered less than successful. However much we may dislike conventional grading, our students still need "carrots and sticks," and they still need a sense of justice. More importantly, they need to be able to experiment and to make mistakes without fear of devastating penalty. In an attempt partially to resolve these tensions, and at the same time to produce a grading system more congenial to the needs of a composition course, we have devised a "new" contract grading system.

Unlike a quantitative contract grading system based on the number of finished essays (for example, five to be eligible for a C, six for a B, seven for an A), our system is qualitative, designed to encourage a great deal of revision. Also, unlike a contract system wherein students decide at the beginning of the course which particular grade they want to work towards and then "contract" with the teacher for that grade, our system allows the students the freedom to decide at any time during the course. A further difference is that students never have to "contract" formally with us.

The Approach

Here's the way our system works: In the course of a semester, every student is required to write seven deliberative essays. Each essay is evaluated by the instructor and placed into one of the following categories:

"publishable"   — A publishable essay is one that makes a clear and perceptive point, is well supported with reasoning and details, is well organized, is written in a mature and appropriate style, and contains only minor mechanical and spelling errors.

"revisable"   — A revisable essay is one that is well conceived and shows considerable evidence of planning, but which fails to execute successfully in one or more of the areas listed in the definition of "publishable"—that is, in terms of support, organization, style, or mechanics.

"re-write"   — A re-write essay is one that fails in one of the following ways:
1) is ill-conceived; makes no consistent or useful point;
2) is poorly constructed and carelessly written; the reader has trouble following the ideas or train of thought;
3) contains so many errors in sentence structure and usage that the message is troublesome to decipher;
4) departs from the assignment in an unacceptable way.

After the essay is returned, the student has several options, depending upon the essay's category. If the essay is a "re-write," a specific due date is assigned (usually a week later) for re-submission. If the essay is "revisable," the student is free to revise it and to turn it in at any time later in the semester, several times if necessary and feasible. (We stipulate that all revisions must be "good faith" revisions—serious efforts to improve the essay toward the category of "publishable.") The only qualification we add is that during the last two weeks of the course, a student may turn in a maximum of two revised essays; a deluge of papers at the end of a writing course is, of course, a composition teacher's nightmare.

The final grade for the course is determined by the number of revisable and publishable essays the student produced in a course organized around six 600–1000-word essay assignments. Our basic "contract" is as follows:

A   four publishable essays and two revisable essays

B   two publishable and four revisable (however, there must be a total of four attempted revisions)

C   six revisable (with at least three attempted revisions)

D   near fulfillment of the C contract

F   serious failure to fulfill the C contract, coupled with a lack of effort

We should pause here for a moment to discuss the importance of revision in our system. Since we rely so heavily upon revision, the student needs to be educated in how to revise. Revision is largely a waste of time if a student is only correcting mechanical errors. Therefore, we impress upon our students that a revision must take into account not merely mechanical concerns, but rhetorical ones as well. Organization, argumentative strategy, and audience appeal all have to be considered by the student during a successful revision. In addition, we inform our students that we will not identify every single problem we see in the paper the first time we evaluate it; to do so would place a great burden on the student and might discourage revision. Rather, we try to indicate major problems in the first evaluation and then move on to other problems in subsequent revisions. We have found that it is crucial to make these revision policies very clear to students from the beginning of the course, so that they know what a "good faith" revision is.

We feel that this grading system is advantageous in several ways. The primary advantage of our system is that it avoids discouraging students with a low grade from the very beginning of the course. The effect of a D or even a low C on a student's initial essay can be debilitating. In fact, a kind of vicious cycle can result. The student receives a D on the first essay and panics; the student envisions being forever doomed to the realm of "d-ness," with no real way to improve the writing. Our system, in that it encourages revision and "writing in progress," offers the chance to learn the nuts and bolts of writing. Moreover, our system offers the psychologically positive opportunity to move from the rewrite to the revisable to the publishable category.

A second advantage is that our system encourages the student to view writing as a process. For too long, composition teachers have functioned too exclusively as evaluators of finished products. We judge the essay, give it its letter grade, and push it back to the student, who files it away in a notebook somewhere and immediately forgets the comments we have labored so faithfully to provide. It is here that we lose an important opportunity to help the student become a better writer. It is much better to take that essay, point out major shortcomings, and allow the student to continue developing ideas in a revision. The procedure certainly injects an element of realism. After all, most of us are rarely satisfied with our own final drafts; in fact, we often wish we could get them back after it is too late.

Thirdly, our system offers the teacher a positive alternative to the letter grade syndrome. It may at first appear that our categories are just another way of saying A, B, or C, but such is not the case. The publishable category may be the equivalent of the A, but the revisable category encompasses both the B and the C ranges (and perhaps at times even the high D). The difference between a B and a C is not always very clear in something as subjective as essay evaluation. However, both the B and the C are distinct from the A. Consequently, should not both require revision in order to be considered publishable?

Finally, our system encourages "real-world" writing, and it discourages "writing-to-the-teacher." The implicit role of the teacher is transformed from that of grader to helpful, sympathetic editor. Incidentally, the system facilitates peer discussion of essays, by focusing comments and criticisms toward possible revisions. A basic requirement of our course is that every student have at least one essay reproduced for every member of the class. That essay is then read out loud by the student (or teacher) and is evaluated by the rest of the class. Typically, the comments of the student's classmates are very helpful and point out areas needing revision. Most often the class then categorizes the essay as Publishable, Revisable, or Re-write. This method helps to keep the student focused on real-world writing, where an audience must be considered.

However, we would be less than candid if we did not admit that there are potential problems with our system. The first, as we have already mentioned, is that the student will fail to understand what revision actually means. Therefore, we spend much class time, especially at the beginning of the course, talking about revision. Secondly, there is a good deal of extra grading; and quite frankly, initially this seemed the greatest drawback for many of us. However, we found that frequently the time spent on evaluating the major weaknesses of each revision was no more than we would have spent on doing a minute evaluation of that "final